W9-BLX-558

TV OR NOT TV

Ronald L. Goldfarb

TV OR NOT TV

Television, Justice, and the Courts

A TWENTIETH CENTURY FUND BOOK

NEW YORK UNIVERSITY PRESS

NEW YORK AND LONDON

NEW YORK UNIVERSITY PRESS
New York and London

The Twentieth Century Fund sponsors and supervises timely analyses of economic policy, foreign affairs, and domestic political issues. Not-for-profit and and nonpartisan, the Fund was founded in 1919 and endowed by Edward A. Filene.

Library of Congress Cataloging-in-Publication Data
Goldfarb, Ronald L.
TV or not TV : television, justice, and the courts / Ronald L. Goldfarb.
p. cm.
"Twentieth Century Fund book."
Includes index.
ISBN 0-8147-3112-0 (acid-free paper)
1. Conduct of court proceedings—United States. 2. Free press and fair trial—United States. I. Title.
KF8725.G65   1998
347.73'05—dc21   97-45289
                                                      CIP

New York University Press books are printed on acid-free paper, and their binding materials are chosen for strength and durability.

Manufactured in the United States of America

10 9 8 7 6 5 4 3 2 1

For H.M.R.
Always my friend

A popular Government, without popular information, or the means of acquiring it, is but a Prologue to a Farce or a Tragedy; or, perhaps both. Knowledge will forever govern ignorance: And a people who mean to be their own Governors must arm themselves with the power which knowledge gives.

9 Writings of James Madison 103 (1910)

A trial is a public event. What transpires in the courtroom is public property.

Justice William O. Douglas,
Craig v. Harney, 331 U.S. 367 at 374 (1947)

CONTENTS

FOREWORD

Courtroom drama, both fictional and based on real trials, became commonplace on television almost from the inception of the medium. This should not come as a surprise: trials have long fascinated audiences. In their own time, the trials of Aaron Burr for treason (twice) and Henry Thaw for the murder of Stanford White, the Scopes "monkey trial," and the trial of the kidnapper of the Lindbergh baby riveted the nation when they took place and continued to fascinate, especially when presented in dramatic form in the theater, on film, and on television. More recently, the national obsession with the televised O. J. Simpson murder trial, and the subsequent cottage industry of books and commentary, startled even the most careful observers of popular culture. Of course, cable television's "Court TV," which provides a steady supply of more prosaic cases, had indicated that there is an apparently insatiable audience, eager to peek through the camera into courtrooms around the nation.

The televising of trials, however, has not been without controversy. A substantial proportion of the bar and the judiciary continue to resist granting such media access. Television cameras, in fact, are still barred from federal courtrooms, and many states are equally strict. The list of issues that trouble those who oppose televising trials is lengthy, involving many complex arguments. But it is fair to say that the most important all focus on the potential for television to affect the behavior of judges, lawyers, and witnesses in a case. In other words, the central question is, Does the camera affect the outcome?

Ronald Goldfarb, himself an attorney, brings unusual credentials to the task of exploring the pros and cons—and the implications—of televising trials. He understands that the heart of the matter is the potential conflict between the constitutional right of the public to know and the press to report and the constitutional protections meant to ensure a fair trial. He makes clear that the differences among experts and judges on this issue do not fit neatly into our normal categories of liberal or conservative—supporters and opponents of television in the courtroom fall into both ideological camps. Goldfarb's book also provides a necessary historical perspective on the current state of the argument. He explains how opinion has shifted over time and how particular trials have affected, at least in the short run, the balance of forces on the issue. His work is comprehensive, discussing both the case for and against cameras in the courtroom and then providing his own thoughtful point of view about what should be a sensible national policy in this area.

For the Twentieth Century Fund/Century Foundation, Goldfarb's study continues a long tradition of exploring the interaction of media and journalism with government and public policy, most recently in our Perspectives on the News series. The issue of universal television coverage of courtrooms cuts across all of these areas. In fact, one of the central questions about such trials relates directly to the election process for important state and local officials; after all, many judges and district attorneys stand for election. (In thinking about this aspect of the issue, keep in mind that public performance at criminal and civil trials became a routine way to develop a political following in the Roman Republic.) Televised trials, therefore, represent "political" photo opportunities for candidates. As such, they may affect not only the way candidates conduct themselves during a trial but also the outcome of some future elections. The obvious counterargument is, "Can it be bad for the public to know more about how officeholders actually perform in the jobs to which they were elected?"

More generally, as Goldfarb makes clear, one cannot rationally discuss the "camera in the courtroom" issue without finding common ground on just what the public interest is in this area. As the pages that follow explain, however, there is no simple answer to this question. For the Fund, then, this book has a characteristic that we seek in all our publications: a quest to understand the issues involved and to assess the best course of action for the nation. While he fairly represents the case on behalf of opponents of court television, Goldfarb concludes with a powerful brief on behalf of universal access.

Goldfarb's argument builds on the traditional right to know embodied in the Constitution and the writings of the founders of the American Republic. But the weight of evidence for his position includes many other considerations, including the inescapable advantages of "seeing for yourself" versus even the most assiduous reporting. Moreover, he suggests that the current resistance to universal televised trials is only a transition phase, a pause while old habits of mind are shed in the wake of the inevitable changes wrought by new technologies. Indeed, the concluding section of *TV or Not TV: Television, Justice, and the Courts* looks beyond the current debate to the future, raising interesting questions about how, as television in the courtroom becomes ever more fully established, we can make it serve the twin causes of justice and the right to know most effectively.

On behalf of the Trustees of The Twentieth Century Fund/Century Foundation, I thank Ronald Goldfarb for his significant contribution to our understanding of this important contemporary issue.

Richard C. Leone, President
The Twentieth Century Fund/Century Foundation
September 1997

ACKNOWLEDGMENTS

The Twentieth Century Fund provided me with a grant that made writing this book possible. For their support, I would like to thank Richard Leone and the board of directors, who made this grant; Kathleen Quinn and Jon Shure, who helped me nurture the manuscript through its evolutionary stages; and Beverly Goldberg, who managed the publication. Their friendly and professional assistance is very much appreciated.

Niko Pfund wisely edited the book and enthusiastically nursed it through its production at New York University Press.

Several law students who worked in my office provided helpful research assistance and I thank each of them: Einar Hernits, Susan Shamoto, and Tom Comerford. Elizabeth Machado helped with my social sciences research. Sean Britain and Lauren Komar assisted in the research on state studies and new technology.

Faculty members of the American University and University of Maryland journalism departments provided important critical assessments that informed the ideas in my conclusion, and they all have my respect and gratitude.

Steve Brill, Jeff Ballabon, Fred Graham, and other staff members at Court TV were gracious and helpful, providing me with information about their work.

Dan Kevles, Erwin Chemerinsky, Leslie Maitland, Carl Stern, Joe Russin, and Dan Hamilton each read a chapter and offered wise advice about it. Denny Heck advised me about Washington State's innovative program. Each was wise, generous, and helpful, and they have my gratitude.

Sharon Kirby began the preparation of the manuscript. Lauren Komar helped the production process in countless ways. Peg Dreibelbis took over and completed it, perfecting a zillion jobs with masterful competence, genuine goodwill, and indispensably sound advice.

INTRODUCTION

In the final two decades of the twentieth century, televised court proceedings have progressed from an outlandish and unthinkable idea to a feasible, if not inevitable, reality. In the past few years, the practice has become commonplace. Yet, many observers continue to voice serious reservations about this trend. Following several highly publicized trials—often criminal cases with which the media and the public became obsessed—much public soul-searching and professional deliberation has ensued about the dangers all media publicity, especially television, pose to the justice system.

Some critics contend that television is inherently a sovereign medium that takes over and changes the subject of its attention. Television is an environment, one of its better practitioners has stated, and like weather it changes and dominates everything. Others argue that the dignity of the trial process is jeopardized and commercialized by television. Many fear that the medium inevitably disturbs the participants in trials, needlessly invades people's privacy, and portrays a distorted picture of justice. The excessive indulgence of the constitutional rights of the press, some argue, unnecessarily prejudices the constitutional rights of defendants to a fair trial.

Most government proceedings are open to the public in this country, and many of these proceedings are televised. The judicial branch has been the last and most reluctant to open its proceedings to media generally, and to television especially. The rationales for this institutional diffidence have varied. At first, television was considered unruly and disruptive. Later objections were based on its commercialism and sensationalism, as well as its pernicious influence on the players in the trial process—defendants, lawyers, judges, witnesses, and jurors.

It is a measure of the antipathy of many members of the bar and the judiciary toward cameras in courtrooms that a champion of freedom like the late Supreme Court Justice William O. Douglas viewed the prospect as an anathema to fair trials.[1] His indictment of televised trials contained four counts, which others would prosecute over the years.

First, Justice Douglas thought that television would cause "insidious influences" upon the administration of justice by intimidating and distracting frail witnesses and goading others to become clowns, and by arousing the emotions of the community. Television would give the press undue influence over the many judges and district attorneys who run for office and who should be insulated from majoritarian pressures. One First Amendment authority also feared that televised trials constitute a form of psychological punishment of an accused.[2] The late Appellate Judge Learned Hand observed, at a time when television was banned from courts, that he could not imagine anything worse than having to endure the pressures of a trial; no doubt, for most people the realization that such an experience was being broadcast widely would add to their anxiety.

Second, Douglas feared that television would transform our deliberative trial process into an inquisitorial spectacle where passion and showmanship replaced the dispassionate search for truth. A televised trial, he thought, was a spectacle just as a trial in Yankee Stadium or the Roman Coliseum would be. He recalled a raucous mass trial in a Cuban stadium, and one in a Baghdad People's Court where seventy defendants charged with an assassination plot were herded into a klieg-lighted pen before a shouting, hand-picked audience. He quoted Juvenal's saying, "Two things only the people anxiously desire—bread and circuses," and another judge's rhetorical comment that "Ordeal by publicity is the legitimate great-grandchild of ordeal by fire, water, and battle."

Third, the Justice argued that the Sixth Amendment's public-trial guarantee was intended for the benefit of the accused, not the press, and never was meant to require every member of the community to see and hear every case: "the historic concept of a public trial envisaged a small, close gathering, not a city-wide, state-wide or nation-wide arena." The core idea behind this amendment, he urged, was and still is to avoid closed and secret trials, not to open trials as widely as possible, nor "to provide the public with recreation or with instruction in the ways of government."

Fourth, Douglas feared that television would cheapen and vulgarize government by denying the sacrosanct dignity of courts and by deflecting the search for truth, a quest that by definition must proceed quietly and without fanfare. Skeptics of television in the courts fear the specter of a three-minute segment covering a local trial sandwiched between a dog food commercial and a pantyhose commercial, to paraphrase one judge.[3] The conventional view of the bar, at least until recently, was that television would transform the temple of justice into crass theater. Gerry Spence, one of America's most successful trial lawyers, believes that television turns "the search for justice into a spectator sport for the amusement of drooling couch potatoes."[4] A related question concerns the commercialization of the justice system: If trials are broadcast, should it be done by the government or by the profit-seeking or nonprofit private sector?

Though the reticence of the bench and bar to allow cameras in courts has been deep-seated and widely shared, it is not unanimous. Not long after Justice Douglas criticized televised trials, an equally respected member of the federal judiciary, D.C. Circuit Court of Appeals Judge J. Skelly Wright, argued for more and better coverage of the justice system by the mass media.[5] Before blaming the press for the sins of the justice system, he thought the bar should correct its own misconduct. Most prejudicial trial publicity derives from out-of-court statements by police and district attorneys about confessions, prior records, and the evil character of defendants, and by defense lawyers "spinning" the media in their clients' interests, all violations of Canon 20 of Professional Ethics, one "more honored in the breach than in the observance."

Judge Wright reminded us that "our most dignified ceremonies are televised, for example, church services and inaugurations," and he called the fears about losing the dignity of trials a "dead-end argument." Furthermore, concerns about the trial participants' right of privacy are misplaced; they "must always yield to the people's right to know." Distortions by the lens are no more likely than those by the pen.

Why not try television in courts, Wright urged, and seek models of excellence, techniques to control excesses, experiments to assess the reality, rather than relying on speculations about the idea. And what better way to experiment, he suggested, than at the top—by televising appellate proceedings, even the Supreme Court. "Our Supreme Court has been called a continuous constitutional convention, reinterpreting for each generation the meaning and application of those fundamental principles on which the nation is founded," he wrote. "It would be a matchless lesson in the meaning of our constitutional rights and principles for the people of the country to hear the decisions themselves."[6]

Judge Wright sided with advocates of television in courts because he thought the new technology would give a truer view of the justice system than that provided by traditional media. The most ardent advocate of the educative power of television in courts, Wright believed that much of the misunderstandings about cases, particularly important Supreme Court cases, are caused by the public's lack of firsthand information about what actually transpires in the courts. He was not the only authority to draw this conclusion. The late Justice Hugo Black complained to me in 1961, before television was allowed in courts, that the press distorted the meanings of the Court's important decisions, resulting in public misperceptions about these rulings. This in turn led, in his opinion, to improper criticism of the Court. The late Justice Oliver Wendell Holmes, Jr., while a state supreme court justice in Massachusetts, wrote: "It is desirable that the trial of causes take place under the public eye . . . because it is of the highest moment that those who administer justice should always act under the sense of public responsibility, and that every citizen should be able to satisfy himself within his own eyes as to the mode in which a public duty is performed."[7]

In 1986, Supreme Court Associate Justice John Paul Stevens

pointed out the historic rationale for open trials. Quoting James Madison, he stated that the First Amendment guarantees more than freedom from governmental restraints. The public's ability to acquire information about the operation of public institutions is a fundamental component of the self-governance contemplated by the framers.[8] In 1989, the U.S. Supreme Court again noted the historic importance of public trials: "While the benefits of a public trial are frequently intangible, difficult to prove, or a matter of chance, the Framers plainly thought them nonetheless real."[9]

Advocates of television in courts claim that the judiciary has been needlessly protectionist, that in all trials (certainly in appellate and civil cases) there is an educative and public interest in observing the issues under consideration and the methods of the justice system. One law professor has suggested that televised trials "are like civics classrooms. . . . Every verdict has educational value beyond the impact on the litigants. . . . It reinforces the norms of society."[10]

The silent camera will portray "the real thing," it is argued, presenting a more accurate and illuminating picture of the justice system than other media. Without courtroom cameras, the public only knows what information a small number of reporters can digest and deliver. And if the justice system is suspect in the minds of many people, so too is the media.

As with all persistently controversial issues, television in the courtroom is a two-edged sword. It is both invasive and informative. Though it brings the trial to the widest possible audience, in doing so it creates pressures and temptations for all participants. Though it reduces community speculations, rumors, and fears about what transpires in the courtroom, it also thrusts the general public (which may possess information the jury may not have) into assessments of specific cases and of the justice system in general. The public as watchdog is an insurance against autocracy; but as an outside influence on a controlled deliberative process, it may also interfere with justice.

History suggests, however, that criticisms about resolutions concerning excessive press coverage of trials betray a fundamental naivete. As legal historian Sir John MacDonnell, long ago noted:

"Often a trial is the one luminous point in darkness. . . . It takes one outside the formulae of the textbooks. Truthfully reported, a trial is a living picture; it brings us nearer to life than the best literature. You hear the voices; it is life itself."[11] Because of the personalities involved and the enormity of the acts and their implications, certain trials invariably become hypnotic mirrors of a society, provide a distillation of its conflicts. Frivolous, base, or squalid motives are not what make these cases gripping, one columnist noted during the O. J. Simpson trial. The media have not forgotten their manners or mission because of their fascination with such cases; a case does not require redeeming social value to warrant media and public interest. While much of the reportage that passes for serious news is actually "speculative, transitory, and more earnest than important," this experienced reporter admitted, "much of what constitutes the frowned upon preoccupation of readers and viewers—the startling crimes and trials, the passions that wreck lives and destroy families and other institutions—goes to ancient, even primal concerns."[12]

———

This book places the question of televised trials in historical perspective. Present concerns about the perceived conflict between media and courts are part of a recurring public debate on the proper balance between an active and informative press and a caring and open trial system, which has engaged American thinkers throughout our country's history. The Bill of Rights protects both the freedom of the press (not its license) and the defendant's rights to an open and fair trial (though not calling for an agora and not necessarily requiring an acquittal). The proper line between entertainment and education, between exploitation and information, between the negative consequences of "in camera" (closed) trials and those of "on camera" trials is not always clear, nor can it be measured with scientific objectivity. And while the concerns about the prejudicial potential of pretrial publicity and actual trial coverage are related, there are important differences. Presently, the rule in our federal courts generally banning cameras stands in opposition to the practice of most state courts, which permit televised trials. Does this dichotomy indicate the flexible genius of our federal system, or the divided thought about a contentious and important issue of public policy and constitutional law?

TV or Not TV traces the key cases that have influenced our collective thinking about televised trials, places them in the broader context of cases dealing with what has been called the free press-fair trial issue, and outlines the prevailing rules in the state and federal courts. The relevant legal and social science studies are presented that bear on the critical concern about whether cameras in courts distort or portray the justice system, and whether they prejudice the quality of justice in individual trials by disturbing the key participants. The many arguments for and against cameras in courts are analyzed in view of the actual experiences to date in jurisdictions that permit televised trials and the lessons to be learned from Court TV's coverage of a remarkable sampling of cases on its own cable channel.

All the arguments that are advanced against televised trials are addressed in this book: the fear of physical disruption; the fear of adverse psychological impact on the trial participants; the potential for exploitation of the justice system for commercial purposes; the fear of prejudicing trials; the invasion of the privacy of witnesses, jurors, attorneys, and others involved in cases. The points advanced by proponents of televised trials are also covered: the educational value of an exposed judicial system, the need for parity in the treatment of print and broadcast media, the need to redefine what a public trial means in this era of advanced technology; the media's impact both inside and outside the courtroom, the need for open government. All these arguments, pro and con, involve defining standards of constitutional law: the freedom of the press, the right to a public and a fair trail. The issue is the relationship between the *quality* of justice and the *visibility* of justice.

I believe it is possible to find a sensible and balanced solution to this cyclical conflict, including a wise approach for dealing with these confounding questions in the next century. As we enter an era of technological sophistication likely to change many past concepts—

What is public? What is information? What is truth?—the fundamental issue must be: How can we best blend new media technologies with our traditional and revered commitment to democracy and justice?

Chapter 1

THE TRIAL OF THE CENTURY

Crime news lies at the heart of one of the more recurring and confounding dilemmas of the twentieth century. The constitutional rights of people charged with crimes to both a "public" and a "fair" trial may present an inherent conflict. If there is too much public attention, that very openness may affect the fairness of the trial. The corresponding press right to cover crime news by its own standard—different from that of courtroom judiciousness—may cause a competing constitutional conflict. As the media become more pervasive and more influential, the potential for conflict between the press's right to present crime news and the defendant's right to a fair and open trial increases.

To compound the conundrum, the two constitutional rights guaranteed by the First and Sixth Amendments may be complementary as well as conflicting. As one federal appeals court judge put it, "the right of fair trial is companion, not servant, to the constitutional guarantee of public trial."[1] The two institutions—press and courts—are mutually reinforcing, and occasionally adversarial. A probing press may expose injustices, assure fair trials, and censure improprieties by judges, police, and prosecutors; the courts may preserve press independence when it is challenged. Erwin Chemerinsky, a University

1

of Southern California law professor, argues that the supposed tension between the First and Sixth Amendments is "illusory." The media informs public debate about important issues, and media coverage of trials "increase[s] the likelihood of fair and just proceedings."[2]

But the constitutional companion can become a villain. This perplexing conflict was described by the late Supreme Court Justice Felix Frankfurter in an appeal of an Indiana murder conviction and capital punishment that was decided by a jury whose impartiality had been prejudiced by intensive pretrial publicity. Motions for a second change of venue and a continuance were denied. In a concurring opinion to Justice Tom Clark's reversal, Justice Frankfurter complained: "This Court has not yet decided that the fair administration of criminal justice must be subordinated to another safeguard of our constitutional system—freedom of the press, properly conceived. The Court has not yet decided that, while convictions must be reversed and miscarriages of justice result because the minds of jurors or potential jurors were poisoned, the poisoner is constitutionally protected in plying his trade."[3] The problem is not new, but it is profoundly important: Its causes and effects are unclear, and its cures controversial.

Originally, the guarantee of an open trial was a common law reform meant to prevent closed proceedings and assure that the public was informed about and could participate in the workings of the judicial system. In the days when the press was neither ubiquitous nor pervasive, the mere presence of the public—albeit a very small and local public—was the means of subjecting government to the scrutiny of its subjects. Few could quarrel with such a democratic notion. But sometimes virtues can evolve into vices when conditions change.

During the nineteenth century, a public of local spectators was supplemented by reporters who came to trials and reported what they observed to a distant reading audience. With the invention of the telegraph, immediate reports of criminal trials could be communicated quickly to larger and more distant audiences. As the media presence and impact grew, problems arose. The very ubiquity of the press threatened to make differences in the kind as well as the degree of publicity pertaining to trials.

From the earliest days of this country's history to the present, there have been excessively publicized criminal trials. Television is only the latest chapter in a long and evolving continuum of institutional and constitutional dynamics.

As early as the mid-1700s, public attention was riveted on dramatic courtroom battles, engaging as much for their entertainment value as for their treatment of vital political issues. The seditious libel case of John Peter Zenger in 1734 has been called no less than "a precedent . . . for the American Revolution and the Bill of Rights."[4] Andrew Hamilton, the most illustrious trial lawyer of the colonial period, argued the case for the defense, and the trial is featured in most collections of great American trials as having helped establish press freedom to honestly (if truculently) criticize government.[5] Indeed, the case arose out of a newspaper war typified by provocative charges and countercharges.

When the jury announced its verdict acquitting the martyred printer, according to one report, "The roar of the crowd seemed to shake the courtroom. Vainly the angry judge rapped for order. . . . The waiting people outside in Wall St. . . . shouted their joy. Broadway answered with resounding cheers."[6] According to another account, "Long before the opening of the court the little room was crowded to its utmost. . . . The majority of the people felt that they had assembled not merely to witness the trial of the printer for libel, but that here the last fight was to be made against the administration which was so arbitrarily oppressive."[7] In striking a blow against censorship, the widely publicized case had a remarkable effect on post-Revolutionary America in places far from the courtroom in New York City. Even in England, accounts of the trial were reprinted far and wide.

Aaron Burr—senator from New York, vice president to Thomas Jefferson in 1800 (after the only tie vote in the electoral college), and survivor of a celebrated duel with Alexander Hamilton—twice successfully defended himself against charges of treason in trials presided over by then Chief Justice John Marshall. His trials in Richmond,

Virginia, are often referred to by both admiring and critical biographers as early examples of the clash between public opinion and judicial dispassion in causes célèbres.[8]

Reports of the trial told how "the throng straining to get in so far exceeded the capacity" of the chamber that the courtroom had to be expanded. Though promising a fair trial, Burr's prosecutor, U.S. Attorney General Caesar A. Rodney, conceded that earlier reports of Burr's alleged conspiracy "have resounded through the newspapers so long and so strongly" that they implanted in the public's mind "the general opinion" that Burr was guilty.[9] Thousands poured into town to observe the trial, "colonies of tents and covered wagons dotted the northern bank of the river," and reporters from every large newspaper in the country sent news of the trial all over the world. Washington Irving covered the trial for the *New York Gazette*.

Crimes of passion particularly have provoked sensational trials and yellow journalism for centuries. What now seems an example of quaint male Victorianism—some would call it early American chauvinism—regularly led to crimes of violence committed to protect the honor of one's spouse or family member who was considered defiled by another man, regardless of the woman's role in that sexual liaison. Those cases, then as now, generated widespread press attention.[10] For example, when in 1859 Congressman Daniel Sickles shot his wife's lover, Washington District Attorney Phillip Barton Key, notable public figures including senators and congressmen attended the trial, and newspapers around the country (including the usually austere *New York Times*), and even as far away as the *London Times*, "commended the honorable nature of the homicide," and finding a dispassionate jury was thus unusually difficult. After Sickles was acquitted, the *New York Post* reported, "extraordinary demonstrations followed the verdict . . . the shouts of the crowd for 'a speech' from Sickles—the offer to unharness the horses from his carriage, that men might take the places of the brutes—the noisy cavalcade rushing and hurrying down the avenue—the gratitude of the old fruit-seller, who presented a basket of oranges to the man 'who had taught him how to defend his family honor' . . . the serenade of the lawyers."[11]

In the late nineteenth century, a time when we might have assumed the media's influence on the justice system was insignificant, judicial causes célèbres captured the public's attention, no less than now. The notorious alienation-of-affection trial of the prominent and charismatic preacher Henry Ward Beecher could have been a modern TV movie. Nationally famous, from a notable family, yet associated with whiffs of scandal, Beecher had clashed with the well-known feminist Victoria Woodhull over standards governing the sexual mores of the times. In January 1875, Beecher was sued by his best friend, an editor named Theodore Tilton, for engaging in an affair with Tilton's wife, Elizabeth.

It was referred to as the trial of the century, an appellation that would be adopted and repeated henceforth time and again, as if the phrase was freshly discovered each decade. The press afforded the case more coverage than any event since the Civil War.[12] The six-month-long trial took place in the Brooklyn City Court. According to one account:

> The proceedings provided the chief entertainment in town. Tickets were black-marketed at five dollars apiece, and as many as three thousand persons a day were turned away, affording near-by saloons a booming business. Prominent politicians, diplomats, and society leaders fought for seats in the courtroom with ordinary curious folk and went without their lunch in order to hold them, or bought sandwiches and soft drinks from vendors. Newspapers assigned as many as ten reporters to the trial. The audience was frequently unruly, having to be silenced by Judge Joseph Neilson for unseemly applauding, hissing, and whispering—there were several arrests for disorderly conduct.[13]

The summations by the two eminent counsels, "contests of classical erudition and oratory as much as they were legal arguments," continued for twenty-five days, and the courtroom audience complemented the barristers' elocutionary efforts with outbreaks of applause. During the eight days of jury deliberation, sizable crowds milled about constantly near the court, neighborhood bars were jammed, and people slept on the grass outside the court. "Reporters clung to lampposts and crowded out onto window ledges with spyglasses. Diagrams of the jury in various postures of debate were printed and analyzed, and each juror's background was studied." When the jury announced it could not reach a decision throngs of reporters besieged "the unfortunate twelve. The courtroom was bedlam."[14]

Beecher's was neither the first nor last of what repeatedly has come to be called the "trial of the century." Stanford White was a "boulevardier architect," a fashionable socialite whom Henry Adams dubbed the Moses of Manhattan's nouveau riche. His extraordinary career seemed straight out of an Edith Wharton novel about rich New York society at the turn of the century.[15] His architectural firm, McKim, Mead, and White, designed several of the majestic public buildings and stately private clubs and mansions of that time and place, including Madison Square Garden and the Washington Square arch. Late in his life, with his business and health failing, White was shot and killed by Harry Thaw, an eccentric millionaire playboy, who was jealous of White's earlier relationship with the actress Evelyn Nesbit, who had later become Thaw's wife. At her husband's murder trial, the actress testified, demurely, that she had been to a great many apartments with Stanford White and believed she had been drugged and seduced.[16]

The 1907 trial was a bonanza of frenzied and feverish journalism, including what has been called "massive and unrelenting character assassination" of White. One report of the case says that "the story was copy catnip."[17] Characterized as a voluptuary and pervert, White's reputation was utterly destroyed by the press. Reporters besieged the Manhattan trial court, and Western Union set up a special office to handle the flow of news about the case and its chief characters. The huge crowds broke all prior attendance records in New York trial history.

After a hung jury, in a second trial in 1908, the defendant was acquitted by reason of insanity and hailed by the public as a hero in an American morality play. E. L. Doctorow included the scandalous trial in his novel *Ragtime*. Earlier, Ray Milland, Joan Collins, and Farley Granger portrayed the three characters in a movie, *The Girl in The Red Velvet Swing*,[18] an allusion to the scene of White's seduction of Nesbit. Press coverage of the seamy details of the lovers' liaisons was so sensational that President Theodore Roosevelt asked the postmaster general to forbid news accounts of the salacious testimony to be transmitted in the mails.[19]

Another "trial of the century" soon followed, and this time radio was the culprit. In the small town of Dayton, Tennessee, in 1925, William Jennings Bryan and Clarence Darrow fought over the teaching of Darwin's theory of evolution in what became known as the Scopes trial.[20] That amazing trial, which captured the attention of distant audiences, pitted Darrow, the country's most notorious defense counsel, against Bryan, one of the country's most famous conservative political theorists and fundamentalist advocates. Bryan was recruited to prosecute a young high school science teacher and coach for violating the state's newly enacted anti-evolution law.

The two nationally famous lawyers (the defendant was simply a pawn in their litigative match) opened the case with cosmic pronouncements: "Bryan announced, 'The trial uncovers an attack for a generation on revealed religion. A successful attack would destroy the Bible and with it revealed religion. If evolution wins Christianity goes.' Darrow retorted, 'Scopes isn't on trial; civilization is on trial. The prosecution is opening the doors for a reign of bigotry equal to anything in the Middle Ages. No man's belief will be safe if they win.' "[21]

On the day of the trial, the courthouse was swathed in Bible-quoting banners, the courtroom overflowed with spectators, and the largest group of journalists anyone could remember seeing at a trial were in attendance. Microphones were set up to broadcast press accounts of the proceedings nationwide and abroad in several languages. One writer reported that the whole town had become "a camp meeting, a Chautauqua, a state fair, a carnival or a belated Fourth of July." Loud "Amens" could be heard periodically during the proceedings from spectators, and applause greeted the lawyers' repartee.

Eventually, the whole trial was moved to the lawn outside the courthouse because the unruly throngs in the courtroom were weakening the floor, which was in danger of collapsing. Five thousand spectators, sweltering in the July heat, stood around or watched from wooden benches, and the press sat at tables nearby. A huge banner proclaiming "Read Your Bible" hung from the building in clear view of the jury, alongside another stating "Read Your Evolution."

After a tumultuous trial, which included Darrow cross-examining Bryan on his literal reading of the Bible, Darrow asked the jury to convict so the case could be appealed. Eventually, the appellate court reversed Scopes's conviction on technical grounds. But along the way, the press had a field day, giving both the protagonists and their important issue unprecedented coverage. However, both sides savored the attention, and the public witnessed an important debate by notable advocates.

The raucous trial of Bruno Hauptmann in 1935 for the kidnapping of the Lindbergh baby offers another classic example of the persistence and growth of press coverage of sensational crimes. Charles Lindbergh was a national hero whose solo transatlantic flight in the *Spirit of St. Louis* made him famous worldwide. His wife, Anne Morrow Lindbergh, was the daughter of a socially prominent banker and diplomat. Their perfect life was shattered when their first child was kidnapped mysteriously from their home in Hopewell, New Jersey.

Bruno Richard Hauptmann, a carpenter who had immigrated to New Jersey from Germany twelve years earlier, was arrested and charged with the kidnapping after a two-and-a-half-year manhunt that became an avidly followed national melodrama. Though the evidence against Hauptmann has since been seriously questioned,[22] the press presumed his guilt from the first headline—"Lindbergh Kidnapper Jailed"—and press coverage was by any standard excessive and prejudicial.

The scene of the trial was a courtroom in the small town of Flemington, New Jersey—designed in 1828 to hold two hundred spectators, but jammed with five hundred—a thirty by forty-five foot room with six pew-like wooden benches and a gallery above for spectators. Curious observers from all over the world came to see what H. L. Mencken called "the greatest story since the Resurrection." The international press arrived in droves, including 350 reporters (William Randolph Hearst alone sent 50) and 130 cameramen. The line was crossed from news to entertainment. Celebrity commentators such as Walter Winchell and Damon Runyon, sports figures such as Jack Dempsey, and theatrical stars such as Ginger Rogers made cameo appearances. Some tourists came to see the trial, others to see the journalists and celebrities.

Telegraph and telephone facilities, set up in empty courthouse rooms to enable correspondents to file their stories quickly created a "cat's cradle of wires." Foreshadowing the docudramas that came later in the century, actors performed the trial participants' roles on radio daily. Hidden movie cameras provided film clips that were shown in movie theaters. Coverage exceeded any comparable event in American history. The press thrust itself into the case, conducting investigations and paying participants for their stories.[23] Thousands of sightseers crowded around the courthouse on Sundays, taking pictures of each other in the jury box and the judge's chair. The trial became "the center of the universe" and "a circus," to quote the *American Mercury*. Novelist Edna Ferber added, "It made you want to resign as a member of the human race."[24] Hauptmann was convicted and later executed, though the excesses of the press in this case resulted in a subsequent ban on cameras in courts that lasted approximately fifty years.

Movies were the next new medium to play a part in the publicity of notorious trials. Films taken by the U.S. Army were used as evidence at the eleven-month-long Nuremberg trials of Nazi war criminals in 1945 and 1946. They also recorded this internationally important historical event, and added a theatrical aspect to the trial. At these International Military Tribunal proceedings, Army newsreels were used as evidence to prove the involvement of key German commanders in the four sweeping offenses charged. The medium itself, to borrow a future phrase, became part of the message, as well as a new and powerful messenger.

Lighting equipment used to film the trials was so intrusive that several defendants in the dock wore dark glasses. Movie newsreels broadcast excerpts and sound bites worldwide. The trials in the heavily draped Courtroom 600 of the Palace of Justice were held not only to punish the guilty, but also to present a public display of justice.

Few would argue with the judgment of the American special prosecutor, Supreme Court Justice Robert Jackson, that the trial was not merely a private litigation, but also the public recounting of a great social question. It was ritualistic; but it was educative, as well.

As with most important social issues in the United States, the propriety of press coverage of trials eventually would be decided by the U.S. Supreme Court. Indeed, in the 1960s the court dealt decisively with press-created bedlam both in pretrial and at trial in the celebrated case of Dr. Sam Sheppard, a Cleveland physician whose conviction for murdering his pregnant wife eventually was reversed on the basis of press interference.[25]

The local law enforcement officials in that case quickly concluded that Dr. Sheppard was guilty, and the press adopted its conclusion and took up an "editorial artillery" of persistent front-page assault on the doctor. A coroner's inquest, held in a school gymnasium swarming with reporters and cameramen, was broadcast, though the defendant and his counsel were not allowed to participate. When his lawyer tried to act he was ejected. Years later, Sheppard's appellate lawyers filed with the Supreme Court five volumes of partisan press clippings calling for Sheppard's arrest and conviction.

The trial atmosphere was even worse. The jury was not sequestered and thus was besieged by mail and the media. Cameras on a helicopter photographed the jury viewing the crime scene. Commenting on the case, outside broadcasters such as Walter Winchell described the defendant as a social menace. The small courtroom was overcrowded with media representatives whose carrying on was unrestrained. Every aspect of the trial was reported and photographed with intensity and partisanship.

Twelve years after the 1954 trial, the Supreme Court reversed Sheppard's conviction because the "massive, pervasive and prejudicial publicity that attended his prosecution" deprived the defendant of a fair trial. The late Associate Justice Tom Clark spent eleven pages of his majority opinion detailing the pretrial publicity and five pages describing the intrusive and virulent publicity and commotion at the trial itself. The press had created a "carnival atmosphere," the Court concluded, and as a result, rather than being a responsible "handmaiden of effective judicial administration" and a guardian against the miscarriage of justice, the press had become the cause of prejudice and passion that the trial court had failed to control. Justice Clark censured the press and the bar and called upon both to take steps to regulate themselves.

Television came late to the free press-fair trial conflict. The medium itself came into public use around mid-century and was soon ubiquitous. In 1997, more than 98 percent of American homes had television sets (over 211 million) and 60 percent had cable channels.[26]

In its early years, television coverage outside the courtroom merely magnified the general problem of press influence on the trial process. Historic bans against broadcasting in courtrooms barred cameras from courts. In the 1960s, some states began experimenting with televising trials, but in 1965 one Texas case led to a Supreme Court decision that temporarily stopped the practice.[27] In *Estes v. Texas*, there was intense local interest in the trial of a financial wheeler-dealer with national political connections. The pretrial hearing was marked by electric cables that snaked through the courtroom, and the whole atmosphere of the trial seemed jeopardized by the presence of the clumsy new equipment. The circumstances played into the fears of traditionalists who doubted television's maturity. The worst fears of critics—that television would disrupt and demean the judicial atmosphere—seemed to be justified. In the *Estes* case, the Supreme Court condemned the practice, while leaving open the question whether television was banned completely or whether only its excesses would lead to reversal of convictions.

A decade and a half later, in the 1981 appeal of a Florida criminal conviction, the Supreme Court again addressed the constitutionality of televised trials. This time, it deferred to the states on the question of permitting and monitoring televised trials. The Court set out constitutional guidelines allowing states to experiment with televised trials under conditions that assured appropriate solemnity. In the following decade, most states did experiment with televising trials. By the 1990s, a twenty-four-hour cable channel was regularly televising hundreds of cases around the country.

In 1995, all the questions about the propriety of television in courts and its impact outside the court in establishing public opinion came to universal public attention in the extraordinary double-murder trial of O. J. Simpson. The year-long Simpson trial was covered on site by more than twelve hundred domestic and foreign reporters; there was daily gavel-to-gavel coverage by Court TV and many other television outlets. The case soon spawned a small library of books and articles, along with saturation news coverage of the case and every tangential issue it raised. One report estimated that a worldwide television audience of 150 million people stopped what it was doing in order to watch the announcement of the verdict.

Inevitably, people referred to the case as the "trial of the century." The crime itself was the stuff of legend, redolent with melodramatic issues to interest everyone—interracial marriage, drugs, sex, domestic violence, the fast Hollywood life. *Los Angeles Times* columnist David Shaw wrote: "The Simpson story combines the sensational and the substantive, the voyeuristic and the visceral. It presses every hot button. It's a Bayeaux tapestry of contemporary American culture."[28] Serious journalists compared it to *Othello*, the Greek tragedies, Theodore Dreiser's novels; some called it a TV game show, the ultimate reality TV.

The case involved a celebrity almost everyone knew and admired. As a football star, O. J. Simpson had won the Heisman Trophy in college, excelled in professional sport for many years, and later was a regular sports commentator on television. In addition, because he appeared in movies and advertisements, he was widely recognized. Finally, because of his charm and good looks, his image was appealing across racial and economic lines. If ever anyone began a case benefiting from a genuine presumption of innocence, despite prosecutors' and police officials' claims that they had a mountain of incriminating evidence, it was the popular Simpson.

The announcement of his ex-wife's murder (and that of her friend Ron Goldman) and his arrest commanded national and international news coverage. A huge, high-tech city of TV and radio equipment (including eighty miles of TV cables) and a community of permanent and roving reporters settled into "Camp O.J." in downtown Los Angeles, and at the later civil trial in Santa Monica, California, for a year-long siege of trial coverage. The additional administrative court costs to California taxpayers to accommodate all this public attention totaled more than $8 million. People were torn between "indignation and fascination," the *New York Times* reported; the trial coverage "hijacked our culture." A national obsession, it "held the nation in thrall for 16 months," the *Los Angeles Times* reported.

The media pursued and was used by everyone having anything to do with the case, and some who had little to do with it. CNN's anchor, Jim Moret, reported, "We were as much a tool and a conduit for each side as we were an investigating arm of our own organization." The *Los Angeles Times* dubbed the media "both players and chroniclers, purveyors of news and pawns of the legal spinmeisters." The tabloid media paid for stories, but were credited by the *New York Times* for having shaped the public perception of the case. With the *National Enquirer* repeatedly breaking stories, the longstanding distinction between the mainstream and tabloid press had become blurred. Network magazine-style shows aired more than a hundred Simpson stories.

With television allowed in the courtroom, the roomful of local citizens was now a global village of viewers who could watch the extraordinarily engaging trial. Most journalists covering the case observed the trial on television screens in the press office in the courthouse. Of the fifty eight seats in the small courtroom, twenty-four were available for the media; seven seats were assigned permanently (to two book authors and five news organizations) and seventeen on a rotating basis. As the *Los Angeles Times*'s Shaw noted, "the media played a pivotal role in this most bizarre drama." As a result of television, the defense attorneys "were trying two cases simultaneously, one in Judge Ito's courtroom and one, through the news media, in the court of public opinion." NBC reported that the intense media scrutiny prompted some witnesses to refuse to testify and others to come forward.

As the trial progressed, and the drive continued to satisfy the public appetites the media itself had created, the accuracy of press coverage was questioned. The Los Angeles Police Department press liaison complained that many press representatives had "lost their compass."

Careless and erroneous stories emerged. Journalists began interviewing other journalists, causing one Court TV anchor to complain about an "echo chamber of errors." ABC's Jeff Greenfield called the case "the Chernobyl of American journalism." "We in the media have met the circus, and we are it,"[29] *Los Angeles Times* reporter Howard Rosenberg concluded.

One reaction to this extraordinary public involvement in a criminal trial was to blame television for the sins of jurisprudence. Whatever one deplored about that case—the court management, the lawyering, the jury verdict—was blamed on the camera that recorded it. The *Washington Times* predicted that the case would provide opponents of court television "with their best weapon in thirty years of trying to put trial television off the air." Indeed, a widespread reaction against cameras in courts followed the Simpson trial. Dissenters, such as former Los Angeles District Attorney Ira Reiner, reminded critics that it was not the cameras in the courtroom that were responsible for all the media commotion. "Indeed, the live camera provides an antidote to some of the media frenzy."[30]

As each new medium has been added to the press coverage of crime news and the trial process, the same questions have been raised about the press's impact upon prevailing notions of the nature of the judicial process. Does the public attention to an investigation and trial preclude a fair trial? Do cameras demean and disrupt courts? Do the participants to the trial process—judges, attorneys, jurors, witnesses—negatively alter their behavior because they are being watched widely?

Often, when a notorious trial captures the public and the press, excesses occur, followed by recriminations and resolutions. What we call the "trial of the century" has become a veritable genre. In addition to the cases mentioned, many others come to mind: the Watergate and Iran-Contra trials, the Chicago Seven case, the Rosenbergs, Alger Hiss, Charles Manson, Jimmy Hoffa, Muhammad Ali, the Berrigans, Patty Hearst, Sirhan Sirhan, and Jack Ruby, to name just a few. Each seemed at the time to be unique in the volume of its press coverage, as well as in the issues raised and the personalities involved.

With the advent of television coverage of trials, the question has become whether differences of degree have created a difference in kind. Critics of the practice believe that television in the courts is the final interference by the First Amendment into the world of the Sixth Amendment. Proponents of the practice believe that, properly administered, television is a neutral mirror, a mannered reflection of reality, the ultimate compromise in a historic dilemma.

—

Sensational trials receive disproportionate attention, whether they are civil or criminal cases. In the classic scenario, a crime is committed, followed by a high-visibility investigation. A suspect is arrested; perhaps this is the guilty party, perhaps not. Newspapers, radio, television, and even motion pictures, in their zeal to bring the offender to justice and to inform the public about the workings of criminal law (not to mention their desire to sell what appeals to the public's appetite), publicize the case extensively. The accused's description, background, prior convictions, statements, and confession are displayed on the front page of newspapers or on television screens. Police and prosecutors make proclamations, and defense lawyers attempt to put a spin on the evolving information. Sides are taken, and partisanship often prevails. Rumors, third-party statements (identified, verified, or not), and editorial opinions all become part of this hodgepodge of public information. Although these facts and opinions may relate to evidence that will later be held inadmissible at the trial, they help to mold the public's attitude toward the crime and the accused. To deny the force of public curiosity about crime news is to ignore reality.

As the technology has improved and its access and pervasiveness have expanded, it has not been unusual for most of the community to know many facts about an accused even before he or she is arraigned, much less tried. In extreme situations, the crime itself has been viewed as it occurred. When Jack Ruby shot Lee Harvey Oswald, 42 million people watched the murder live on their television sets, and 90 percent of the adult population saw repeat broadcasts within a few hours. Before Rodney King's assailants ever came to trial, probably a larger American public had repeatedly seen the videotapes of his beating. O. J. Simpson's long, strange Bronco ride on a Los Angeles highway before his arrest was seen by a vast network of viewers, but the videotapes—which many felt were damning evidence of his consciousness of guilt—inexplicably were not shown to the jury by the prosecutors at the trial.

Press coverage of sensational trials may inform a concerned public about events it has a legitimate interest in understanding (the Iran-Contra prosecutions for government malfeasance, for example) or about the quality of its justice system (that it is not racist, for example). In this regard, the coverage may improve public understanding of the justice system and protect defendants from abuse by the state.

But the press's motives for its trial coverage may also be less wholesome and noble. Trial by newspaper and television often is based upon salability, curiosity, and opinion. The media are interested in selling crime news, and the public is interested in learning about it. But trial by jury is based on standards of relevancy, competency, and veracity. The court, basing its decisions on the rules of evidence, determines what evidence shall be admitted, and the jury decides whom to believe. Thus, the community as a whole may get one view of the case through the mass media while the jury gets another through the judicial processes of the trial. If the result of the judicial inquiry is not in accord with public opinion, as shaped by the press, confidence in the judicial system may be impaired. As the Supreme Court noted, it would be the grossest perversion of the rationale offered by late Associate Supreme Court Justice Oliver Wendell Holmes, Jr., for the First Amendment's protection of free speech, to suggest that it is also true of the thought behind a criminal charge "that the best test of truth is the power of the thought to get itself accepted in the competition of the market."[31]

When a trial has sensational aspects, public interest is intense. Divorce and adultery (Woody Allen), butchery (Jeffrey Dahmer), insanity (John Hinckley), passion (Lorena Bobbitt), scorned love (Jean Harris), drugs (Marion Barry), and politics (Sacco and Vanzetti, Alger Hiss, the Chicago Seven) sell. They appeal to the public's prurient, morbid, or elemental curiosities. Everyone becomes a vicarious juror. Courtrooms are packed. Agents of the press are everywhere. A generally undignified and turbulent atmosphere often prevails in the precincts surrounding the formal world of jurisprudence.

What happens when courtroom cameras are added to the mix and notorious trials are broadcast worldwide? Celebrity and notoriety of a new dimension is added to all the other pressures on trial partici- pants. The actual triers of the case may be threatened by interested parties or by partisan members of the public. Parties or spectators may attempt to discuss the case with jurors, necessitating procedures to keep them incommunicado. Judges, too, may be pressured by strong community views.

As such trials progress, the press continues to flood the public with reports and opinions. Public opinion polls are taken to determine the "popular" outcome. If jurors are not kept in seclusion throughout the trial (itself a problematic practice), these activities will probably come to their attention. The police and prosecution often make state- ments to the press, or "leak" information to it. The defense may be inclined or forced to reply in kind. Such a climate of public opinion shaping is hardly conducive to the detached, deliberative, or rational thought that is the ideal at trials.

After the trial, the judge, jurors, and counsel may be vilified for their part in the proceedings. Participants may make public state- ments; the winners, losers, witnesses, and jurors may write books and appear on popular interview shows. Witness the post-trial scram- ble for attention and payoff after the Simpson trial.

The pressures then shift to the appellate courts. Since the appeals courts are not as directly connected with the action in the case, such pressure may have less impact on their decisions. However, in some cases, such as the Rosenbergs' appeal of their capital sentence, the public pressures on an appellate judge can be intense. This is so even in civil cases. Imagine the community pressures a chauvinistic public put on the Cleveland judge considering a requested injunction against the Browns' owner Art Modell's plan to move his football team to Baltimore!

What is the "public interest" in the administration of justice? Is a public burlesque the only alternative to Star Chamber secret trials? Is the proper antidote to in-camera proceedings on-camera appearances?

A 1950 case highlights the dilemma that arises from this clash of fundamental liberties. A radio broadcaster was held in contempt of court for announcing on his news program that a man had been arrested for committing a despicable crime, and that the suspect, who had previously committed a similar crime, had confessed. His report was accurate. When the accused was brought to trial, his confession and previous conviction were vital evidence. As a result of the great public interest in the crime, the widely heard broadcast had a pervasive impact.

The broadcaster appealed his contempt conviction to the Supreme Court, and it was reversed.[32] In a unique twist, opposing amicus curiae briefs were filed by two civil liberties groups. One favored conviction of the contumacious broadcaster, arguing that the defendant's right to a fair trial must be of uppermost concern. The other brief sought acquittal, urging that in any conflict such as this, freedom of the press should prevail. Is there an alternative between these extremes, or must one choose either the rock of censorship or the whirlpool of prejudiced trials?

One might be inclined, at least viscerally, to believe that since something must be done, and since the accused can do little to quell publicity (some, of course, seek it for their own ends), the communications media either must exercise self-restraint or take the chance of being restrained by the courts. Press protestations about the importance of First Amendment policies have been called "pious platitudes," and their promises to curb excesses no more than questionable contrition. Proposed press restrictions, however, are fraught with constitutional perils as great as those arising from any interference with the right to fair trial.

One reason the venerable free press-fair trial conflict is particularly perplexing is that it is not one between right and wrong, but rather between right and right. In such a contest, no wise observer wants there to be a loser. As the late Associate Justice Hugo Black wrote in one such case, "For free speech and fair trials are two of the most cherished policies of our civilization, and it would be a trying task to choose between them."[33]

Indeed, the more vigorous and influential the press, the more likely that the trial process will be fair; and the more independent the trial system, the safer will be the press that describes its workings. As the late Chief Justice Warren Burger wrote in 1986, "It is difficult to disagree in the abstract with the court's analysis balancing the defendant's right to a fair trial against the public right of access. It is also important to remember that these interests are not necessarily inconsistent. Plainly, the defendant has a right to a fair trial but, as we have repeatedly recognized, one of the important means of assuring a fair trial is that the process be open to neutral observers."[34]

The confounding question arises when the free exercise of one fundamental constitutional right conflicts, or seems to conflict, with the operation of the other. Does television's portrayal of the judicial system at work cause unfair trials by altering the trial's atmosphere and the participants' behavior? There are public policy questions, as well, about televised trials—complex questions of taste, commercialism, traditions, and goals.

Paradoxically, in broadcasting to a dispersed and distant audience, an invisible camera seems to present a more precise and complete portrayal of the proceedings than is possible in traditional reporting by print reporters or broadcasters. They, too, are present in court; their summaries are necessarily subjective, diluted, and incomplete versions of what actually transpired; and their actions—for better or worse—raise the same questions as does the television camera.

—

The following chapters describe the evolution of the law regarding free press and fair trials, present the status of cameras in American courts at the end of the twentieth century, explore the basis for the widespread fears about courtroom cameras, and conclude with recommendations for balancing two important rights so that they can be exercised in a compatible and mutually helpful fashion.

Chapter 2

THE FREE PRESS, THE FAIR AND PUBLIC TRIAL

A CONSTITUTIONAL CONUNDRUM

Within a few years of the adoption of the Constitution, the First Amendment was added to provide a bulwark against actions by the federal government abridging freedom of the press. In 1925, the Supreme Court ruled that freedom of the press was "among the fundamental personal rights and liberties protected by the due process clause of the Fourteenth Amendment from impairment by the states."[1] Few rights are more firmly established in American law. Though there is little to question about the principle, however, its application has caused vexing, recurring confrontations.

At the time the printing press was invented, absolute monarchies controlled most of Europe. The Tudors and Stuarts reigned in England. The press was considered to exist solely as a servant of the state. Truth was second to efficient government, and efficient government meant complete compliance of subjects to the will of the rulers. Most of the press was government owned. Private publishers were controlled by the Crown through grants, which could be revoked at pleasure. Since, under this view, the state was superior to the individual, knowledge was best passed on to the people through a controlled press fostering unity of thought. Under this authoritarian scheme, there was no room for criticism of the state or its leaders.[2]

The rigid and strict contempt rules enforced in England today are remnants of this inhibited notion of the meaning of a free press.

Toward the end of the seventeenth century, the spread of literacy, the growth of private enterprise, and the development of democracy brought an end to royal monopolies over the press. Still, government reasserted its authority by prosecuting individuals for treason and sedition if they printed information inimical to the state, and for contempt if their publications were thought to interfere with justice.

The beginning of the eighteenth century saw a refocusing of the relationship between government and its subjects, led by thinkers such as Milton and Locke in England and Jefferson in America. Their libertarian philosophy was based on the theory that human beings were rational actors capable of advancing their own best interests.[3] According to this philosophy, society would make the right decisions through the competition of individual ideas. Individual judgments should be based on a choice among opinions competing in a free marketplace of ideas. The press was seen as an extralegal check on government. Thus, publishers should be able to report facts harmful to the government, if true.

A more conservative view, expressed by William Blackstone,[4] equated freedom of the press with the mere absence of prior restraint. A much broader understanding of this freedom was developed in the United States, where a free press was considered an agent in the search for truth and a check on government, as well as a medium of entertainment. Nonetheless, some limitations, such as laws prohibiting libel and obscenity, remained as press restrictions.

The spirit of free press has always been vigorous in America. The original colonies, anxious to throw off the authoritarian yoke of the English king, demanded complete freedom of the press. Jefferson articulated this demand when he urged that the press be free, no matter how obnoxious its product.[5]

Out of this laissez-faire climate grew a libertarian theory referred to as the social responsibility view of the press. If the press enjoys special privileges under a democratic government, it consequently owes an obligation to society. The nature of the press's moral duties has never been clearly stated. Yet, with the growth of the press into a giant business and the rise of public educational standards, critics have complained that the accumulation of the press power in the hands of a few has resulted in selfishness, sycophancy, and superficiality. The worst and most mendacious media march under the same flag as the best and brightest. The appropriate ethical standards for the mass media are constantly debated, but rarely determined by government. The overarching concern is that "any agency capable of promoting freedom is also capable of destroying it."[6]

Judicial treatment of freedom of the press has followed a changing course in the United States. Some policymakers, such as the late Supreme Court Justice Hugo Black, have considered First Amendment freedoms absolute.[7] The general tendency, however, has been to balance First Amendment freedoms against other conflicting values. The eminent law professor Zechariah Chafee, reporting in the mid-twentieth century for an influential Commission on Government and Mass Communications, concluded that press freedom, though one of the most important values of a free society, is not absolute. Chafee also questioned whether the modern centralized press was what Milton envisioned in the *Areopagitica*.[8]

Legal controls on the press's coverage of trials historically have fallen into several categories. The doctrine of constructive contempt permitted judicial sanctions against newspapers that interfered with the administration of justice. Bench and bar rules proscribed certain kinds of press practices in courts. And judicial procedures—continuance, change of venue, challenges of jurors, instructions, sequestration—have been used to filter out nonjudicial influences on trials. As a last resort, convictions may be reversed in cases where these filtering procedures fail to prevent prejudice at trial.

THE CONSTRUCTIVE CONTEMPT DOCTRINE

Since the early eighteenth century, judges have summarily punished mischief that affected the administration of justice through the doctrine of Anglo-American law called *constructive contempt*.[9] It has been applied against the press about a hundred times in the past 175 years, though it has fallen into disuse toward the end of this century.[10] The doctrine was first rationalized by British judges "to keep the streams of justice clear and pure" so that courts could preserve justice for those before it. In some cases, the power was enlisted to punish the press for criticizing the judge himself, or as the institutional euphemism put it, "the court itself." Newspaper publishing was "a perilous adventure," the British jurist Lord Goddard admonished in one such case.

The English rule today is still more harsh than its American counterpart, no doubt due to the different prevailing standards (not the least of which is the First Amendment) governing courts and press in each country. The press has a more freewheeling tradition here, though it has had its share of battles with hostile judges.[11] Use of the constructive contempt power against the American press has been sporadic and usually, on appeal, unsuccessful. Initially, American law embodied the English common law rule. Since 1831, statutes have sanctioned as contempt misbehavior in the presence of the court, "or so near thereto" as to obstruct the administration of justice. But the Supreme Court has drastically cut the range of this law, for example, by interpreting the "or so near thereto" clause as a *geographical* rather than a *causal* limitation. Since most press publications (at least in the era before television) occur neither in nor near the court, the power to punish contemptuous publications has been effectively eliminated in the United States by judicial interpretation, if not by the First Amendment directly.

The Supreme Court has applied the "clear and present danger" test in some constructive contempt cases to bar convictions of newspapers, generally finding that the free discussion of the case did not impede the defendants' right to a fair trial. Indeed, the present effect of these collective cases has been to give the press virtual immunity from contempt convictions in these situations.

BENCH AND BAR RULES

During the first decades of the twentieth century, radio and cameras captured the highlights of notorious trials, though the American Bar Association (ABA) opposed the practice, declaring that it "shocks our sensibilities."[12] In the aftermath of the media madhouse during the Hauptmann trial for kidnapping the Lindbergh baby, the organized bar and judicial administrators called for codes of professional responsibility.[13] In 1937, Canon 35 of the Canons of Judicial Ethics was adopted, which called for "fitting dignity and decorum" in court, barred taking photographs in the courtroom during sessions and recesses, and forbade the broadcasting of court proceedings. These practices, the Canon declared, "detract from the essential dignity of the proceedings," degrade the court, and create misconceptions in the public's mind. ABA committees issued opinions condemning the broadcasting of trials as unfair to the parties.[14] This standard became entrenched in the law as a result of the *Estes* case in 1965, a development that is described in the next chapter.

In 1952, Canon 35 was amended to add television broadcasts of court proceedings to the earlier ban because they "distract the witness in giving his testimony."[15] This ban was interpreted rigorously, even barring judges from appearing on a commercial television program that simulated or recreated a judicial proceeding.[16] The only exception to the ban was court-supervised ceremonial naturalization proceedings.[17]

In 1972, the ABA adopted Canon 3A(7) of its Code of Judicial Conduct, which replaced Canon 35 of the Code of Judicial Ethics. This canon confirmed and readopted the ban on television. Most states adopted rules that mirrored Canon 3A(7), and when those rules were challenged, state courts upheld them.[18] However, in 1978 the Conference of State Chief Justices adopted a resolution "advocating state experimentation with camera coverage."[19] States began to experiment,[20] and eventually the practice was approved by the U.S. Supreme Court (see chapter 3).

Following extensive experimentation in thirty-eight states, ABA Standard 8–3 was enacted in 1982. It removed the ban and replaced it with a general rule inhibiting unrestricted camera coverage of state court cases, but permitting it in "the sound discretion of the trial court pursuant to an expressly formulated set of rules enacted by the appropriate judicial supervisory authority."

The federal courts have been more restrictive. In 1944, Congress passed Rule 53 of the Federal Rules of Criminal Procedure, which banned taking photographs or radio broadcasting during criminal trials in the federal courts. That ban was reaffirmed by the Judicial Conference of the United States in 1962, 1980, and 1994. However, as Court TV's lawyers have urged, Congress could change its mind and repeal Rule 53, even if the Judicial Conference did not change its policy, since "Congress has undisputed power to regulate the practice and procedure of federal courts."[21] Congress has oversight powers over the federal courts' rule-making, and it has the power to legislate. Therefore, it could repeal Rule 53 and permit cameras in courts.

A bill has been proposed to do just that. H.R. 12–80 would give the presiding judge in any federal court discretionary power to permit "photographing, electronic recording, broadcasting, or televising" court proceedings over which he or she presides. Called the "Sunshine in the Courtroom Act," it would apply to civil and criminal trials and appeals. The proposed law gives the U.S. Judicial Conference the authority to promulgate advisory guidelines. Constitutional scholar Alan Morrison agrees that Congress has the power to pass a statute amending Rule 53, but points out that the separation of powers doctrine forbidding one branch of government from interfering with the activities of another coequal branch could lead to a standoff.[22] The Supreme Court would then have to rule on its own refusal to follow the mandate of a new Rule 53.

PROTECTIVE PROCEDURES

The law has developed a number of filtering devices designed to block out whatever prejudicial effects pretrial information published about a criminal case might have on a jury. These procedures are intended to serve as a screen to keep nonjudicial particles out of the carefully regulated atmosphere of the jury trial system. Of course, they are not 100 percent effective or there would be no free press-fair trial problem.

"The theory of our system," Justice Oliver Wendell Holmes wrote, "is that the conclusions to be reached in a case will be induced only by evidence and argument in open court, and not by any outside influence, whether of private talk or public print."[23] Nonjudicial evidence that could not be allowed at trial must not come to the jury's attention through any other avenue. Moreover, public pressure should not be brought to bear upon prospective jurors, who are, again in Justice Holmes's words, "extremely likely to be impregnated by the envisioning atmosphere." Justice Felix Frankfurter put it this way: "Precisely because the feeling of the outside world cannot, with the utmost care, be kept wholly outside the courtroom, every endeavor must be taken in a civilized trial to keep it outside."[24]

In the courtroom, special requirements must be met to protect the lay decision-makers on the jury. The general purpose of this aspect of the law—to ensure that jurors are not exposed to knowledge or influence about a case except that which emerges at trial—has been interpreted rigidly by most observers. One commentator, somewhat unrealistically, has said: "The minds of a jury may be likened to 12 test tubes," in that they are not to be used for important careful experiments when they are soiled by foreign elements.[25]

The law attempts to guarantee impartial juries through four procedures: (1) the motion before trial to change the venue (location) of the case; (2) the motion before trial to delay the case to a later date; (3) the voir dire examination of prospective jurors by the judge and counsel at the beginning of the trial to determine their freedom from bias or prejudgment; and (4) the judge's instructions to the jury at the end of the presentation of the case. A number of other remedies are also discussed below.

Continuance and Change of Venue

Continuance and change of venue are procedures developed in the common law and adopted everywhere in the United States by constitution, statute, or rule of court. These procedures seek to abate the potentially adverse effects of publicity by either delaying the trial until things cool off, or by moving it to a location where the presumed influence of the press and public feeling would be less likely, if not totally absent. That a defendant is constitutionally guaranteed a speedy trial in the place where the crime is supposed to have been committed has not been considered an objection to these two procedures, which are designed for the defendant's benefit. The rationale behind continuance is that the right to delay for good reasons is part of the inherent power of courts to hear and determine cases. The rationale of the change of venue is that it is a means to a constitutional end—trial by an impartial jury.[26]

The rationale behind the change of venue procedure was articulated by a Minnesota court in a highly publicized romance-murder case:

> Courts can do little to restrain news media from printing or broadcasting what they claim is news, but when it appears that the public has been subjected to so much publicity about a case that it seems unlikely that a fair trial can be had in the locality in which the trial normally would be held, the court can and should see to it that the trial is transferred to another locality in which it is more probable that a fair trial can be had.[27]

The U.S. Supreme Court endorses the same rule and applies a balanced, practical rationale for it. The jury must be impartial, but not entirely ignorant of the facts of a case:

> In these days of swift, widespread and diverse methods of communication, an important case can be expected to arouse the interest of the public in the vicinity, and scarcely any of those best qualified to serve as jurors will not have formed some impression or opinion as to the merits of the case. This is particularly true in criminal cases. . . . It is sufficient if the juror can lay aside his impression or opinion and render a verdict based on the evidence presented in court.[28]

In some places a defendant may move for a change of venire—that is, ask that a new panel of jurors be brought in from another area. This procedure is designed to serve the same purpose as the change of venue without the difficulty of moving the trial itself. It is thought that there is a public interest in trying cases in the community where the crime was committed in order to maintain public confidence in the criminal law process by keeping the process visible.

The related, but somewhat different, idea behind the continuance has been described in these words:

> While a change of venue is designed to avoid local prejudice by transferring the case out of the community, and will therefore be of value only when the hostile feeling has not permeated the jurisdiction, continuance, which involves removal in time from the focus of the prejudice against the defendant, will be appropriate where this hostility exists throughout the jurisdiction but can be expected to fade within a reasonable time.[29]

As much sense as these two techniques make, they are not used frequently and are in fact of questionable value in causes célèbres—those very cases where they are most likely to be sought. The press is so ubiquitous nowadays that it can rekindle interest in a case of strong public interest that has been moved or delayed. Decades ago, a federal court in New York admitted: "Modern means of news communication have taken away many of the reasons for the transfer of the cause célèbre which may have existed 50 years ago."[30] Whenever and wherever notorious cases are tried, the publicity will follow.

Moreover, once community feelings about a case are aroused, they may persist on their own. Thus, the late Judge Learned Hand said in response to motions for continuance and change of venue in the famous Communist trials in New York City:

> That such feeling did exist . . . is indeed true; but there was no reason to suppose that it would subside by any delay which would not put off the trial indefinitely. The choice was between using the best means available to secure an impartial jury and letting the prosecution lapse. It was not as though the prejudice had been local, so that it could be cured by removal to another district; it was not as though it were temporary so that there was any reasonable hope that with a reasonable continuance it would fade . . . we must do as best we can with the means we have.[31]

The dilemma is that where these remedies may be most needed, they are least likely to work. Indeed, arguments about invoking these procedures to move or delay trials may compound the difficulty they set out to solve—further publicity about the case ensues and the problem spirals.

Another difficulty with these two procedures is the hesitancy of courts to use them. Whether judges are skeptical about the potential prejudicing effect of press publications (in other contexts they are not), or merely hesitant to pass their problems on to other judges, they frequently deny motions for continuances or changes of venue. Proof of more than a juror's exposure to publicity is required by most judges. But how can any but the wealthiest and most resourceful defendants or their lawyers show more?

Judges have refused to grant continuances or changes of venue until it becomes clear that selection of an impartial jury is impossible, adopting a wait-and-see approach to complaints about prejudicial publications. Once a jury is empaneled, they argue, why continue a case or change its site? The fact that the jury has been empaneled is the best proof that an impartial jury could be found. Other courts have indulged in seesaw logic, denying a motion for change of venue on the ground that continuance was the appropriate remedy, and vice versa. The courts do not grant these motions simply because there has been significant publicity about a case.

Continuances are rarely allowed on the grounds of prejudicial publicity, and then only when there are extraordinary circumstances. For example, continuances were ordered in a case where excessive pretrial publicity arose out of a prior legislative investigation, and in another case where public interest was so intense that lynch mobs were formed, houses burned, and the National Guard was eventually needed to restore order. Nevertheless, one bafflingly imaginative court denied a requested continuance on the theory that if jurors would perjure themselves, or public officials would indulge in misconduct, they would do so without public pressures, too. Another court denied the remedy because it feared that granting a continuance might create a greater harm by arousing the public about the lethargy of the judicial process.

The motion for a change of venue is based upon less subjective criteria than continuance. Ordinarily, the party seeking change of venue must accompany the request with affidavits attesting that the climate of public opinion in that community precludes a fair trial. This practice often leads to a battle of affidavits between the prosecution and defense, the former claiming the virginal virtue of the prospective jury panel or that the defendant is shopping for a favorable forum, and the latter arguing the complete corruption of the prospective jury panel by public pressures and yellow journalism. Sometimes public-opinion polls are offered as proof of the need to remove a trial to another, less prejudiced community.

Even when they are granted, both remedies are less than totally satisfactory. The defendant will have been caused delay, expense, and inconvenience, and will have been forced to sacrifice the constitutional right to a speedy or a local trial.

Even so, somewhere between sensational cases of nationwide notoriety and the overwhelming majority of routine trials where prejudicial publicity is not a problem, there are some contentious cases where continuance and change of venue could perform a real service. Even in some highly publicized cases, initial community excitement and animus may abate with the passage of time. And even with the pervasiveness of the modern-day news media, some localities will be less absorbed and opinionated by news of crimes than the localities in which they occurred. I've prosecuted sensational cases, including one retrial after a hung jury, and learned that, even in these unusual circumstances, with a little ingenuity impartial juries can be empaneled. The Supreme Court itself has admonished that until the courts have used the devices available to them to cancel any impact on jurors that may have been caused by the press, verdicts will not be upheld and the press will not be restricted.

Voir Dire

In voir dire examination, both sides may question prospective jurors chosen at random from the jury rolls in an attempt to find an impartial panel to try the case—at least in theory. In reality, each side wants a favorable panel rather than a totally impartial one.

If it can be established through formal questioning by the judge, the plaintiff or defense counsel, or the prosecuting attorney that pretrial publicity has caused a juror to form an unalterable opinion about the case, that juror can be challenged for cause. Challenges for cause are available in all jurisdictions and are unlimited in number. If a challenge for cause is overruled, the juror may nonetheless be challenged peremptorily. Every jurisdiction allows some peremptory challenges, for which no cause need be proved. The number of peremptory challenges allowed usually is determined by statute in civil cases, and by the penalty for the particular crime in criminal cases.

The federal courts have varying procedures for challenges: some allow counsel to question the jurors in voir dire examination, with the judge remaining passive (eleven states follow this procedure); others allow counsel to conduct pretrial questioning after the judge has questioned the prospective jurors (twenty-nine states); some provide only for questioning by the judge and allow none by counsel (ten states). In these latter cases, counsel ordinarily may submit questions for the judge to ask.

Here again, what seems like a logical solution is not necessarily a workable one. The courts apply Judge Learned Hand's do-as-best-we-can approach. As the Supreme Court has stated:

> The theory of the law is that a juror who has formed an opinion cannot be impartial. Every opinion which he may entertain need not necessarily have that effect. In these days of newspaper enterprise and universal education, every case of public interest is almost, as a matter of necessity, brought to the attention of all the intelligent people in the vicinity, and scarcely any one can be found among those best fitted for jurors who has not read or heard of it, and who has not some impression or some opinion in respect to its merits. . . . [T]he court will practically be called upon to determine whether the nature and strength of the opinion formed are such as in law necessarily to raise the presumption of partiality.[32]

In one notorious criminal case, a federal court stated that voir dire is more than a charade and that a juror's word must be accepted at face value. It would be too cynical to believe that jurors would consciously hide their partiality and prejudices, the court stated. Despite the fact that every individual who enters the jury box brings his or her own personality and point of view with them and may not be exempt from the general feelings prevalent in the society, these individuals are trusted to lay such thoughts aside once they take their oath. "If there be human frailty," the court concluded, echoing Judge Hand, "we must do as best we can with the means we have."

Unfortunately, the subtle psychological question of whether or not notoriety has prejudiced a prospective juror is for the most part left to the juror. It seems unlikely that jurors would recognize their own personal prejudices—or, knowing them, would admit to them. However, since there are no empirical data to contradict a declaration of detachment, their word is ordinarily the determining factor. Moreover, the more prejudiced or bigoted the jurors, the less they can be expected to confess forthrightly and candidly their state of mind in open court. The more naive or sincere juror, who might be likely to discard prior knowledge for the purpose of their decision-making duty, would probably be more ready to acknowledge his or her state of mind and thus be challenged.

A further practical problem looms. The more publicized and notorious the crime, the more cumbersome and self-defeating the examination of prospective jurors becomes. When community sentiment becomes inflamed about a horrible crime, it can take weeks to find a suitable panel of jurors. Many members of the bench and experienced trial lawyers recognize that voir dire questioning in sensational cases may be suicide. As Justice Frankfurter said of one case: "every time defense counsel asked a prospective juror whether he had heard a radio broadcast to the effect that his client has confessed to this crime or that he has been guilty of similar crimes, he would by that act be driving just one more nail into [the defendant's] coffin. We think, therefore, that remedy was useless."[33] The risk of antagonizing the jury, or of bringing to its attention unfavorable facts about which it may have had no knowledge, vexes even the most adroit and expert trial attorney. In cases such as the Oklahoma City bombing, few potential panelists could be found anywhere who were free of all information and feelings, and the very questioning of prospective jurors underscored the notoriety of the offense.

The purpose of challenges is to allow each side to attempt to find a fair jury. Counsel questions prospective jurors and makes their choices on the basis of instinct and experience or the advice of experts. Trial lawyers differ in their estimates of the efficiency of the examination. One study of voir dire, based on a series of jury cases in a midwestern federal district court over a year and a half period in the late 1950s, concluded that voir dire examination generally is perfunctory and ineffective in weeding out unfavorable jurors or eliciting crucial data about prejudice. Jury panels resisted the procedure and displayed less than complete candor.[34]

The juror's preconception of guilt will disqualify him or her if its source is direct and its strength is entrenched. Personal knowledge about a case is a basis for disqualification; rumor, general sentiment, or exposure to newspaper reports need not be. Aside from the practical problem with voir dire, there is a theoretical problem in that the line between these two areas is thin and unclear. No juror can adjudge a case without preconceptions. Moreover, if such a person existed, he or she would not be an ideal juror, since the function of the jury is, in part, to apply the mores and sentiments of the community to the law. A juror cannot and should not come to the process untouched by human concerns. As one court said: "Trials cannot be held in a vacuum hermetically sealed against rumor and report. If a mere disclosure of the general nature of the evidence relied on would vitiate a subsequent trial, few verdicts could stand."[35]

Instructions

Along with these filtering procedures, the law provides another purification process—instructions by the court. The judge usually instructs the jurors at the outset of a trial not to expose themselves during the trial to press comments about pending cases. And at the conclusion of the trial the judge will ordinarily tell the jury what it may consider in reaching its verdict, and what it must ignore. W. S. Gilbert described this procedure in *Trial by Jury*:

> *Now, Jury men, hear my advice—*
> *All kinds of vulgar prejudice*
> *I pray you set aside:*
> *With stern judicial frame of mind,*
> *From bias free of every kind,*
> *This trial must be tried.*

The hope is that whatever deleterious effect the press may have had upon a jury's impartiality will be cured by the court's admonition. Thus, in theory, the judge is supposed to be able to wipe out any effects of press reports, personal comments, or knowledge of facts never received in evidence.

There is reason to be skeptical about the efficacy of instructions. The late Judge Jerome Frank equated the practice with Mark Twain's anecdote of the young boy who was told to stand in the corner and not to think about a white elephant. He called reliance on such "ritualistic admonitions" an unrealistic way to cure defects in the composition of a jury. "The futility of that sort of exorcism is notorious," he said. And the late Supreme Court Justice Robert Jackson believed that "the naive assumption that prejudicial effects can be overcome by instructions to the jury . . . all practicing lawyers know to be unmitigated fiction."

Nevertheless, courts regularly allow the question of a fair trial to turn on this ritual, arguing or pretending that the judge's instructions vitiate the effect of any improper knowledge that may have come to the attention of the jury. And great deference is given to the trial judge's discretion by the appellate courts. Furthermore, in long and complicated cases, juries are sometimes confused or annoyed by the court's instructions. It is therefore questionable whether juries are generally scrupulous in heeding the court's instruction.

But courts cannot simply give up when there has been pretrial publicity about a case. As Judge Charles Clark wrote in 1951: "Trial by newspaper may be unfortunate, but it is not new and, unless the court accepts the standard judicial hypothesis that cautioning instructions are effective, criminal trials in large metropolitan cities may well prove impossible."[36] Then, as now, the problem was not a new phenomenon. Years before, Justice Holmes had pointed out that if the mere opportunity for prejudice or corruption was enough to raise a presumption that they existed, it would be hard to maintain jury trials. Another judge pointed out: "The mere fact of unfavorable publicity does not of itself raise a presumption of prejudice. The prejudice must have manifested itself so as to corrupt due process."[37]

Other Protective Procedures

A number of other available procedures are intended to prevent or correct interference by the press with fair trials. Blue ribbon juries—special panels usually composed of a more sophisticated, better-educated class than the ordinary jury—have been used occasionally to ensure that the careful rules of the court control the trial of an unusually complicated or controversial case. It has also been suggested that a defendant who fears a prejudiced jury should be allowed to choose trial by a judge or by a panel of judges.[38] This is predicated on the viewpoint that judges can be exposed to outside pressures and nevertheless try cases fairly. Sometimes the law does allow a defendant to waive his constitutional right to trial by jury, but where it is permitted the court and prosecution must agree.

Recently, courts have resorted increasingly to sequestering juries to avoid exposure to publications during trials. This procedure is expensive, disruptive, and takes its toll on jurors. Whether juries resent the government or develop hostility toward the defendant for inconveniencing them is beyond proof. But one thing is sure: no one likes the practice and it remains a device of last resort, used only in unusual cases.

In cases where extraordinary public pressure surrounding a case has injected outside influences into the trial atmosphere, a jailed defendant may seek habeas corpus relief where all else fails. However, this remedy is technical, cumbersome, prolonged, and used only in flagrant situations. Nevertheless, it can be used (as it was in the *Sheppard* case) to allow the Supreme Court to scrutinize the atmosphere surrounding state court trials and assure that constitutional standards of due process have been met.

CORRECTIVE PROCEDURES

Courts may declare a mistrial, reverse a conviction, or order a new trial on the ground that press influence has deprived a defendant of a fair trial. New trials have been granted for such incidents as mob dominance during trial, an unfair atmosphere in the court itself, and misconduct on the part of jurors. Courts are more likely to grant new trials where the government contributed to the adverse publicity. Of course, these procedures are not cures; they are merely devices to undo injustices already done.

In essence, American law does not guarantee that it will always be possible to find an impartial jury. Indeed, such a goal might be unattainable. However, it does aspire to assure that no defendant's conviction will be upheld if the jury was not impartial.

Where press mischief before the trial does contaminate the proceedings, courts have reversed the conviction rather than punish the press. The classic example of this was a 1951 Florida case, *Shepherd v. Florida*,[39] where sensationalistic press coverage caused the Supreme Court to reverse a state criminal conviction. Four "Negro men" (so described by the court) had been charged with raping a white girl. Virulent and persistent pretrial newspaper coverage reported a confession (never offered at the trial) and called for the death penalty. The fevered press coverage surrounding the case contributed to a mob mentality that resulted in torched homes and vigilantism. On the basis of the trial record, the Supreme Court condemned the circumstances of the conviction, noting that these prejudicial influences on the jury led to the inescapable conclusion that the defendants were prejudged as guilty. Convictions like these, Associate Justice Robert Jackson wrote, do not meet civilized concepts of due process of law.

Pretrial publicity does not always lead to convictions, or even to prejudice. Sometimes a press report actually becomes critical evidence (exculpatory or incriminatory) at a later trial; sometimes it informs the community with extrajudicial information that the subsequent jury is not able to consider. Neither Jack Ruby's brazen execution of Lee Harvey Oswald, nor Rodney King's infamous beating by overzealous Los Angeles policemen, nor O. J. Simpson's live-broadcast Bronco ride were the first or only example of television pervasively portraying acts that juries might later be called upon to weigh as evidence at a criminal trial. The U.S. Supreme Court dealt with this very issue in a 1963 case.[40]

The felony murder conviction and death sentence in that case—

involving a killing during the course of a bank robbery—were reversed because the trial judge improperly denied the defendant's motion for a change of venue. The defendant's confession while in jail was filmed and broadcast widely and repeatedly over local television. Jurors who had seen the film were not challenged, and the judge allowed them to sit. This episode, the Supreme Court ruled, denied due process of law and the basic right to be tried in court under constitutionally circumscribed conditions, and not in jail.

The problem caused by an unruly and disruptive press at the trial itself is easier to cure, and for the past thirty years the guidelines have been clear. The bedlam in notorious cases such as the Hauptmann trial is clearly inconsistent with civilized notions about judicial decorum. It is easier for courts to control the press in the courtroom than in the community, where controls might violate the First Amendment. Since the landmark *Sheppard* case,[41] convictions are reversed when press misconduct occurs at the trial itself.

The Supreme Court issued its *Sheppard* decision on June 6, 1966. In an opinion delivered by then Associate Justice Tom Clark, the Court held that the trial judge in the *Sheppard* case had failed to protect the defendant from "massive, pervasive and prejudicial publicity that attended his prosecution," and that therefore Sheppard "did not receive a fair trial consistent with the Due Process Clause of the Fourteenth Amendment." This was not the appeal of a contempt conviction against the press, but rather an appeal of the defendant's conviction itself, long after it had been originally upheld (the original trial was in 1954).

Justice Clark pointed out that all aspects of the problem of prejudicial publicity were present: participation by public officials, physical intrusions on the participants to the trial (including the defense counsel, the defendant, and the jury), and intensive national coverage. All these elements combined, along with "virulent publicity," to create an environment in the courtroom which the Court described as a "carnival atmosphere" and a "Roman holiday for the news media."

Clark then discussed the legal doctrine appropriate to this situation: "A responsible press has always been regarded as the handmaiden of effective judicial administration, especially in the criminal field," he wrote, pointing out that "The press does not simply publish information about trials but guards against the miscarriage of justice by subjecting the police, prosecutors, and judicial processes to extensive public scrutiny and criticism." He noted the unwillingness of the Supreme Court to use its contempt power to limit directly the traditional freedom of the news media to report about the process of justice. However, he added the qualification that legal trials cannot be carried out like elections, through the use of meeting halls, radios, and newspapers. He reminded us that the Supreme Court has always insisted that criminal cases must tried in a public tribunal, "free of prejudice, passion, excitement, and tyrannical power." The Court's description of the details in the *Sheppard* case demonstrated that the requisite calmness and solemnity of the courtroom were absent, and that there were good reasons to believe that the jury's verdict might not have been based solely on the evidence received in open court.

The Court added that it is not necessary to show specific prejudice in deciding this question, noting that our legal system "has always endeavored to prevent even the probability of unfairness." Justice Clark held that in the *Sheppard* case "the totality of circumstances" demonstrated a lack of the requisite trial fairness. The Court also pointed out that the available, ordinary legal techniques for filtering out prejudice at trial were not used by the judge in that case. The motion for a change of venue was denied; the jury was not sequestered; moreover, no adequate instructions were given to the jury not to read or listen to published news of the case. The trial judge did not make appropriate arrangements to control the actions of the news media; thus, Sheppard was deprived at his trial of the proper judicial serenity and calm to which he was entitled.

The Court placed the responsibility for balancing the competing demands of the press and the law with the courts. Justice Clark's opinion referred to a New Jersey Supreme Court murder case[42] that led to a court rule governing the conduct of state lawyers and police. The rule drew extensive national comment and caused considerable concern among local press and public officials. It banned prosecutors and their lawyer staff members from making statements to news media about alleged confessions or inculpatory admissions by the accused, or to the effect that the case is "open and shut" against the defendant, or with reference to the defendant's prior convictions or arrests. Statements such as these have the capacity to interfere with a fair trial and would not be countenanced. With respect to prosecutors, detectives, and members of local police departments who are not members of the bar, such statements would be deemed an improper interference with the due administration of criminal justice and would constitute conduct unbecoming a police officer, warranting discipline by proper authorities.

The ban applied to defense counsel as well. The right of the state to a fair trial was not to be impeded or diluted by a defense lawyer's out-of-court assertions to news media on the subject of his client's innocence. The proper place to settle the issue is the courtroom. Comments by the defense before or during the trial that have the capacity to influence potential or actual jurors to the possible prejudice of the state would be impermissible.

The New Jersey judge who issued the rule concluded that it would not impinge upon freedom of the press. The implication of his opinion was clear: the bar and the police had better clean their own houses through internal controls or the courts would do it for them, through their judicial powers of contempt and their control over the bar, with the power to censure and even to disbar attorneys.

A fundamental error in the *Sheppard* case, according to Justice Clark, was the trial court's failure to use its power to control publicity. Available procedures, he ventured, "would have been sufficient to guarantee Sheppard a fair trial." The Court enumerated specific steps that the trial judge could have taken to avoid press interference with the judicial process. The presence of the press could have been restricted when it appeared to be acting in a prejudicial or raucous manner. The trial court should have adopted strict rules governing reporters' use of the courtroom. The number of reporters could have been limited, and their physical location could have been set up in a less disruptive way. The press's conduct in the courtroom itself could have been controlled more strictly by the judge.

But mainly, Justice Clark believed, the court should have made efforts to control "the release of leads, information, and gossip to the press by police officers, witnesses and the counsel for both sides." Emphasizing that the inflammatory publicity derived more directly from the court's lack of control than from the press's overindulgence, Clark's opinion suggested that the trial judge "might well have proscribed extra-judicial statements by any lawyers, party, witness, or court official which divulged prejudicial matters." Had the judge, other court officers, and police placed the interest of justice first, the news media soon would have learned to be content with the task of reporting the case as it unfolded in the courtroom, rather than piecing it together from extrajudicial statements.

Observing that the reversal of a case is merely a palliative and not a cure, the Clark opinion called upon trial courts to "take such steps by rule and regulation that will protect their processes from prejudicial outside interferences. Neither prosecutors, counsel for defense, the accused, witnesses, court staff, nor enforcement officers coming under the jurisdiction of the court should be permitted to frustrate its function."[43] Indicating that the bar should clean its own house before it criticizes the press, the majority opinion concluded: "Collaboration between counsel and the press as to information affecting the fairness of a criminal trial is not only subject to regulation, but is highly censurable and worthy of disciplinary measures."

It is more difficult to evaluate the impact of publicity in those cases where there are no disruptions in the courtroom by reporters or by camera equipment, but only the fear that the very presence of the unseen eye of television, decorously and quietly transmitting the image of the trial to a vast audience, in and of itself is prejudicial. That subject is treated in chapter 4.

THE RIGHT TO A PUBLIC TRIAL

The Sixth Amendment's equally venerable and important guarantee that in all criminal prosecutions the accused must have a "public" trial and "an impartial jury" is no less vital a part of a democratic society. Originally a protection against the federal government, it was applied to the states through absorption into the Fourteenth Amendment.[44] This provision also raises questions, even among its adherents. Can an informed jury also be an impartial one? Who has the right—in addition to the accused—to claim access to a courtroom based on the public trial guarantee? The press? The public?

The concept of a public trial is a carryover from English common law. Two different legal procedures developed in Europe and England. In traditional Roman judicial procedure, examination was performed in secret. However, in England, according to one noted historian, "the genius of publicity dominates over its antagonist."[45] One feature of common law English justice is that all judicial trials are held in open court, to which the public has free access.[46] English lawmakers determined that publicity in the administration of the law on the whole was worth more to society than it cost.[47]

The phrase *public trial* is not found in Sir Edward Coke's *Commentary on the Magna Charta* nor in Sir John Fortescue's *De Laudibus Legum Angliae* (1464–1470); nor is it mentioned in the English Petition of Right in 1621 or the 1689 Bill of Rights. It was considered a common law privilege.

Although the exact date of origin of the public trial right in English common law is unknown,[48] several documents provide insight into its history. An early reference to the right to a public trial is found in Sir Thomas Smith's *De Republica Anglorum* (1565).[49] Smith wrote, in the parlance of the times, "Evidences of writinges be shewd, witnesses be sworn and heard before them [the jury] not after the fashion of the civill law but openly, that not only the Judges, the parties and as many as be present may heare what ech witnesse doeth say." He also wrote that a trial "is doone openlie in the presence of the Judges, the Justices, the enquest, the prisoner and so manie as will or can come so neare as to heare it." In recounting criminal proceedings, Smith reported: "In the towne house, or in some open or common place, there is a tribunall or place of judgement made aloft upon the highest bench."

Sir Matthew Hale's *History of the Common Law of England* (1670) notes that evidence is given "in the open court and in the presence of the parties, counsel and all by-standers." Hale viewed this as a valuable feature: "the excellency of this Open course of evidence to the jury, in presence of the judge, jury, parties, and counsel, and even of the adverse witnesses, appears in these particulars. That it openly, and not in private before a commissioner or two, and a couple of clerks; where, oftentimes witnesses will deliver that which they will be ashamed to testify publickly."[50]

Blackstone, citing Hale, also applauded public trials: "the open examination of witnesses viva voce, in the presence of all mankind, is much more conducive to the clearing up of truth than the private and secret examination before an officer or his clerk, in the ecclesiastical courts and all that have borrowed their procedure from the civil law: where a witness may frequently depose that in private which he will be ashamed to testify in a public and solemn tribunal."[51]

The change to open trials was provoked as much by a desire to eliminate command influences by authorities as to secure publicity about trials. It seems that Parliamentary opponents of the Star Chamber did not regard its secrecy and closed proceedings as particularly reprehensible; they were more concerned about its unchecked and arbitrary exercise of power.

Neither the Petition of Right, presented just before the Star Chamber was abolished, nor the Bill of Rights, enacted when the Stuart dynasty was expelled, has anything to say about the right of public trials. Similarly, the famous speech of Lord Andover against the Star Chamber does not mention secrecy of trials. Thus, while an open and public trial is considered a historic safeguard against tyranny, this right was not much considered among the noted historians of the "rights of Englishmen." As legal historian Max Radin noted, "It is likely that the word 'public' was introduced into the list of the rights of free men from the statements in HALE and BLACKSTONE, without very much concrete example in mind of what publicity implied and without a clear idea of what it was meant to secure."[52]

Nevertheless, the American colonists, steeped in Hale and Blackstone, certainly considered the open and public trial of the English common law a venerable liberty. A right to speedy and public trial found formulation in the laws of almost every state, either in charters or in state constitutions, and, of course, in the federal constitution.

According to Radin, "What happened, then, was that a traditional feature of English trials, more or less accidental, was carried over into the American system, and since it was relatively ancient, was treated with the reverence which so many other elements of the common law received."[53]

What of the right to a fair, as well as public, trial? William the Conqueror brought this practice to England. After the Norman Conquest, primitive criminal processes, such as trial by ordeal, gradually declined and the modern notion of trial by jury arose in their place. This method of trying cases came not from ancient customs, but from the exercise of royal prerogative by the Frankish kings, who set up inquests to discover the extent of royal rights and interests in the community, primarily in financial matters.[54] This practice later included inquiries into criminal offenses.

Inquests or assizes, forerunners of the grand jury, became the usual procedure in criminal matters by the end of the twelfth century. Indictment by an inquest created a presumption of guilt. By the thirteenth century, to give the accused a chance to rebut the presumption, he was asked to "put himself upon the country." This meant that the accused would accept the decision of the community on the question of guilt, as it was given by his neighbors on the jury. The exact time when this second, adjudicative (as opposed to investigative) jury developed is not known. By 1302, the defendant was permitted to challenge any juror who sat on the "petit jury."

The members of both types of early juries were chosen specifically for their knowledge of the events in the case, not for their ignorance of relevant information—as is the standard today. By the sixteenth century, however, the historic "witness" style of jury gave way to a procedure in which the litigants produced the evidence upon which a jury free from prior information about the issue relied. This technique, originally used only in civil cases, was extended to criminal trials by 1700.[55]

The petit jury gained independence as a result of the decision in *Bushell's* case.[56] In that case, a juror who ignored a direction by the Crown to bring in a verdict of guilty was jailed after the jury had acquitted the defendant. The juror brought a habeas corpus petition and was freed. Thereafter, the jury was free to decide as conscience and the evidence warranted, not as the government commanded.

In a landmark case in 1649, John Lilburne, accused of high treason before a Special Commission of Oyer and Terminer, demanded and received the right to a public trial.[57] In another renowned case in 1681, a judge responded to the jury's request in the Earl of Shaftesbury's trial to examine witnesses in private: "But certainly it is the best way, both for the king, and for you, that there should, in a case of this nature, be an open and plain examination of witnesses, that all the world may see what they say."[58] Although the jury protested, fearing prejudice to the king if the examinations were conducted publicly, the judge held his position. "It will be no prejudice to the king to have the evidence heard openly in court; or else the king would never desire it."

Opinions abound about the original justification for a public trial. After reviewing the lack of prisoners' rights in seventeenth-century England, one commentator concluded that Hale was thinking not of the rights of the accused when he recorded his history of the common law of England, but rather of the effectiveness of the trial process.[59] The public trial guarantee in English common law was created by officials and most likely expedited convictions, not acquittals.[60] The records of Lilburne's 1649 trial (in which the accused demanded and received the right to a public trial) and the Earl of Shaftesbury's 1681 trial (where the judge overruled the jury's request to examine witnesses in private), however, dispute the theory that the guarantee of a public trial served only to expedite the trial process.

Other legal historians have concluded that a public trial serves to benefit the accused. According to Joel Prentiss Bishop, "In some circumstances, only by an open trial can fair dealing be secured to one unjustly pursued."[61] Witnesses will be less apt to lie in public, and thus defendants wrongly accused will benefit from public trials. "Evil men shrink from the light; and the fear from exposure may restrain them in public from what they would gladly do in private." The American constitutional commentator Thomas M. Cooley elaborated on this theme of protecting personal liberty: "The requirement of a public trial is for the benefit of the accused, that the public may see that he is fairly dealt and not unjustly condemned, and that the presence of interested spectators may keep his triers keenly alive to a sense of their responsibility and to the importance of their functions."[62]

The colonists in America firmly believed in trial by jury. During the Revolution, the Continental Congress granted to the inhabitants of each colony the right to public trials by "their peers of the vicinage,"[63] the right to counsel, and the right to present witnesses. These rights also appeared in state constitutions, and were eventually incorporated into the federal constitution. Most state constitutions also grant the accused the right to a speedy, public, jury trial. The basic aim of these constitutional rights is to ensure the right to a fair trial in open court. "Today almost without exception every state by constitution, statute, or judicial decision requires that all criminal trials be open to the public."[64]

Although part of our common law heritage, it was not always clear to whom the right of public trial belongs. Since the Constitution speaks of this right with respect to the criminal defendant, it appeared to be his or her personal privilege. Yet some cases implied that this privilege also belongs to the public at large.[65] Even if the public does have a right to be present at criminal trials, however, we have no historic working definition of "the public." The audience at most trials is composed of courthouse denizens and unemployed citizens interested in observing the workings of justice, or those with a personal interest in what is transpiring. Such limited public observation of criminal trials, along with press coverage reaching a wider audience, is rationalized as a means of instilling public respect and confidence in the justice system.

American constitutional history provides perspective—but not answers—to current quagmires. The Constitution was adopted only after agreement was reached to amend it to include a bill of rights. Concerned about potential abuses of government power, citizens wanted a document reserving specific rights to the people.[66] James Madison was elected to Congress on the platform that he would propose a bill of rights, and he introduced a list of amendments to the House of Representatives in the First Congress.[67] These amendments included several of the provisions already adopted in existing state constitutions. Although considerable debate ensued over several other amendments, there was little controversy over the passage of what eventually became the Sixth Amendment.

The *Annals of Congress* indicate that the meaning of a "public" trial was not debated. On August 11, 1789, the First Congress addressed the seventh proposition (later the Sixth Amendment). "The committee then proceeded to consider the seventh proposition in the words following: in all criminal prosecutions the accused shall enjoy the right to a speedy and public trial."[68] The only debate concerned the right of the defendant to delay the trial, but this right was not passed. The right to be tried in the state where the offense was committed was adopted and the provision was amended. The House then adjourned, conducting no further discussion on the amendment, and no debate about the right to a public trial. The lack of debate can be attributed to the fact that the right to a public trial had already been included by many states in their own constitutions.

After its approval in the House, the provision was considered by the Senate. Although there were changes made to the other amendments, the provision for the right to a public trial remained intact.[69] No opposition was reported,[70] and the provision ultimately became the Sixth Amendment. The states ratified these amendments in 1791.

The right to a public trial has been documented in this country as early as 1677 in the *Concessions and Agreements of West New Jersey*, which had been conveyed to Quakers interested in establishing a settlement in the New World as a way to escape persecution in Restoration England.[71] One of these Quakers, William Penn, became a trustee for Edward Byllinge. He sponsored the settlement in Burlington in 1677 and became instrumental in shaping the political ideas in West New Jersey. It is unclear whether Penn himself, as his biographers claim, or Byllinge drafted the *Concessions*.[72] That document adopted Quaker notions about government and contains clauses guaranteeing private rights, including provisions that trials should be conducted fairly. Chapter XXIII states: "That in all publick courts of justice for tryals of causes, civil or criminal, any person or persons, inhabitants of the said Province may freely come into, and attend the said courts, and hear and be present, at all or any such tryals as shall be there had or passed, that justice may not be done in a corner nor in any covert manner."

In 1776, the Pennsylvania Declaration of Rights provided for a speedy public trial by an impartial jury of the county in all criminal cases.[73] The Vermont Declaration of Rights (1777) also contained a provision protecting the right to a public trial. Other states followed suit, so that by the time Madison drafted his proposed amendments, the idea of a public trial had already been accepted by the states and their citizens.

While this document contained the first guarantee of the right to a public trial in the United States, the belief in the right to a public trial was not a new concept. Although the Quakers may have been inspired by the injustices they suffered in Restoration England, the concept of a right to a public trial originated in the early English common law system upon which our country's laws were based.

The U.S. Supreme Court has wrestled repeatedly with the concept of the public trial. In one early case, it held that "whatever other benefits the guarantee to an accused that his trial be conducted in public may confer upon society, the guarantee has always been recognized as a safeguard against any attempt to employ our courts as instruments of persecution. The knowledge that every criminal trial is subject to contemporaneous review in the forum of public opinion is an effective restraint on judicial power."[74] In a 1980 opinion, the Court stated that "the early history of open trials in part reflects the widespread acknowledgment, long before behavioral scientists, that public trials have a significant community therapeutic value. Even without the experts to frame the concept in words, people sensed from experience and observation that, especially in the administration of criminal justice, the means used to achieve justice must have the support derived from public acceptance of both the product and its results."[75]

The public trial question has been considered by the Supreme Court in a series of decisions over the past twenty years arising from state criminal prosecutions in New York,[76] Virginia,[77] Massachusetts,[78] Georgia,[79] and California.[80] The first of these cases, *Gannett*

Co., Inc. v. DePasquale,[81] arose out of a pretrial hearing to suppress evidence (confessions and certain physical evidence) in a murder prosecution in Rochester, New York. The trial judge had granted the defendants' motion to exclude the press and public on the ground that the inevitable publicity would preclude their getting a fair trial. Neither the prosecutor nor the reporter in attendance when the motion was made objected, though the Gannett company, a newspaper publisher, later appealed the trial judge's decision to close the courtroom.

The late Justice Potter Stewart wrote the Court's majority opinion, holding that "members of the public have no constitutional right under the Sixth and Fourteenth Amendments to attend criminal trials." Aside from the fact that the public trial provision of the Sixth Amendment does not mention pretrial proceedings, the Court ruled, the public interest in the trial was adequately preserved by the public availability of the transcript and the right of the press to report about the trial itself. Incidentally, the Court added the observation that the Sixth Amendment right of a defendant to a public trial "does not guarantee the right to compel a private trial." The right to waive a constitutional right does not include the right to insist on the opposite of that right.

Recognizing the public interest in the Sixth Amendment, the Court ruled, does not create a constitutional right on the part of the public. "In an adversary system of criminal justice, there is a public interest in the openness of the administration of justice. The interest includes assuring the impartiality of trials and officers of the court, deterrence to perjury, eliciting witnesses, and educating us about the justice system. That interest is protected by the participants in the litigation."

A concurring opinion by the late Justice Lewis Powell raised a question that would lead to further litigation regarding the constitutionality of closure. Agreeing that the public trial feature of the Sixth Amendment is for the benefit of defendants, he urged that a reporter's interest in the judicial system, as an agent of the public, is protected by the First Amendment. Justice Powell admonished that a flexible accommodation of First and Sixth Amendment rights is desired, in which neither is subordinate to the other, and that trial judges should pursue every means to protect defendants' rights to fair trials without impinging on the press's right to cover those trials.

Justice William Rehnquist used his concurring opinion to disagree with Justice Powell, urging that the First Amendment creates no right of access to judicial or other governmental proceedings. "The Constitution does no more than assure the public and the press equal access once government has opened its doors." Other justices weighed in with their thoughts on whether the majority opinion answered or reserved for another case the question of whether the First Amendment guaranteed the press access.

The Supreme Court soon confronted that very question, in 1980, in *Richmond Newspapers v. Commonwealth of Virginia*.[82] There, in the third retrial (fourth trial) of a second-degree murder case in a rural Virginia county, the defendant moved that the trial be closed so prospective witnesses could not be informed about what had transpired at the present trial. The prosecutor agreed, and the judge cleared the courtroom. The trial went forward.

The press appealed the closure, but the Virginia Supreme Court upheld the trial judge. The earlier *Gannett* ruling had been criticized both by the press and in professional journals as unclear, ambiguous, and confused. If *Gannett* determined that the Sixth Amendment public trial guarantee did not give the press or the public access to a pretrial hearing, nor did it give the accused a right to a private trial, could a criminal trial be closed at a defendant's request without proof that closure is necessary to assure a fair trial? The U.S. Supreme Court agreed to review the law on this subject.

In the *Richmond* majority opinion, the late Chief Justice Warren Burger traced the venerable historical origins of the Anglo-American practice of public trials, a rule of the common law since time immemorial: "[A]t the time when our organic laws were adopted, criminal trials both here and in England had long been presumptively open. This is no quirk of history; rather, it has long been recognized as an indispensable attribute of an Anglo-American trial." Such a rule resonates today because it assures a therapeutic community involvement in the justice system; deters bias, perjury, and partiality; and provides the key to public respect and confidence in its government. "The crucial prophylactic aspects of the administration of justice cannot function in the dark; no community catharsis can occur if justice is done in a corner [or] in any covert manner." An educative value also exists, the Court noted. "People in an open society do not demand infallibility from their institutions, but it is difficult for them to accept what they are prohibited from observing."

The Court endorsed a comment by an earlier Supreme Court (1947) that "A trial is a public event. What transpires in the courtroom is public property,"[83] and thus "the public has a deep interest in trials."[84] In the age of the global village, the media has become the surrogate for the public; and the Supreme Court has acknowledged that "without some protection for seeking out the news, freedom of the press could be eviscerated."[85] Thus, the Court ruled, though not stated in the amendment explicitly, "the right to attend criminal trials is implicit in the guarantee of the First Amendment." Absent a proven overriding interest, a criminal case must be "open to the public."

Richmond was "a watershed opinion," in the words of Associate Justice John Stevens' concurring opinion, in determining that the acquisition of news has an independent constitutional protection, different from the constitutional rights of an accused.

A Massachusetts case soon raised a question about how *Richmond* should be interpreted. *Globe Newspaper Company v. Superior Court for the County of Norfolk* dealt with a Massachusetts law requiring trial judges to exclude the press and public from criminal trials for sex offenses involving young victims. In a multiple-rape trial, the judge closed his courtroom in order to preclude potential psychological damage to the three underage crime victims who had waived their rights to statutory closure. When the *Globe* appealed this ruling to the U.S. Supreme Court, the late Justice William Brennan's majority opinion held that the state mandatory closure rule violated the First Amendment.

The Court conceded that the general constitutional rule stated in *Richmond* did not provide an *absolute* right of access to the press and the public in criminal trials. Rather, any limitations the states do impose must be justified by weighty, compelling governmental interests—and even then, only narrowly tailored limitations would be approved in a case-by-case balancing of interests. Thus, the Massachusetts law was declared unconstitutional, despite the fact that the trial had concluded (the defendant was acquitted) by the time the Supreme Court issued its opinion. The state ban was too rigid to meet the constitutional requirement of the *Richmond* decision, which created a presumption of openness.

Chief Justice Burger and Associate Justice Rehnquist dissented, complaining that the majority opinion was "a gross invasion of state authority," and that it created "a disturbing paradox" that permits closure to protect the sensibilities of young defendants, but not for the benefit of young crime victims.

The issue arose again in a 1984 Georgia antiracketeering case.[86] In *Waller v. Georgia*, the government moved to clear the courtroom during a pretrial hearing to suppress wiretap evidence in order to protect the privacy of people other than the defendants mentioned on the tapes. The court closed the hearing to everyone except the parties, lawyers, witnesses, and court personnel. The hearing lasted seven days, only two and a half hours of which dealt with the wiretaps. After they were convicted, the defendants appealed, questioning the propriety of the closed hearing.

Justice Lewis Powell's majority opinion restated and clarified the court's position distilled from the prior recent cases: "[T]he right to an open trial may give way in certain cases to other rights or interests, such as the defendant's right to a fair trial or the government's interest in inhibiting disclosure of sensitive information. Such circumstances will be rare, however, and the balance of interests must be struck with special care."

Justice Powell also noted that "the explicit Sixth Amendment right of the accused is no less protective of a public trial than the implicit First Amendment right of the press and public." The values warranting this public interest in open trials are no less pertinent in suppression of evidence proceedings, Justice Powell added. These hearings often are a crucial component in a case and can raise important questions about police and prosecutorial conduct and judicial responsibility. As with trials, open hearings tend to discourage perjury and encourage witnesses to come forward.

In the *Waller* case, the government failed to prove an overriding interest in a closed hearing and the court did not pursue alternative solutions to the problem raised, and thus the closure was deemed improper.

In 1986, in *Press Enterprise Co. v. Superior Court of California, Riverside County*, the Supreme Court considered another state curb on full press access in a criminal trial, again involving a preliminary hearing (it lasted forty-one days). In a criminal case charging a nurse with murdering twelve patients with massive doses of a heart drug, the trial judge thought national publicity of the prosecution's case (no defense witnesses were called) would have been prejudicial and unfair to the defendant. The California Supreme Court held that the First Amendment did not apply because a preliminary hearing is not a criminal trial.

The U.S. Supreme Court, in a majority opinion by Chief Justice Burger, ruled that "the qualified First Amendment right of access to criminal proceedings applies to preliminary hearings." Without a specific finding that substantial prejudice would follow from open proceedings, not a mere "conclusory assertion," the First Amendment precludes closure. A dissent by Justices Rehnquist and Stevens argued that in preliminary hearings, if the states use reasonable criteria, limited periods of closure may be reasonable where the demonstrated need outweighs the value of public attendance. The court also noted that the right to a public trial applies in civil as well as criminal cases.[87]

In 1990, a federal appeals court in Oregon, following the two-part test—that the proceeding traditionally has been open and that publicity would curb government misconduct—ruled that the press must have access to all documents in plea agreements because such agreements often replace criminal trials.[88]

The most recent U.S. Supreme Court opinion on this subject (in 1993) arose out of a criminal preliminary hearing in Puerto Rico.[89] A local rule stated that all such hearings were to be held privately unless the defendant requested otherwise. A reporter for a local newspaper, *El Vocero de Puerto Rico*, asked to attend, was denied, and appealed.

In overruling the Puerto Rico Supreme Court's approval of the local privacy rule, the U.S. Supreme Court followed its 1986 *Press Enterprise* ruling,[90] which required preliminary hearings to be open to the public because they are essentially comparable to trials. The high court reaffirmed its *Press Enterprise* rule that: "If the interest asserted is the right of the accused to a fair trial, the preliminary hearing shall be closed only if specific findings are made demonstrating that, first, there is a substantial probability that the defendant's right to a fair trial will be prejudiced by publicity that closure would prevent and, second, reasonable alternatives to closure cannot adequately protect the defendant's fair trial rights."

Federal courts do not equate all preliminary proceedings with criminal trials, however. The Ninth Circuit denied investigative reporters the right to examine sealed FBI search warrants and affidavits filed with the trial court during an ongoing criminal investigation into fraud and bribery in national defense contracting.[91] The public need for an uninhibited investigation outweighed its need for access to these documents before the indictment and trial, the court ruled. While openness informs the citizenry and monitors government misconduct, courts will not permit it to undermine or frustrate investigations, invade people's privacy, or jeopardize the integrity of the criminal justice system. For this reason, the secrecy of grand jury and jury deliberations and internal court communications are not considered violations of the First Amendment.

In the past decade, the lower federal courts have allowed partial closures that were deemed justifiable and were "narrowly tailored to serve the interests for which they were ordered." For example, partial closure was permitted to protect a witness who feared harm or harassment if required to testify in public,[92] to protect a minor witness who was embarrassed to testify at a rape trial,[93] and to avoid disorder.[94]

Where plea agreements include references to ongoing investigations, those references will be protected.[95] And, where there is a compelling public interest in qualified closure—as under the Federal Victims Protection and Rights Act provision protecting children by limiting identification of children victims—nondisclosure is permitted.[96]

The current rule was summed up in two Ninth Circuit Court of Appeals decisions reviewing two notorious West Coast criminal cases.[97] The First Amendment's qualified right of access to the press and the public, which applies to pretrial proceedings and documents, is justified when there is a history of openness that contributes to the proper functioning of government proceedings. In the case of grand jury proceedings, for example, the answer would be no; with petit juries (their operations, not their deliberations) the answer would be yes. Even then, those who wish to seek closure on fair trial grounds must satisfy three tests. First, proof must be offered that without closure there would be "a substantial probability that irreparable damage to [defendant's] fair-trial right will result." Pervasive publicity alone will not automatically lead to that conclusion, as notorious cases like Watergate and Abscam proved. Second, a substantial probability must be demonstrated that less drastic alternatives to closure will not adequately protect the right to a fair trial. Third, closure must, in all likelihood, effectively protect the defendant from the harm perceived.

———

In addition to the defendant's Sixth Amendment right to a public trial, and the concomitant First Amendment right of the public at large, the Sixth Amendment explicitly guarantees defendants the rights to a speedy trial by an impartial jury, to be represented by counsel, and to confront witnesses testifying against them. These elements collectively have been referred to as the "right to a fair trial." A trial is deemed "fair" if the defendant is not prejudiced by the trial process itself or by outside influences.

The critical question, then, is whether the pervasiveness and power of television's coverage before and during trials necessarily corrupts the trial process and thereby makes trials unfair. To make the question more confounding, consider its inverse: When should the rationale of a fair trial—as contrasted with the right to a public trial—be deemed to encompass the idea that a defendant has the right to deny the public access to a trial?

Regardless of the original justification of a public trial, the Supreme Court has recognized a separate public right of publicity, distinct from the protection of the rights of the accused. For example, in discussing the concept of pretrial publicity, the Supreme Court has determined that even pervasive, adverse publicity does not invariably lead to an unfair trial.[98]

The Constitution is rooted in fundamental principles, but these principles must evolve with changing realities. New technological advances led to new media, which raised new questions whose answers must be found in current applications of venerable principles. A prizewinning 1953 essay on the free press-fair trial question effectively illustrated how the then-modern media (essentially before the era of television) affected historic notions of a "public" trial: "One person in the city state of Athens could by word of mouth be the conscience and the gadfly of the state. The New England town meeting could draw into the democratic process the entire community. Such personal participation is no longer possible. The media of mass communication must be the vital link between the people and the government."[99]

In its decisions, the Supreme Court has referred repeatedly to the constraints of logic and experience on this issue. Applying this measure of logic and experience today, one must concede that the notion of what is a "public" trial has flip-flopped over the centuries almost 180 degrees. Practices have gone from secret proceedings in a finite judicial chamber to televised trials reaching a potentially infinite public. If "contemporaneous review in the forum of public opinion" is the necessary restraint of government power, as the Supreme Court said as long ago as 1948,[100] if an open judicial system is the means by which the people maintain control over their political institutions, if the law is an evolving process that must absorb life as it exists in the present, and if all these premises are well-established principles — what is the proper role of television in courtrooms? That question cannot be answered definitively by the Constitution's Bill of Rights. Instead, we must turn to the evolving standards of professional conduct as they struggle to adapt to the new situations raised by the explosive growth of communications technology.

Chapter 3

CAMERAS IN THE COURTS

THE EXPERIMENT

W hen television began covering public affairs at mid-century, it was met at the courthouse door by almost unanimous professional cynicism about its place in courts. The American Bar Association and powerful and prestigious judicial committees had passed edicts against it, and only a few states (Texas, Colorado, and Oklahoma) permitted any coverage at all. Inevitably, a case eventually came to the U.S. Supreme Court questioning the very constitutionality of cameras in courts.

That landmark litigation, *Estes v. Texas*,[1] argued and decided in 1965, arose out of a notorious swindling case in which a Tyler, Texas, judge changed the venue and allowed a continuance, but permitted televised broadcasts of parts of the trial over the defendant's objection. After an unruly two-day pretrial hearing on the defendant's motion to ban television, the trial proceeded with hidden cameras broadcasting live only the prosecution's arguments and the verdict, though excerpts of the proceedings were also shown in the news summaries. The Texas appeals court approved the trial judge's actions.

A closely divided U.S. Supreme Court reviewed the conviction on constitutional grounds. Several opinions were written, and the differences between them were as important as they were revealing. Justice Tom Clark wrote the Court's majority opinion, in which Chief Justice Earl Warren and Justices William Douglas and Arthur Goldberg concurred. Justice Potter Stewart wrote a dissenting opinion, joined by Justices William Brennan, Hugo Black, and Byron White. The 4–4 tie was broken by a separate opinion from Justice John Harlan, who concurred with the Clark opinion but expressed reservations that left questions about the ultimate meaning of the Court's ruling.

The majority opinion held that even limited televising and broadcasting violated the defendant's Fourteenth Amendment guarantee of due process of law because it deprived him of a fair trial. The Court noted the history and meaning of both the "public" trial and the "fair" trial requirements of the Sixth Amendment and considered how those rights meshed with the freedom of the press guaranteed by the First Amendment. Noting that the legal profession feared the presence of television in courts, the Court concluded that it was not necessary to demonstrate specific prejudices resulting from television coverage. The simple fact of the camera's presence was prejudice enough: "The prejudice of television may be so subtle that it escapes the ordinary methods of proof, but it would gradually erode our fundamental conception of trial."

The Court disagreed with the argument that "psychological considerations are for psychologists, not courts, because they are purely hypothetical." The majority of justices thought, as Justice Douglas wrote, that television creates "insidious influences" on the trial process. Admitting that the impact of television cannot be evaluated objectively, the majority nonetheless decided that its presence would inevitably lead to distractions, conscious or unconscious effects on jurors, witnesses, and even on judges (who as a rule run for election), as well as harassments and indignities for defendants. "Trial by television," the majority warned, is "foreign to our system," and thus an inherent denial of due process of law. "No one could forget," one opinion proclaimed, "that he was constantly in the focus of the 'all-seeing eye' . . . the evil of televised trials . . . lies not in the noise and appearance of cameras, but in the trial participants' awareness that they are being televised."

Commercialism and politicalization were clearly on the minds of some of the justices. They were disturbed that the coverage of the trial was interrupted by commercial ads. They compared televised trials to the Soviet Union's trial of the American U-2 pilot, Francis Powers, which had become a kind of televised political theater. They worried that a televised trial was akin to a trial in Yankee Stadium, where showmanship would overwhelm fairness and essential due process of law. They alluded to recent mass public trials in other countries such as Cuba, which had shocked the consciences of fair-minded observers.

Admitting that the press has been "a mighty catalyst in awakening public interest in governmental affairs" and "informing the citizenry," the Court concluded that the guarantee of a "public" trial is for the benefit of the defendant, not the press. Television reporters were to be allowed inside courtrooms, as are print reporters, but they could not bring their cameras any more than newspaper reporters can bring typewriters or printing presses. If this comparison sounded disingenuous, the Court did add that when the art of the new medium advances to the point that its presence is not hazardous to the fairness of the trial, "we will have another case."

Joining Justice Clark in a concurring opinion that would have gone farther, Justices Warren, Douglas, and Goldberg argued that the "televising of criminal trials is inherently a denial of due process." They urged that the time was appropriate "to make a definitive appraisal of television in the courtroom." A dignified setting for a trial is a crucial component of the required essential fairness of the criminal justice process, they stated. Television diverts trials; it has an inevitable impact on the participants, singling out those defendants whose trials are covered; and, the justices feared, it "gives the public the wrong impression" by detracting from the dignity of the trial.

Noting the prevailing almost unanimous condemnation of televised court proceedings, the Warren opinion concluded that the "guarantee of a public trial confers no special benefit on the press, the radio industry or the television industry. A public trial is a necessary component of an accused's right to a fair trial and the concept of public trial cannot be used to defend conditions which prevent the trial process from providing a fair and reliable determination of guilt."[2]

The majority of justices in *Estes* conceded the usefulness of tele-vision, but drew a rhetorical line in the dust: its activities may not extend into the "hallowed sanctuary" of the courtroom. Ironically, the chief justice accompanied his critical conclusions about the evil impact of cameras with a selection of seven photographs of scenes at the *Estes* trial. For some purposes, even he agreed, a picture is worth more than words.

Justice Harlan's concurring opinion was more hospitable to the positive potentials of television and more tentative about how far the Supreme Court should go in proscribing future practices. Hoping to balance the need to protect against the mischievous potential of television with the need to permit states to experiment with novel practices, Harlan concluded that only "in this case" did the former considerations outweigh the latter. He remarked that if and when the day arrives that television can cover courtroom trials without causing an unfair trial, the Court's conclusion in *Estes* should be reexamined.

That reservation was key because the dissenting opinion of Justices Stewart, Black, Brennan, and White argued that their colleagues who had joined in the Clark opinion had wrongfully allowed their per-sonal views to escalate into "a per se constitutional rule." The subject of television's artfulness is a variable, subject to "continuous and unforeseeable change" that "may be modified tomorrow," they noted. None of the dire consequences that the majority of judges predicted occurred in the *Estes* case, they pointed out; indeed, "there is nothing to show that the trial proceeded in any other way than it would have proceeded if cameras and television had not been pres-ent." These four dissenting justices were not willing to reach a con-stitutional conclusion banning television on theoretical grounds because to do so would impose on the press "a burden of justifying its presence," contrary to the presumption of the First Amendment: "If what occurred did not deprive the petitioner of his constitutional right to a fair trial, then the fact that the public could view the pro-ceeding on television has no constitutional significance."[3]

To make the dissenter's point emphatically clear, Justice Brennan added his own final words to the Court's *Estes* opinion: "Today's decision is *not* a blanket constitutional prohibition regarding the televising of state criminal trials." But as a practical matter, it was widely debated by interested observers whether the *Estes* ruling really precluded all television in all courts. This uncertainty prevailed for a decade and a half.

Some states conducted limited experiments with courtroom cameras in the years following the *Estes* decision. Florida, Washington, and Alabama were the first to launch pilot projects; soon nineteen states allowed some electronic coverage of court proceedings. Florida particularly allowed coverage of a variety of cases, civil and criminal, trial and appellate, in whole and in part. There was gavel-to-gavel coverage of several cases in 1979, 1980, and 1981, including that of serial killer Ted Bundy, as well as less notorious cases. The public responses and professional reactions to those experiments were favorable.

Under the Florida rule, access was at the complete discretion of the presiding judge, and few cases were televised. Lawyers and station managers for the Post-Newsweek station in Miami (Channel 10) devised a strategy to seek a rule from the Florida Supreme Court allowing presumptive access for electronic media. Noting that with the development of compact, low light-level cameras, videotaping was actually less disruptive than sketch artists with easel and chalk, the station's counsel, Talbot D'Alemberte, an eminent Florida attorney who would later become president of the American Bar Association and of Florida State University, proposed a prototype rule to the Florida Supreme Court, which had supervisory control over its courts' procedures.[4]

The Florida Supreme Court held a hearing to demonstrate the new technology. The court ordered a one-year trial period,[5] after which it conducted a survey of judges and participants, seeking their evaluations of the experiment. As a result, the court issued its present presumptive access rule, which other states would soon emulate.[6]

D'Alemberte takes pride in that episode of creative legal engineering: "it took a court," he wrote me, "with great intellectual confidence to make the decision which placed an enormous number of judicial proceedings at risk of displacement by the U.S. Supreme Court," which at that time was operating under the precedent of the *Estes* case.

A case of local notoriety in Florida, which eventually was appealed to the U.S. Supreme Court, again raised the *Estes* question of whether the mere presence of television at a criminal trial creates a constitutional prejudice to defendants. In 1981, the Supreme Court used that opportunity in *Chandler v. Florida*[7] to clarify its sixteen-year-old decision in *Estes* and to promulgate a new and clear rule: Television may be permitted in courts, so long as there is no specific evidence of actual prejudice resulting from it.

The precedential case arose out of a burglary of a Miami Beach restaurant. The crime had several intriguing features: the burglars were policemen; the key prosecution witness was an amateur radio operator who happened to overhear and record the delinquent cops' conversations over their police walkie-talkies during their burglary. Because the defendants objected to any televising of their trial, the trial judge—operating under Florida's new experimental rule—permitted the televising of the prosecution's key witness but not of the defense case, and allowed coverage of both closing arguments.

The convicted defendants appealed their conviction to the Florida Supreme Court on the ground that the presence of a television camera deprived them of their constitutional right to a fair trial. The Florida high court ruled that "due process does not prohibit electronic media coverage of judicial proceedings per se," even though neither the First nor the Sixth Amendments "mandate entry of the electronic media into judicial proceedings." The Florida Supreme Court based its ruling on the premise that it had supervisory authority over its state courts.

The ruling was appealed to the U.S. Supreme Court. Among the many advisory comments to the court was an amicus brief filed by PBS and its Florida affiliates, pointing out that *Estes* was decided when television was still in its infancy. By 1981, the technology had advanced and states had accepted the implicit invitation of the *Estes* opinion to experiment. Furthermore, the majority of Americans regarded television as "the most credible communications medium." The amici pleaded the public policy arguments favoring coverage of court cases. Justice and the appearance of justice require public observation of the system in action. The camera is the technological surrogate for public attendance at trials. Observation of the judicial process elevates public understanding of this important and complex part of government, promotes discussion of the legal system, fosters confidence in it, serves as a check on official corruption, improves the quality of judges and trial lawyers, protects the accused, and provides the public a prophylactic or therapeutic sense of participation in the system. The amicus brief also listed various examples of its coverage of judicial proceedings in Florida between 1977 and 1980, including gavel-to-gavel coverage of splashy murder cases, ceremonial judicial proceedings (investitures), appellate arguments, interviews, documentaries, and clemency hearings. It placed this process in an impressive noncommercial and educational context, and cited a university study concluding that "television does not disrupt trial proceedings."

The defendants' lawyer argued to the U.S. Supreme Court that the mere presence of cameras in the courtroom was inherently prejudicial and thus deprived his clients of a fair trial and due process of law.[8] Although he could offer no proof of this claimed prejudice, he argued to the high court that "human nature and common sense" make it clear that "people act differently, posture differently, pose differently when they know they're on TV"; we don't need psychological studies to confirm such an obvious conclusion. "[W]e all know," he argued, "that timid people become more timid, nervous people become more nervous, people who are not used to being in a courtroom can only have their anxiety exacerbated by the presence of a television camera." He also argued that there is a likelihood that people—particularly jurors—will conclude that what is televised is more important than what is not.

On behalf of the Florida Supreme Court, the state attorney general argued that public scrutiny of the trial courts has an educative effect. Constitutional law should not be predicated upon conjecture about possible prejudicial effects, he urged, but only upon demonstrated reality. Florida's experience with televised trials, the Attorney General noted, had been positive. It is better for citizens "to see the actual image and hear these portions of testimony" than "to depend on the interpretation that a news commentator might like to give it." It is the essence of federalism that states should be allowed "to experiment with novel ideas," he argued. He also pointed out that television had become more "serene" and "commonplace" since the *Estes* decision. Seventeen states and the conference of chief justices supported Florida's position in amicus briefs.

The U.S. Supreme Court agreed with Florida, concluding that it would not interfere with the state's decision unless a particular constitutional deprivation resulting from particular, proven practices was demonstrated. The Court used the *Chandler* case to clarify the law governing televised trials and to end the debate over the meaning of the divided and debated *Estes* decision: "It does not stand as an absolute ban on state experimentation with an evolving technology, which, in terms of modes of mass communication, was in its infancy in 1964 when *Estes* was decided, and is, even now, in a state of continuing change." Recalling Justice Louis Brandeis's jurisprudential comments in a 1932 case that the rights of states to experiment in social and economic areas is "one of the happy incidents of the federal system" and noting that Supreme Court justices "must be ever on our guard, lest we erect our prejudices into legal principles," the high federal court deferred to the Florida Supreme Court. Since no specific evidence was offered to prove that the presence of the television camera hampered the defense or deprived the defendants of an impartial jury in the *Chandler* case, and there was no basis for the Supreme Court to supervise the Florida courts without proof of a constitutional deprivation, the conviction was upheld.

The *Chandler* ruling stated that generalities or abstract fears about the potential risks of televised court proceedings would not be sufficient for a constitutional objection. Potential mischief to the judicial atmosphere is no basis for interfering with careful state experimentation with the administration of its trial process. Scientific evidence from the limited surveys to date did not definitely demonstrate the truth of prevalent fears that cameras in courts would inevitably make more harrowing the timid witness's experience, more cocky the defense advocate who thrives in the limelight, more pluming the political prosecutor, or more self-conscious the presiding judge. Agreeing that such effects would be as deleterious to the judicial process as physical disruptions, the Supreme Court refused to interfere without proof that these problems had occurred in the particular case in question.

So long as trial courts are vigilant in safeguarding defendants' rights by the range of procedural curative devices (change of venue, continuance, sequestration, etc.) available to prevent publicity from prejudicing cases, the Supreme Court ruled, there is no basis to find constitutional impediments. Indeed, two justices in the *Chandler* case—Potter Stewart and Byron White—wished to construe the high court's decision as a complete reversal of the *Estes* decision.

STATE RULES

In *Chandler*, the Supreme Court harkened back to the late Justice John Harlan's key concurring opinion, which created the majority in *Estes*, that "We must judge television as we find it." How *do* we find the status of television in courts in the era after the early days of state experimentation?

After the *Estes* case in 1965, Colorado was the only state that allowed any electronic media in courts. During the 1970s and after, other states conducted their own limited experiments, the one in Florida which led to the Supreme Court's *Chandler* decision being the most notable. After *Chandler*, the American Bar Association modified its hortatory rule, Canon 3A(7), to allow for televised trials. By 1990, most states had studied their judicial systems and devised various procedures that permitted some form of televised trials under specific guidelines assuring judicial supervision and control of local practices.

The experiences in the states that experimented with televised trials were both similar and illuminating. In 1973, the Supreme Court of Washington authorized a pilot project permitting televised trials.[9] The results were widely praised, and in 1976 the court permitted cameras in the courtroom permanently, in both trial and appellate courts, as long as the coverage did not distract the participants or jeopardize the dignity of the proceedings.[10] Coverage of witnesses, jurors, or parties who expressed objection was prohibited. In 1991, the provision giving participants the option of not being filmed was omitted.

In 1978, the state conducted a survey of 111 superior court judges asking for their opinions and experiences with video cameras in their courtrooms. Of the 111 judges, only 41 had any direct experience. Of that group, 34 reported a positive experience, while only 7 reported negative responses. One judge explained his negative experience in a murder trial as follows: "Whether it was real or not, at 3:30 or 4 o'clock in the afternoon of each day, when all the cameras and reporters were absent from the courtroom, it seemed as if there was a general easing and relaxing of previous tension and a sigh of relief seemed to breathe through the crowded court." In contrast, another judge, who also had tried a first-degree murder trial, had this advice: "I would suggest that any judge who anticipates having cameras in the courtroom, take the opportunity before trial to casually discuss the set up with the camera men or reporters so that it is clear that both sides understand the other's position on that particular case. I did and found this to be very beneficial." The report concluded that the data gathered "appears to support a continuation of allowing cameras in the courtroom."

From 1977 to 1978, Florida conducted a sample survey of participants' attitudes about trials involving electronic media and still photography coverage in its courts.[11] (No attempt was made to determine the comparable reactions of participants of trials that did not involve media coverage.) Of the 2,660 witnesses, attorneys, court personnel, and jurors sampled, 62 percent responded. Sixty-nine percent of the attorneys, 67 percent of the witnesses, 65 percent of the court personnel, and 78 percent of the jurors surveyed had either favorable or very favorable experiences during their court service when cameras, photographers, and related equipment were present. The majority of jurors, witnesses, and court personnel concluded that the presence of cameras during the trial was not at all distracting. In contrast, 59 percent of the attorneys felt that cameras were at least slightly distracting. One attorney, who said that "television has absolutely no place in the courtroom," thought that the cameras diluted the jury's attention and diverted it from what he felt to be the crucial point of the case. One witness believed that as a result of the camera coverage, "the attorneys act as though they are competing for an Emmy and witnesses get too nervous, affecting testimony."

As of May 1, 1979, Florida permitted coverage in all civil and criminal courts, with television coverage subject only to the authority of the presiding judge. Exclusion is possible where it can be shown that the proceedings would be adversely affected because of a "qualitative difference" between electronic and other forms of coverage.[12] Of course, in 1981, as a result of the U.S. Supreme Court's *Chandler* ruling, the national rule was formulated in some measure on the basis of Florida's experiences.

In 1978, Wisconsin appointed an eleven-person committee to monitor and evaluate the use of courtroom audio and visual equipment for a period of one year.[13] Eight years earlier, a similar twelve-person committee had split evenly on the question of allowing television cameras to broadcast judicial proceedings.[14] The 1978 committee conducted its study by polling all 181 circuit court judges and by distributing questionnaires to attorneys, judges, jurors, and witnesses who were involved in televised trials. They also used graduate and law students as court observers.

All three methods of observation produced similar results. Of the 181 circuit court judges polled, only 55 replied. Forty-four of them stated that they supported televised trials and that televising the proceedings did not cause any unfair trials. Only eight judges were opposed to the use of photography in the courtroom.

The majority of attorneys, judges, jurors, and witnesses who responded to the questionnaires stated that the audio and visual equipment had no bearing on the outcomes of their trials. One juror stated, "When the trial was going, I was oblivious to them. When we came back in [to the jury box] you'd say, 'Oh, the cameras are there,' but I got too absorbed to notice them." One of the court observers reported that, "Overall, the media equipment did not appear to be obtrusive."

The verdict was not unanimous. When asked what effect media coverage had on a 1978 arson trial, the prosecuting attorney replied: "I would like to say none, but I might hedge to a degree. Since the jurors were isolated, they were not exposed to [media reports]. I think the fact that they were there indicated the significance or importance of the trial, and might have been a signal [to the jurors] to be more scrutinizing and careful to come up with a decision."

The committee concluded that televising trials is "in the public interest" and should be permitted in the state's courtrooms. The committee quoted a statement (made in another context) of the late Associate Justice William O. Douglas in 1947: "A trial is a public event. What transpires in the courtroom is public property. . . . Those who see and hear what transpires can report it with impunity. There is no special prerequisite of the judiciary which enables it, as distinguished from other institutions of democratic government, to suppress, edit, or censor events which transpire in proceedings before it."[15]

The committee proposed twelve specific rules to govern the use of audio and video equipment in the courtroom. In addition, it made two recommendations to the Wisconsin Supreme Court: that the Supreme Court should permanently adopt the committee's proposed rules; and that radio broadcasting, still photography, and television cameras should be allowed into courtrooms, provided that the rules of the Court are strictly adhered to, and specifically that the presiding judges have wide discretion to assure fair trials.

Since July 1, 1979, all trial and appellate courts in Wisconsin have allowed radio broadcasting, still photography, and television coverage of both criminal and civil matters, subject to the adopted regulations.[16]

In 1980, Massachusetts created a fourteen-member advisory committee to oversee the experimental use of cameras and recording equipment in its courtrooms.[17] Cameras and recording devices were permitted in both trial and appellate courts for the two-year experimental period. The advisory committee's primary concern was that television coverage of pretrial hearings, such as arraignments and bail hearings, could prejudice potential jurors. During this period, thirty-eight out of sixty-nine cases involved television coverage.

After the completion of a murder trial in Dedham, Massachusetts, which received television coverage, the jurors and witnesses were given questionnaires to assess the effects of media coverage on the trial. Of the thirty-nine witnesses, 62 percent thought that the presence of a television camera did not interfere with the conduct of the trial, 17 percent disagreed, and 21 percent were undecided.

The committee highlighted a positive ramification of the media coverage in the courtroom. The combination of television and print media seemed to maximize the exposure of the trial to the general public: "It seems that the two media are playing complementary roles in such trials, the television capsulizes the day's latest developments in the evening, and the newspaper the next morning follows up with detailed presentation and analysis." The committee recommended continued use of camera and recording apparatus in courtrooms, with the presiding judge having a large degree of discretion to assure a fair trial.

As of January 1, 1983, electronic coverage has been permitted in Massachusetts trial and appellate courts. In addition, the use of electronic or photographic media to present evidence, for perpetuation of a record, for the purposes of judicial administration, and for the preparation of educational materials was allowed when authorized by court rules.[18]

In January 1978, the Minnesota Supreme Court allowed coverage of its proceedings by cameras on an experimental basis for an indefinite period of time. On March 18, 1981, various media groups petitioned the court for either a permanent rule or a two-year experiment that would allow media coverage in trial and appellate courts. The petitioners, including radio and television stations, newspapers, and journalism associations, appeared before the Minnesota Advisory Commission on Cameras in the Courtroom, which in turn submitted its report to the state supreme court.[19]

In its January 1982 report, the commission concluded that television technology had become sufficiently advanced as to be relatively unobtrusive. However, the commission also noted that no empirical evidence exists to support the position that cameras in the courtroom are either detrimental or beneficial to the judicial process. It is impossible to reach conclusions regarding the impact of television coverage on the trial participants, the report stated, because relevant data is based on "opinion, behavioral theories, unprovable suppositions and personal prejudices." The commission concluded that the petitioners had failed to sustain the burden of showing that they were entitled to the access they requested.

While not favoring a permanent rule, the commission did recommend that video and audio coverage of trial proceedings be allowed on an experimental basis for a period of two years. The commission also recommended that all participants in the experiment be requested, if not required, to provide feedback to the Supreme Court. The experimental period was then extended to January 1, 1994. Presently, trial coverage is permitted on a case-by-case basis. Camera coverage has been allowed in Minnesota appellate courts since April 20, 1981.

On March 1, 1982, Arizona began a one-year experimental period during which electronic and still photography of public proceedings was permitted in all state courts. The decision to permit coverage was within the sole discretion of the presiding judge. Prior to this one-year period, media coverage had only been permitted in the appellate courts for about two and a half years.

A committee was established to conduct a very structured study during the experimental period.[20] The study addressed five major areas of concern: physical disruption, prejudicial publicity, selective coverage, psychological impact, and procedural delay. Detailed questionnaires were sent to 440 jurors, witnesses, court personnel, judges, and attorneys, 75 percent of whom responded. Fifty-eight percent of all respondents thought that the continued coverage of trial court proceedings would be beneficial. Eighty-two percent of the judges and attorneys responding stated that in their opinion jurors were not more sensitive to public opinion due to the presence of the media. Forty percent of the judges responding thought that the presence of the equipment and its operator in the courtroom made them personally more attentive.

As a result of the committee's favorable review, the Arizona Supreme Court issued an order on June 30, 1983, permanently allowing electronic coverage of proceedings in all state courts.[21]

A 1980 report of a Maryland judicial committee considered whether to extend media coverage to court proceedings.[22] The committee noted that the use of still cameras presented a greater potential for physical disruption than the operation of video equipment because of the noise and movement associated with still photographers.

Indeed, the report noted that a video camera would likely remove most media from the courtroom, thereby decreasing any distraction from reporters writing on notepads, sketch artists drawing, or the clicks of print photographers' cameras.

The report expressed confidence that jurors could accomplish their job in spite of camera coverage: "it is our experience that jurors bring to the court and deliberation rooms a very strong sense of the importance of their task and responsibility for their decision, and it is unlikely that unobtrusive, extended coverage in a dignified setting will adversely affect their attention to the case or their vote on the outcome." The report also noted that undue apprehension on the part of witnesses could be thwarted "if care is taken to ensure that a proper setting is maintained." To accomplish this, the report recommended giving judges broad discretion to control any "circus-like atmosphere" that might be created by the cameras and lights.

While acknowledging that the presence of a video camera places additional responsibilities on trial judges, the report noted that most judges' opposition decreased after having had experience with a televised trial. The committee also believed that any additional public pressure on judges resulting from TV coverage would not substantially affect judicial decisions.

The Maryland Court of Appeals passed a permanent rule in May 1984 permitting coverage of civil trials.[23] Coverage of appellate civil proceedings remains on an experimental basis. State legislation prohibits coverage of all criminal proceedings.

Hawaii conducted its first televised trial in 1982.[24] The one-day case involved a misdemeanor theft tried before a jury. Only one camera was allowed during voir dire and the trial, and the footage was not released to the media. All parties had consented to the presence of cameras. After deliberating for three hours, the jury returned a verdict of not guilty.

Immediately after the jury's verdict, survey questionnaires were filled out by fourteen prospective jurors, twelve jurors, one alternate juror, and three witnesses. The prospective jurors were seated in a public gallery with camera coverage. Two-thirds of the prospective jurors responded "very unfavorable" to the presence of the cameras.

However, the actual juror responses were more favorable. The contrast between the two juror groups was highlighted by their responses to the question of whether they would be reluctant to serve as a juror solely because of the presence of television cameras. Some of the prospective jurors said they would be reluctant. But all the actual jurors said they would not be reluctant to serve again. When asked if they were afraid that some psychological, reputational, physical, or financial harm would come to them as a result of the camera coverage, the prospective jurors were divided in their answers. But all thirteen of the real jurors answered no. Two of the witnesses reported that they were aware of the camera but were not distracted. The third witness reported he never was aware that a camera was present.

On December 7, 1987, after a four-year experimental period of audio-visual coverage of all state courts, the Hawaii Supreme Court ordered permanent extended media coverage of state proceedings.[25] The permanent rules required prior consent of the judge for coverage of trial proceedings; however, consent is not required for coverage of appellate proceedings.

In Nevada, experimental coverage of trial and appellate proceedings began in April 1980.[26] After the completion of this one-year experimental period, a report was prepared by the state Administrative Office of the Courts. In collecting data for the report, surveys were sent to every court in Nevada and distributed to judges, attorneys, media representatives, and witnesses.

Judges and attorneys were by far the most supportive of cameras in the courtroom; 75 and 70 percent, respectively, were completely or slightly in favor of the experimental rule. Witnesses were least in favor of cameras in the courtroom; 45 percent were slightly or completely opposed. In addition, 48 percent of judges reported that witnesses were extremely distracted, and half of the judges reported that a party or witness objected to the media's presence in the courtroom. One attorney commented that media coverage affects witnesses adversely, if at all. One witness stated that the presence of cameras made him feel like he was on trial rather than the defendant. Finally, an administrative concern voiced in the report was that witnesses who were waiting to testify could hear and see the testimony of other witnesses on monitors in the halls, thus nullifying the witness exclusion rule.

The report concluded that the overall reaction to the presence of cameras in the courtroom was positive and recommended that a yearly evaluation should be conducted by a standing committee on cameras in the courtroom. Following an eight-year experimental period, media coverage was permitted on a permanent basis in both trial and appellate courts as of April 1988. The consent of the participants is not required. The issue of coverage is placed at the discretion of the presiding judge, except for proceedings that are made confidential by law.[27]

In Alaska, prior to 1985 it was necessary to get the defendant's permission before news coverage was allowed; defendants rarely agreed. A judicial rule changed this practice, and after July 1, 1985, Alaska's courts were open to the general public via television. In January 1988, after a three-year initial period of experimentation, the Alaska Judicial Council submitted a report on the impact of news cameras in the state courts to the Alaska Supreme Court. The court then ordered a ten-year experimental period during which news cameras were allowed in appellate and trial courts.

After the earlier experiment, the judicial council favored news cameras in Alaska courtrooms on a permanent basis, provided a plan was established to promote smooth relations between the judicial branch and the media. The council recommended in its report:

1. The media should be able to challenge a denial of access;
2. Witness's objections to cameras should be considered on a case-by-case basis;
3. Judges should have discretion to assure a fair trial;
4. Camera access should be assumed.[28]

As of January 15, 1990, media coverage has been extended to all Alaska trial and appellate courts in criminal and civil matters, though some restrictions do apply.[29] The consent of all parties is required in most family proceedings. Jurors may not be filmed or photographed except during the return of the final verdict. Victims of sexual offenses are protected from news coverage. Anyone who violates these rules of the Alaska Media Plan is subject to suspension of their media privileges for up to one year.

In Virginia, in 1987, broadcast of judicial proceedings was permitted on an experimental basis in both trial and appellate courts for two years. Prior to 1987, television cameras were permitted in courtrooms for the sole purpose of preserving the court record. During the experimental period, cameras were to be allowed in the Supreme Court, the Court of Appeals, two circuit courts, and two general district courts.

The focus of the state study was on the presiding judges, since they would be affected on a daily basis by the presence of cameras in their courtrooms.[30] Surveys were sent to the 127 active circuit judges. Seventy-four of those responding concluded that the presence of cameras in the courtroom had a negative impact on the judicial system, while only ten thought that they had a positive impact. Among the judges' chief complaints was that the experimental program had resulted in sensational, biased, and distorted coverage. Also, the judges believed that the purpose of the media during the experimental period had been to entertain, rather than educate, the public.

The study concluded that the negative effects of cameras in the trial courtroom far outweigh any positive or educational effects. Television coverage of appellate proceedings was so rare during the two-year experimental period that the impact was deemed insignificant. As a result of the findings of this study, the experimental period was extended. After three additional years of experimentation, legislation was passed in March 1992 allowing permanent extended media coverage of trial and appellate proceedings for criminal and civil matters, subject to some limitations. Coverage of jurors and certain witnesses is prohibited, along with coverage of adoption, juvenile, child custody, divorce, spousal support, sexual offense, and trade secret hearings, as well as hearings on motions to suppress evidence.[31]

In Maine, in 1993, a special state advisory committee conducted a two-year survey of the effects of cameras in the courtroom on participants in two courthouses.[32] Ten trials, fourteen arraignments, five bail hearings, three pleas, and thirteen sentencings were covered.

Questionnaires were sent and responses received from thirty-eight judges, twenty-one prosecutors, sixteen defense attorneys, and eleven court personnel. Forty-nine out of eighty jurors responded and eighty-four out of one hundred fifty witnesses responded.

The researchers, an advisory committee of appointed judges, lawyers, and consultants, reported that the performance of judges and attorneys was not affected by camera coverage. Rather, most ignored the cameras and focused on their work. No evidence of playing to the cameras was witnessed. The researchers also found that witness anxiety dissolved after witnesses were informed that they would not be shown on camera. Finally, the researchers found that witness anxiety, reported in nearly 20 percent of cases, could not be eliminated completely, but it could be abated by allowing the trial judge to exclude particular witnesses from coverage. The advisory committee concluded that "there is no evidence that substantive rights or outcomes were affected by the presence of cameras inside the courtroom."

When the Maine Supreme Court reviewed this 1993 report, it issued an order on July 11, 1994, authorizing extended media coverage of trial courts in all locations on a permanent basis.[33]

New York State has an extensive and well-documented history of experimental coverage in its trial courts. Television was permanently adopted in state appellate courts on January 1, 1981, with no experimental period. That same year, an experimental program for coverage of trial proceedings was ordered but never implemented because it violated Section 52 of New York's Civil Rights Law, which bans coverage when witnesses appear or may appear under subpoena. This rule is still in effect today.

On December 1, 1987, the New York state assembly and senate passed bills permitting experimental coverage in civil and criminal trial court cases. At the end of the two-year period, Chief Administrative Judge Albert M. Rosenblatt submitted a report on the effects of audio-visual coverage on the conduct of judicial proceedings.[34] His study included a survey of 1,095 witnesses, attorneys, judges, and media personnel. Of the judges surveyed, 60 percent had favorable opinions of media coverage. However, 15 percent of the judges thought that the equipment and personnel detracted from the dignity of the proceedings.

Several attorneys commented that audio-visual coverage infringed on the privacy rights of witnesses and the constitutional rights of the defendants. Also, expert witnesses, who were initially nervous in front of cameras, worried that cameras would inhibit and cause anxiety to nonexpert witnesses. The recommendation of this 1989 report, to adopt a permanent statute allowing coverage in state trial courts, was modified in favor of extending the experimental period.

The New York State Defenders Association strongly criticized the 1989 report,[35] characterizing it as a myth. The association pointed out that the survey research did not account for the psychological effects of cameras on trial participants and also noted numerous methodological flaws.

In 1991, a New York advisory committee conducted a similar survey which collected evaluation forms from 922 trial participants. More than 90 percent of the trial judges surveyed reported that audio-visual coverage was either neutral or nondistracting, and 94 percent of them thought that coverage had no effect on the fairness of the proceedings. Only 38 percent of the attorneys responding favored cameras in the courts, while 37 percent reported that they thought that the cameras made the atmosphere of the courtroom tense. Almost all of the jurors surveyed (98 percent) stated that they felt no pressure to acquit or convict as a result of the media coverage. Also, 81 percent of the jurors thought that coverage did not effect the fairness of the proceedings or, if it did, did so in a positive way. The study recommended a permanent rule allowing media coverage in trial courts, but once again the experimental period was extended.

In 1994, the Committee on Audio-Visual Coverage of Court Proceedings echoed the recommendations of the 1989 and 1991 studies. The committee's study consisted of analyzing comments of trial judges, complaints and violations regarding camera coverage, applications for camera coverage, prior studies, statutes in other jurisdictions, and the findings of public hearings. This third, and most recent, recommendation for permanently allowing cameras in New York trial courts also was rejected, and the experimental period in New

York was extended again, this time to June 30, 1997. New York's ten-year experiment, endorsed by three legislative commissions created to study its effects, ended on June 30, 1997, despite recommendations that the practice of televised trials be made permanent.

In state after state, the results were similar. Initial skepticism was replaced by general acceptance after actual experiences with television. While all states were careful to attempt to gain insights about the impact of television on the trial participants, not a single state that tried the practice rejected it. Uniformly, these participants concluded that earlier fears were misplaced. The experience in Tennessee exemplifies the trend away from bans and restrictive conditioning of courtroom broadcasting. Until 1995 Tennessee banned cameras from courts unless all parties in a case agreed—and they rarely did, according to a local report.[36] But the state supreme court's administrative office conducted a year-long study of the subject and recorded comments from attorneys, judges, media, and the public. As a result of its report, the court decided to conduct a one-year pilot program in 1996 allowing cameras and recording devices, and thereafter to decide whether to make the new rule permanent.[37] Under the experiment, judges had discretion to allow television, as well as the responsibility to assure decorum and to protect jurors and children from exposure. After a year, the rule was made permanent.

States proceeded cautiously, implementing rules to control the conditions under which televised trials would be implemented. The nation-wide experience could be viewed as a classic example of federalism at its best, with states operating as local laboratories for experimentation, subject to the Supreme Court's oversight in balancing the broad constitutional issues by which the state experiments would be ultimately measured.

In 1996, Indiana became the forty-eighth state to drop its ban on courtroom cameras when it permitted televising the arguments in its supreme court, leaving only South Dakota, Mississippi, and the District of Columbia continuing the ban. The experiment will provide a basis for evaluating whether to expand cameras into other courts in Indiana.[38] Early indications are that the experiment has been successful. The chief justice stated that the practice increased public understanding of how courts work. The deputy attorney general who gave the first televised argument (a capital punishment case) reported that the cameras were not a distraction: "it was if [they] weren't even there." The defense counsel agreed, as did a state supreme court spokesman.

The Radio and Television News Directors Association (RTNDA) reviews annually the experience of the forty-eight states that allow television in courts.[39] Its results are charted in Table 1 and in Appendix A.

Presently, forty-five states have permanent rules that permit some forms of television trial coverage; six states have experimental rules (four of these have both permanent and experimental rules). Forty-two states permit cameras in both the trial and appellate courts; in all but two states, the rule applies in both civil and criminal cases. One state, Pennsylvania, only allows coverage of civil trials. Two states, Maryland and Texas, allow trial and appellate coverage only in civil cases. Four states (Delaware, Idaho, Illinois, and Louisiana) permit coverage in civil and criminal cases, but only in appellate courts. Forty-one states permit cameras in criminal trial proceedings; of those, only five require the consent of the defendant.

Not every case is eligible for coverage. All states that have experimented with television in courts have preconditions or limitations on the coverage allowed. These conditions fall into various categories. The first involves the permission of certain trial participants. Forty-seven states require the court's consent (in twenty-nine states prior consent is an absolute condition; in eleven states prior notice is an absolute condition; thirteen states do not require *prior* consent or notice, but do require the court's consent). Five states require the defendant's consent in criminal trials. The prosecution's consent is required in three states and not required in thirty-eight states. The party's consent in civil cases and criminal appeals is required in eight states and is not required in forty-one states. The consent of the counsel in civil trials and all appeals is required in five states and not required in forty-four. The consent of witnesses in civil and criminal trials is not an absolute condition anywhere, though there are nu-

Table 1. Summary of Expanded Media Coverage of State Courtroom Proceedings

A=Appellate courts   P=Permanent rules
Au=Audio only   S=Supreme Court only
B=Background shots only   St=Still photography only
C=Certain types of cases only   T=Trial courts
D=Day(s)   U=Upon approval of judge;
E=Experimental rules   or, unless juror objects
N=No   Y=Yes

State	Civil	Criminal	Court's consent required	Notice to court required	Party's consent required	Coverage of participants limited	Coverage of jurors	Certain matters excluded
Alabama (P)	T,A	T,A	Y	—	Y	Y	B	Y
Alaska (P)	T,A	T,A	Y	1D	C	N	N	N
Arizona (P)	T,A	T,A	Y	—	N	N	B	Y
Arkansas (P)	T,A	T,A	N	N	Y	Y	N	Y
California (P)	T,A	T,A	Y	—	N	N	N	N
Colorado (P)	T,A	T,A	Y	1D	N	N	B	Y
Connecticut (P)	T,A	T,A	Y	13D-A 3D-T	N	Y	B	Y
Delaware (E)	A	A	N	Y	N	N	—	N
District of Columbia	—	—	—	—	—	—	—	—
Florida (P)	T,A	T,A	N	N	N	N	Y	N
Georgia (P)	T,A	T,A	Y-T/A N-S	—	N	Y	B	N
Hawaii (P)	T,A	T,A	N,A	N	N	Y	N	Y

State								
Idaho (P,E)	T,A	T,A	N-A Y-T	N	N	N	N	Y
Illinois (P)	A	A	N	5D	N	N	—	N
Indiana	—	—	—	—	—	—	—	—
Iowa (P)	T,A	T,A	Y	14D	C	Y	B	N
Kansas (P)	T,A	T,A	N	7D	N	Y	B	N
Kentucky (P)	T,A	T,A	Y	—	N	N	Y	N
Louisiana (P)	A	A	N	20D	N	N	—	N
Maine (P)	T,A	T,A	Y	—	N	Y	N	Y
Maryland (P)	T,A	A	Y	5D	N-A Y-T	Y	Y	Y
Massachusetts (P)	T,A	T,A	N	Y	N	N	B	Y
Michigan (P)	T,A	T,A	Y	3D	N	Y	N	N
Minnesota (P,E)	T,A	T,A	N-A Y-T	1D-A	N-A Y-T	Y	N	Y
Mississippi	—	—	—	—	—	—	—	—
Missouri (P)	T,A	T,A	Y	5D	N	Y	N	Y
Montana (P)	T,A	T,A	N	Y	N	N	Y	N
Nebraska (P,E)	T(Au),A	T(Au),A	N	N	N	N	—	Y
Nevada (P)	T,A	T,A	Y	3D	N	N	B	N
New Hampshire (P)	T,A	T,A	Y	—	N	Y	U	N
New Jersey (P)	T,A	T,A	Y	—	N	Y	B	Y
New Mexico (P)	T,A	T,A	N	1D	N	Y	N	N
New York (P,E)	T,A	T,A	Y	7D-T	C	Y	N	Y
N. Carolina (P)	T,A	T,A	N	N	N	Y	N	Y
N. Dakota (P)	T,A	T,A	Y	3D-A 7D-T	N	Y	N	N

TABLE 1 (Continued)

State	Civil	Criminal	Court's consent required	Notice to court required	Party's consent required	Coverage of participants limited	Coverage of jurors	Certain matters excluded
Ohio (P)	T,A	T,A	Y	1D-S	N	Y	N	N
Oklahoma (P)	T,A	T,A	Y	—	C	Y	U	N
Oregon (P)	T,A	T,A	N-A	—	N	Y	N	Y
Pennsylvania (E)	T	—	Y-T	—	N	Y	—	Y
Rhode Island (P)	T,A	T,A	Y	N	N	N	B	Y
S. Carolina (P)	T,A	T,A	Y	Y	N	N	B	N
South Dakota	—	—	—	—	—	—	—	—
Tennessee (P)	T,A	T,A	Y	2D	C	Y	N	N
Texas (P)*	T,A	A	Y	—	Y	N	—	N
Utah (P)	T(St),A	T(St),A	Y-A	2D-A	N	Y	B	N
Vermont (P)	T,A	T,A	N	N	N	N	B	N
Virginia (P)	T,A	T,A	N	N	N	Y	N	Y
Washington (P)	T,A	T,A	Y	—	N	N	Y	N
W. Virginia (P)	T,A	T,A	Y	—	N	N	Y	N
Wisconsin (P)	T,A	T,A	N	3D	N	Y	B	Y
Wyoming (P)	T,A	T,A	Y-T	1D-T	N	Y	N	N

*Further categorizations of trial coverage are not included here because guidelines have not been issued yet.

Note: All states in which coverage is indicated permit audio and video coverage for radio and television, plus still photography.

Source: Copyright © 1997 by the Radio and Television News Directors Association. Used with permission. *News Media Coverage of Judicial Proceedings with Cameras and Microphones: A Survey of the States,* January 1, 1997. The full text of this publication should be consulted for a more detailed

merous limited conditions in seventeen states. The witnesses' permission is not required at all in twenty-nine states. Eighteen states prohibit coverage of jurors; seventeen states limit the coverage of jurors, and six states have no rules regarding coverage of jurors.

Most state rules require advance notice or requests to the court before television coverage is allowed. In twenty-one states, no particular time frame is prescribed; seven states require one day's notice; fourteen states require between two and seven days; three states require seven days' notice; and eleven states have no notice requirement at all.

Most states exclude specific kinds of cases or categories of witnesses from television coverage. For example, thirteen states limit coverage in adoption cases, fifteen in child custody cases, and fourteen in divorce cases. Eighteen states limit coverage of juvenile proceedings. Ten states limit coverage of notices to suppress. Nine states limit coverage of police informants, six of relocated witnesses, and fourteen of sex crime witnesses. In cases where trade secrets are involved, eleven states limit witness coverage. Eleven states limit coverage of undercover agents, and three limit coverage of witnesses in orphans court.

Finally, there are specific limitations on broadcasting certain types of hearings. In camera proceedings are not covered in five states; proceedings before clerks of court and magistrates in one state; probable cause proceedings in two states; minor (age) witnesses in four states; notices to dismiss in three states; voir dire hearings in eleven states; notices for acquittal and for directed verdicts in two states; in limine proceedings in two states; witnesses in jeopardy of being hurt in one state; hearings on the admissibility of evidence in one state, of domestic disputes in two states, and of arraignments in one state.

Though there is little chance that the presence of cameras will prejudice the parties or the judicial process in appellate cases, and though the educational potential of appellate proceedings is obvious, more trials than appeals have been televised.[40] Since most requests to televise proceedings are initiated by the media, they are missing a tactical advantage by ignoring this opportunity. Cynics are likely to presume that broadcasters are less interested in the edifying issues in appeals than they are in the more entertaining features of notorious trials.

A notable example of the successful televising of the appellate process began quietly and inconspicuously in Olympia, Washington, in 1993. A former state legislator, Dennis L. Heck, started TVW, a twenty-four-hour, free, daily cable channel. In 1995 TVW began to broadcast gavel-to-gavel live coverage, like C-Span, of legislative sessions, executive boards and commissions, public events and ceremonies, and appellate legal arguments before the state supreme court to millions of viewers. It also provides audio archives of these arguments on the Internet. With funds provided by the state legislature, matched by grants from individuals, corporations, and foundations, TVW reached 1.5 million people in 643,000 households in its first year of operations.

The basic impetus behind TVW is to make the workings of government more accessible to the people. The nonprofit company's founder has no interest in expanding the company or selling franchises in other states; his only interest is in assisting other states that want to follow TVW's initiative in their jurisdictions. When network television and newspapers shrank their coverage of the state's business (despite trends toward openness in government proceedings), and polls showed strong and broad-based public interest in unedited coverage of government operations, Heck started the Washington Public Affairs Network. Drawing on the experiences of C-Span and the six states that provided gavel-to-gavel coverage of nonjudicial branches of government, using start-up funds provided by the Washington legislature, and exploiting the relatively low cost of transmitting through an optical fiber cable infrastructure, TVW was able to provide statewide programming over cable in less than two years.

When TVW began, Heck presumed the courts would resist any participation with the planned network. To his surprise, the administrator of the state courts asked him: "Why did you leave us out?" Heck met with the supreme court's Bailiff, Jack Day, and they quickly and easily worked out ground rules (never written, everything was done with a handshake). The justices unanimously approved the plan.

Several shoebox-sized robotic cameras are placed strategically in the courtroom and operated from a control room across the street. Video and audio signals are carried by fiber-optic cable. This is done so unobtrusively that one attorney was surprised to learn that his argument had been broadcast. The voice-activated cameras are pointed at the speakers' heads—attorneys arguing, judges questioning; there are no dramatic follow-up shots, nor do cameras zoom in on speakers.

The justices support coverage of their court's proceedings enthusiastically. One justice campaigned on the issue of open hearings. Another helped TVW get the legislature to support and fund the project. A third justice endorsed it before the state bar association. One justice was pleasantly surprised when he was approached by an umpire at a little league baseball game who complemented and thanked him for his interesting questions in a case that had been televised.

For those cynics who feared that only sensational cases would attract public attention and that legal issues would make dull programming, Washington's experience teaches a lesson. A variety of important issues were presented to the public in the forty cases televised in the first year. Cases were argued on such subjects as whether an employee could be fired for violating a company rule when he assisted a citizen taken hostage, the application of the state's restitution laws, what procedures should govern the prosecution of juveniles and mentally ill defendants, the operations of the state discrimination laws, the constitutionality of certain criminal procedures, the legality of term limits for elective office, appropriate labeling of music with profane lyrics, whether hate crime laws offend freedom of speech guarantees, and the application of product liability and legal malpractice laws. The coverage was edifying and dignified. Through it, a broader public has come to know more about its legal and judicial system. No longer is the operation of the government in Washington open only to the view of those in Olympia. The TVW model is, in the enthusiastic words of its annual report, "A serendipitous blend of the wisdom of our founding fathers and the technology of the 21st Century."[41]

This network is not interested in ratings, so it does not select sensational cases, nor does it provide interpretation and analysis. It simply covers deliberations thoroughly, without sound bites or editorial commentary. Like the televising of entertainment and sports, full coverage presents "the real thing," not a journalist intermediary's version of what happened. Interactive capabilities will give viewers the choice to tap into a database that provides additional background about the case. Free access is provided to educational institutions for classroom use, but TVW denies use of its programs for commercial or political purposes.

A permanent video record is provided to the state archive. Audio records of these arguments are available, live, on the Internet. This extensive coverage of state supreme court cases provides Washington's citizens (and people outside the state, as well) with information about its government, the knowledge required for democracy to work best, and it does so for relatively low costs (the annual operating TVW budget is $1.7 million; start-up capital expenditures were $1.5 million).

Several other states have sought TVW's assistance in laying plans to adopt comparable programs. In 1996, Michigan followed the Washington model. Through its nonprofit state cable network, MGTV, oral arguments before the state supreme court are now broadcast statewide. This state model provides impressive evidence against the U.S. Supreme Court's rationale for its historic and adamant opposition to the expansion of television into the high court.

THE FEDERAL RULE

Despite Justice Brandeis's admonition that Supreme Court justices should not elevate their personal views into constitutional doctrine, and the nearly unanimous trend in the states to permit televised trials, the federal judicial establishment has continued its historic ban regarding television in federal courts. In no small measure, this resistance to change is due to the antagonism of succeeding chief justices who head the Judicial Conference, the administrative rule-making and advisory agency of the federal judiciary. It is ironic that federal judges who are appointed for life and who wield awesome powers are most resistant to being observed publicly, while state judges, many of whom are elected, may be observed widely through the televising of judicial proceedings.

Since 1946, Federal Rule of Criminal Procedure 53 has barred television from federal courts in criminal cases. The Judicial Conference, mirroring the American Bar Association's Code of Judicial Conduct, promulgated Canon 3A(7) banning all televised trials. Following the *Chandler* case and the evolving experiments in the state courts during the 1970s, media organizations petitioned the Judicial Conference to reexamine its rule, but it refused.

In 1988, a Judicial Conference committee recommended a pilot program to experiment with television in courts. Eventually, in 1990, the Conference began a three-year pilot program. Federal trial courts in Indiana, Massachusetts, Michigan, New York, Pennsylvania, and Washington and appellate courts in the Second and Ninth Circuits volunteered to be in the pilot program. Controlled by the presiding judges, limited to civil cases, and subject to specific guidelines, the pilot program began in July 1991 and continued until the end of 1994. During the experimental period, courts approved 82 percent of the 257 media applications to cover trials.

The Federal Judicial Center monitored the program for the Judicial Conference.[42] Its anecdotal findings were clear and persuasive. Neutral judges presiding in these trials drew favorable conclusions from their experiences. Participating judges and lawyers observed little or no effect of the cameras on the trial participants or on courtroom decorum. The media were cooperative. And state court evaluations of their experiences disclosed that most participants reported "minimal or no detrimental effects on jurors or witnesses."

The report conceded that the surveyors could only record, through their questionnaires and interviews, the perceptions of the participants (jurors, witnesses, lawyers, and judges were questioned), but could not measure actual effects. Did television motivate witnesses to tell the truth? Did it violate their privacy or make them unwilling to testify? Did it distract them or make them nervous? Or did it make them more attentive, more responsible? Were attorneys better prepared, more theatrical, more courteous? Were judges more attentive and courteous, more inclined to be uncontroversial? Was the public educated about courts? There were no answers to these questions. Nor were the appraisers of the experiment able to measure differences between a control group and a second group to determine whether the absence of media made a difference in the results. But the anecdotal reports in the survey were informative and quite positive.

In all, 324 days of coverage during the two-year period were considered. This included fifty-six trials and a scattering of miscellaneous proceedings—twenty-seven pretrial hearings, four bankruptcy cases, twenty-four appeals, injunction and show-cause hearings, and even a judge's swearing-in ceremony. The two largest categories of these civil cases were civil rights and personal injury cases.

Perhaps the most revealing conclusion came from the interviews with the participating judges. Preconceived negative concerns seemed to be assuaged by their actual experiences with electronic coverage. The surveyors concluded that the "judges apparently experienced these potential effects to a lesser degree than they had expected," and thus their changed attitudes could be attributed to actual experiences rather than any changed general attitude toward the media. Since there is scant empirical proof that problems are caused by the mere presence of television, and the debate has been limited by these perceptions, these changed perceptions based on actual experiences are revealing.

The same was true for attorneys (plaintiff and defendant lawyers). Those who responded to the study questionnaire generally ended up with more favorable attitudes about electronic coverage (28 percent were more positive, 4 percent less so, 68 percent unchanged).

The evaluators also conducted telephone interviews with judges, media representatives, and involved court staff. Generally, those questioned thought that the guidelines were workable and that the pooling arrangements worked smoothly (requiring fewer media members in the courtroom). Interestingly, most of the judges concluded that "audio and visual access enhanced news coverage" and that the coverage was "more beneficial and realistic than conventional coverage," despite the fact that it was selective (key testimony, opening and closing remarks, verdicts) and was requested when there were "high profile" litigants, cases of local interest, or broad issues were involved. Media representatives agreed: "Video tells a much better story than a sketch artist's rendition—one can see when a judge gets angry and the facial and body expressions of the parties." However, the surveyors' report about their content analysis adds weight to cynics' claims. The study concluded that "the stories did not provide a high level of detail about the legal process," but rather were used to accompany reporters' narration and reinforce and illustrate their commentary. Of course, there was no gavel-to-gavel coverage in any of these cases.

The federal study also commented on twelve state studies of the effects of electronic media on witnesses and jurors, mostly in state criminal cases. These studies showed that few witnesses or jurors reported being distracted or nervous as a result of the media. In all twelve states—Arizona, California, Florida, Hawaii, Kansas, Maine, Massachusetts, Nevada, New Jersey, New York, Ohio, and Virginia—television had caused no distractions to jurors, nor did it influence jury decision-making. Television coverage did not lead jurors to conclude that the case was important, nor did the presence of television make jurors less willing to serve. The states' findings (strong in every case, overwhelming in some places such as California and New Jersey) supported the Judicial Center staff's recommendations. Other states' studies reviewed by the Judicial Center in its survey, though not cited because their methodologies were deemed insufficiently rigorous by the Center staff, "tend to report results that are similar to our findings and other state court findings." Thus, the federal surveyors concluded that the results of these state surveys were consistent with their own findings in the federal experiment that electronic media caused either no deleterious effects or "only to a slight degree."[43]

As a result of the federal experiment and the Judicial Center's appraisal of it, the research staff made several recommendations to the Judicial Conference. Federal trial and appeals courts should provide two-camera access to civil proceedings subject to the careful guidelines followed in the experiment. Because extended coverage enhances the educational function of the judicial process, gavel-to-gavel coverage with two cameras should be required. Permanent camera facilities should be refined and used.

When the Judicial Conference met (in closed session, as is its practice) in December 1993 to review the staff evaluation of the pilot program and consider its recommendations, it asked for a supplemental report dealing with three questions. First, the Conference wanted to know why the evaluators relied on surveys of judges and attorneys, rather than of jurors and witnesses. Second, it inquired what other studies by various states had determined about the impact of television on jurors and witnesses. Third, it asked what the costs would be to install permanent electronic media facilities in federal courtrooms.

The responding staff report replied that jurors and witnesses were not well-situated to make valid judgments about the effect of electronic media on themselves.[44] State surveys, the response continued, confirmed their findings that most trial participants thought electronic media presence had no or minimal detrimental effect on jurors and witnesses. Finally, the report stated that the cost of equipping each federal courtroom for electronic media would be between $70,000 and $120,000.

Despite the results of the experiment and the recommendations of the staff, the prohibition against televised coverage of civil and criminal proceedings was not changed. As the *New York Times* reported, the federal experiment "assuaged some deep-seated fears about the impact of television in the courtroom," but it "won few enthusiastic converts, and the issue remains a subject of heated debate."[45] The experiment "ultimately fell victim to a yawning cultural gap between the Federal judiciary's self-image and the exigencies of television news. . . . The judges were offended . . . at being used as backdrops or visual aids for the self-styled experts and talking heads of network news."[46] Steve Brill, Court TV's founding impresario, wryly observed the irony that the judges "threw out their own evidence" from "their own in-house think tank."[47]

Recent years, however, have seen cracks in the wall of resistance to cameras in the federal courts. The first appeared in 1996, in a civil case in the federal trial court in New York City. The case, *Marisol v. Giuliani*,[48] involved a class action on behalf of eleven plaintiffs against the city's Child Welfare Administration (the mayor and the governor were parties, as well) asking Federal District Court Judge Robert J. Ward to appoint a receiver to reorganize and run the beleaguered and long criticized agency.

The facts giving rise to the case were egregious—an abused five-year-old girl had been starved, locked in a closet, and horribly brutalized in a foster home where there was drug dealing, violence, and neglect. The city agency knew of the conditions in this home, but had returned the child to her foster mother's custody. Children's rights organizations brought the lawsuit seeking a top-to-bottom reform of the controversial agency, as had happened in other cities— the District of Columbia, Kansas City, and Philadelphia—where institutional negligence was proven. The child advocate groups charged the New York City agency with lack of accountability, swollen caseloads, untrained caseworkers, poor supervision, inadequate resources, and mismanagement.

Court TV asked the court for permission to televise the complete oral arguments by the lawyers. The plaintiffs agreed to the request, but the defendants opposed it, arguing that the public could not comprehend the procedural aspects of the case and the legal nuances of the arguments. The city attorneys said they would not oppose televising the trial itself, but did fear the implications of televising the pretrial arguments.

Counsel for Court TV urged that the various district courts each have their own intramural regulations regarding cameras in their courts, and those regulations are not overruled by the Judicial Conference recommendations on the subject generally. Television and children's rights advocates argued that people ought to be informed about the abuses that were being questioned. As one children's advocate remarked: "The more these issues are aired publicly, the better." Broad cultural changes originate, she argued, from an informed and attentive public, and television would help that cause. The lawyer for Court TV added: "This civil rights action raises one of the most significant issues in American social and political life today." A case of such profound public importance should be witnessed by the public, he argued.

Judge Ward agreed that "the public interest would be served" by televising the two-hour proceedings. He acted under his court's local rule and did not consult with the Judicial Conference before making his ruling. The court was not willing to conclude, as the government attorneys had suggested, that the public was unable to grasp the meaning of the information communicated—a rather arrogant notion to press upon any court, and one which, if true, commentators on both sides of the case could correct on Court TV.

A *New York Times* editorial called Judge Ward's decision "an act of judicial independence"[49] that challenged the view that the Judicial Conference effectively banned cameras in federal courts. The editorial argued that Judge Ward's ruling was in the public's interest and urged Congress to rethink the statutory ban on cameras in all criminal cases.

Soon thereafter, in April 1996, Court TV asked permission of another federal judge in New York City to televise an oral argument of a pretrial motion.[50] The hearing pertained to a class action civil case, *Katzman v. Victoria's Secret Catalogue*, charging the Victoria's Secret company with discriminatory pricing of its mail order catalogue. Court TV relied on local Rule 7, which allows that court to establish local rules, as well as its prior experiences in televising fifty-one federal cases. The plaintiff supported the motion; the defendant opposed it.

Court TV's attorneys pointed out that three New York studies evaluating experiments with televised trials demonstrated that they enhanced public education about the justice system and legal principles and raised the level of other press coverage. They argued that because there could be no witnesses or jurors, motion arguments are more akin to appeals than trials. And they stressed that Court TV's gavel-to-gavel coverage avoided the commonly advanced criticism that sound bites distort the public perception of court proceedings.

In granting the motion, Judge Robert Sweet clarified the tangle of contradictory rules governing this situation. The Federal Rule of Civil

Procedure 83(a)(1) allows federal district courts to make rules governing their practices. Rule 7 was adopted by the Board of Judges of this court pursuant to its power—indeed, the power of all congressionally established courts—to "prescribe rules for the conduct of their business."[51] The Judicial Conference, while declining to follow the recommendation of its task force to allow the televising of federal civil trials and appeals (in September 1994) left to the eleven individual Courts of Appeals (in March 1996) the right to decide whether to permit televising appellate arguments. The Conference urged the Circuits to "abrogate any local rules of court" that defied its hortatory position; but as Judge Ward noted in his *Marisol* opinion, the Conference's position, however influential, does not in fact supplant the governing local rule adopted by that trial court.

Thus, in this New York district at least, the individual judges have the discretion to permit cameras in their courts. Other courts in other districts having similar rules may, too, and now there is precedent for their doing so. Judge Sweet concluded that there is "a presumptive First Amendment right of the press to televise as well as publish court proceedings, and of the public to view those proceedings on television."

The importance of the *Marisol* and *Katzman* precedents is that they demonstrate to the other ninety-four federal district courts that the judicial conference policy on cameras in courts does not override practices permitted under local rules. One recent article stated that fourteen out of the ninety-four districts have rules permitting judges to allow cameras, but sixty-six districts ban cameras.[52] The *Marisol* and *Katzman* cases were the first times cameras were permitted in federal courtrooms after the federal experiment ended in 1994. New York was one of the districts that had participated in the successful federal experiment. However, both broadcasts were of civil cases, and the federal ban still applies to criminal trials. The coverage involved strictly oral arguments by lawyers, and not examination of witnesses before a jury. But the two cases do provide precedents for judges in districts having local rules permitting cameras in limited situations to depart from the recommended total ban without seeking permission from the Judicial Conference.

The issue arose again in a sexual discrimination and wrongful employment termination case in which neither party objected to Court TV's application to televise the trial, though the defendant's law firm was concerned about sensitive testimony concerning salaries.[53] Although its trial record is public, the court reasoned, there is nonetheless a distinction between the availability of information and the broadcasting of it. Using a kill switch to control what was and was not transmitted, thus allowing sensitive testimony to be blocked, the court allowed broadcast coverage.

In 1996, the Eastern District Court of New York followed the Southern District's rulings in the *Marisol* and *Katzman* cases.[54] Court TV had petitioned to televise the arguments of motions in a case where the estates of two victims of gunfire sought damages against firearms companies. Despite pressures from the Judicial Conference, that court interpreted Rule 7, permitting judges to decide the appropriateness of televised proceedings, to allow Court TV to intervene and broadcast arguments in a case. "[T]he public should be permitted and encouraged to observe the operation of its courts in the most convenient manner possible, so long as there is no interference with due process, the dignity of litigants, jurors, or witnesses, or with other appropriate aspects of the administration of justice," Judge Jack Weinstein ruled. About the revolutionary influence of television, Judge Weinstein wrote: "In our democracy, the informed tend to be more robustly engaged in public issues. Information received by direct observation is often more useful than that strained through the media. Actually seeing and hearing court proceedings, combined with the commentary of informed members of the press and academia, provides a powerful device for monitoring the courts."

Despite its adamant refusal to end its ban of television trials, the Judicial Conference voted on March 12, 1996, to allow each of the thirteen circuit courts to decide for themselves whether to allow television coverage of appellate arguments. The vote was close, 14–12; it applies to civil cases, but it is unclear whether it changes Federal Criminal Procedure Rule 53, which bans cameras in federal criminal trials. At the time, one respected judicial proponent of televised appeals stated, "There are no witnesses, no juries, and it's a fairly brief proceeding for every case." A critical colleague replied that the practice threatened judges' privacy.

In permitting the individual circuits to decide about coverage in their own courts, the Judicial Conference strongly urged each Circuit Judicial Council not to permit television coverage of district courts under their supervision and "to abrogate any local rules of court" that conflict with the Conference's 1994 decision not to permit televised trials—a direct retort to the recent rulings in New York. The Conference reminded that it feared "the intimidating effect cameras may have on some witnesses and jurors."[55]

As the principal policy-making authority of all the federal courts, the Judicial Conference has persuasive, though not determinative, powers. It exhorts and influences, but it may not legislate or command. Ten days after the Conference's pronouncement, the Ninth Circuit (covering nine western states and headquartered in California) approved televised coverage of all cases except direct criminal appeals and extradition proceedings. As one of the two appellate courts in the earlier federal pilot program, the Ninth Circuit had positive experiences and already had developed guidelines to cover these situations. The chief judge of the Sixth Circuit recommended that his fellow judges vote to permit cameras, stating "I don't see a problem in appellate courts."

In June 1996, the First Circuit passed a resolution to continue the ban, as did the Seventh Circuit. One judge commented that he was affected by the O. J. Simpson case, "where the lawyers and judge were seen by many as being preoccupied with the media." Another judge protested that "the public should be able to see what's going on in the courtroom. In today's world, the only practical way of seeing what's going on in the courts is through television."[56]

The American Judicature Society, a prestigious and venerable private organization of ten thousand judges, lawyers, and private citizens with a special interest in the court system, publicly endorsed the U.S. Judicial Conference policy allowing the thirteen circuit courts to adopt rules permitting the televising of appellate proceedings. The Society's executive vice president and director, Frances K. Zemans, argued that the Conference recommendations did not go far enough:

"We urge all federal appellate courts to enhance public knowledge about our legal system by allowing broadcast coverage. . . . We're glad to see the Judicial Conference move beyond the negative buzz about televised court proceedings generated during the O. J. Simpson trial, but we'd like to see them move farther and faster by allowing coverage of federal trials, not just appellate arguments. . . . [I]n today's world, television is the most effective way to bring the public into court. We hope this action by the Judicial Conference is a signal that the movement toward allowing cameras fuller access to our courtrooms is regaining momentum."[57]

The Supreme Court, while refusing to ban televised state trials on constitutional grounds, has consistently refused to endorse televising its own proceedings. In the *Estes* case, even liberal members of the Warren Court voiced their objections to any television of trials. Chief Justices Burger and Rehnquist, opposites on the judicial spectrum from the Warren Court, have clearly condemned the idea of televising the Supreme Court's appellate arguments. In 1996, Associate Justice David Souter stated to a House Appropriations Subcommittee that there would be television in the Supreme Court "over my dead body," and his colleague Associate Justice Anthony Kennedy agreed with this conclusion, although in less dramatic rhetoric. One insightful reporter commented, that "the Justices cherish their privacy, . . . and have no wish to become electronic visitors to the nation's living rooms."[58]

———

Whatever the future of televised trials in the United States, and whatever the disagreements over its role, impact, and limitations, the American judiciary has far more extensive experience with this medium than any country in the world. De Tocqueville wrote long ago that America was a country uniquely involved with its laws and lawyers; perhaps the public's interest in televised trials is the latest expression of this phenomenon. Other countries have fundamentally different legal and trial systems, and varied policies about the openness of their trials. Few places outside the United States have had any experiences or dispositions to experiment with cameras in courts.

The few that have made exceptions to banning cameras in courts have done so infrequently.[59]

Canada's historic ban on cameras in courts has only recently been lifted to permit televising two Supreme Court cases, and a two-year limited experimental project began in 1994. Mexico has open trials and no ban on cameras. While it has permitted film excerpts of cases to be broadcast, there have been no televised live trials. In most Latin and Central American countries, even if trials are open to the public, cameras are banned and only snippets of trial proceedings are permitted to be shown after the fact. The most notable televised trials abroad were in Israel, which as a general rule bans cameras (the court can permit filming); there, in the Eichmann and Demjanjuk war crime trials, which were televised worldwide, the educational and historical message overwhelmed all previous regulations. The more autocratic the government structure—Japan, China, and Korea, for example—the more decisively cameras have been forbidden. Yet, even countries with more democratic traditions, such as the Czech Republic and Denmark, are very conservative on this subject and generally deny the filming of court proceedings. Some countries allow exceptions in rare instances—archival usage of cases of historical interest (in France), unusual constitutional issues of public interest (Germany), and one network (in Italy) that broadcasts trials regularly when the judge and parties agree. With rare exceptions such as these, the general rule around the world has been no television in courts.

The American experience with televised trials, whatever its limitations and despite concerns over its implications, is in the forefront in involving the public in the country's courts and justice systems. The trend is clearly and increasingly toward more common acceptance of television in courts. As technology improves, administrative problems are eliminated, and the practice becomes more widely accepted, it is difficult to imagine a reversal of this trend. Indeed, as the new century arrives, the Supreme Court may well face the question of whether television has a constitutional right to be in all courts, subject only to reasonable judicial controls in the interests of justice.

Chapter 4

A Thing Observed,
a Thing Changed

What is the Impact of Television
on Trials?

There is an unstated presumption that the use of a television camera in a courtroom inevitably affects the trial participants. Lawyers primp, witnesses fret, judges pose, jurors are pressured—or so common wisdom has it. As a result of these supposed reactions by trial participants, the justice system is thought to be disturbed, if not perverted. However logical and sensible this presumption may seem at first glance, very little unequivocal evidence exists to prove it. Major policy decisions must be based on more than intuition, especially when—as in the context of cameras in courts—there are profound constitutional implications.

Few studies have tested the hypothesis that courtroom cameras change behavior; such a hypothesis is difficult to prove or disprove. However, anecdotal experiences with televised trials seem to indicate that the widespread fear of cameras may be unfounded. In the state and federal surveys of trial participants, described in chapter 3, once-skeptical critics of the idea generally expressed satisfaction with the practice after actually experiencing it in real cases.

Before Florida adopted its model rule, which led to the *Chandler* decision and which other states would later emulate, the Florida Supreme Court conducted a survey to assess its one-year pilot experiment with cameras in courts.[1] It was a post hoc sample survey of 2,750 participants' attitudes and perceptions, admittedly eclectic and nonscientific, but telling in its results. Though most of the state court judges were unsympathetic with the notion, response levels were high and most concerns about televised trials were addressed. Little effect on the dignity of the proceedings was noted. Distractions were negligible. Neither the truthfulness of witnesses nor the concentration of jurors seemed to be affected. Participants were somewhat conscious of the presence of the cameras, and some were slightly nervous, but both jurors and witnesses thought they were more responsible in their actions. Little difference was noted between television and print media representatives. The supervising justices added their comments that "we found no adverse effect upon the participants' performance or the decorum of the proceedings."

In 1995, Court TV commissioned a survey of judges who had presided over the three hundred civil and criminal trials it had broadcast from federal and state courts in thirty-two states during its first four years of cable coverage.[2] The judges were asked whether Court TV personnel were courteous, respectful of the court and its processes, dressed appropriately, or did anything they shouldn't have done, and whether cameras impeded the fairness of the process or portrayed trial events so as to contribute to public understanding of the legal system. The judges were also invited to make any other comments they wished.

A large majority (71 percent) of the judges (197 of the 278 questioned) responded positively to Court TV's presence, and their comments provide important insights to the questions commonly raised about the impact of cameras in courts. A California judge said, "After the first five minutes we didn't even notice the camera in the courtroom." A Texas judge reported: "I confess to having some significant concerns prior to the beginning of trial, but was actually reassured by another judge who had been televised by Court TV. That judge had advised me that actually Court TV's professionalism had brought the level of other media personnel to what he believed was a higher professional standard. My experience was very similar."

A solid majority (65 percent) concluded that television coverage "helped convey the events of the trial in a way that contributed to the public's understanding of the legal system." A New York judge stated that the jury told him "the cameras did not interfere with their responsibilities." A Denver judge noted that the audience seemed to learn about the judicial system. A Michigan judge concluded that the television coverage provided "a very large public service"; it provided a better way to see how courts work than relying on a reporter's version, one of his colleagues added. A Florida judge praised television's educational capacity. And a Mississippi judge added, "The courts belong to the public, and the public has the right to see what we do."

How valid are these anecdotal assessments? Are they the best evidence that can be gathered on the subject? Are there more thorough and reliable sources that illumine the impact of television on trials?

———

There are lessons to be learned from social science research. Social scientists are concerned with the validity of their techniques of observation, and some of their considerations bear on the question of cameras in the courts.

In doing research, scientific observers are alert to the impact their presence has upon the groups being observed. It is likely that observers cannot avoid having some degree of influence on the groups they observe; the question always is, How much does the form of observation influence the behavior of the observed?[3] How much does the very act of observation change or distort the reality? The reliability and legitimacy of a social scientist's findings may be affected by the reaction his or her work elicits from the people or groups being observed.

There are various research methods of observation, ranging from participatory to strictly observational,[4] the latter coming closest to the camera in the courtroom. The behavior of those observed in a research situation is termed "reactivity." The important issue in social science research is the extent to which the subjects demonstrate certain behavior simply because they are being monitored.[5]

In some academic circles, questions have been raised about the validity of some observational research.[6] An example is the criticism of the conclusions advanced in anthropologist Margaret Mead's celebrated book about the sexual habits of young Samoan girls. One critic claimed that her findings were unreliable because they were obscured by her faulty field research techniques. He argued that Mead's preconceived ideas and attitudes toward the girls influenced their behavior and responses, and thus invalidated her findings.[7]

Much modern criticism is based on the fundamental question of how much one's history, gender, race, and experiences may distort one's observations. In a post-O. J., post-deconstructionist world, we have come to realize that standards of justice are perceived differently according to the social biases of the perceivers. Blacks and whites, men and women, to resort to the most obvious examples, judge the "facts" in a trial differently because their perceptions of the same "facts" are refracted through fundamentally different personal lenses. The surveys of public opinion about the O. J. Simpson verdict made this insight very clear. Thus, some scientists acknowledge in their work "the omnipresence of the uncertainty principle," that the act of observing a phenomenon inevitably changes it. They seek scientific objectivity through insisting on the most scrupulous, noninferential, nondisruptive techniques of observation.

But an additional question must be asked: If observation affects behavior, how do we know whether it affects it negatively or positively? Some experts believe that observation increases socially acceptable behavior and decreases negative behavior. Even if an observer is not present, if people are aware that some form of observation is taking place they react to being observed.[8] Human beings alter their behavior through self-monitoring, and thus may be, to use the prevailing terminology, "self-reactive."[9] Studies have confirmed that observed subjects amplify their socially beneficial behavior and suppress their adverse behavior under scrutiny.[10]

That we exercise self-control when we are watched is hardly a shocking revelation. An example of this fact was related to me by author Bettyann Kevles. Because radiologists make errors in reading X-rays, an experiment was conducted to determine if miss rates could be improved.[11] A comparison was made between accuracy rates in ordinary circumstances and in situations where the radiologists' reads were observed by another doctor or their data was reviewed by a computer. In the latter situations, accuracy rates went up. Yet, however logical this conclusion may be, it is at war with the presumptions about what kind of behavior cameras provoke among trial participants. My personal experiences as a trial lawyer suggest to me that judges behave better when they are observed, and more idiosyncratically when they operate in imperious isolation. Of course, the degree of reactivity is variable, and what positively inhibits one observed subject may negatively stimulate another.[12]

In addition, researchers have concluded that a process of acclimation to the presence of observing outsiders may alleviate initial influences and restore normalcy in observed groups.[13] The impact of being observed gradually diminishes, and thus so does the reaction of the observed.[14] That would explain the comments of participants in televised trials who remarked that the camera quickly became as invisible as a piece of courtroom furniture.

Researchers also have noted that the degree to which an observer does or does not conflict with—or provoke anxiety and disrespect in—those being observed affects the latter's reaction. In this respect, there are significant differences between the cameras in the courtrooms and the reporters outside covering the cases. The former are relatively anonymous, passive participant-observers, to use social science categories, and do not interact directly with the observed; the latter are active and interfering agents, who often cause open and hostile conflicts with the people observed. Recall common scenes of pushing reporters and hoisted broadcasting equipment on courthouse steps, and compare that scene with the invisible camera in the courtroom.

One insight, derived from social science research techniques, is relevant to questions about the impact of televising court proceedings. It is a syllogism. Observational data collected by observers creates reactive effects on the observed. The observers' involuntary selectivity and interpretation distorts the object observed. Any observer's ability to witness all aspects of any phenomenon is thereby limited to some extent. Therefore, however imperfect the courtroom camera may be in portraying a scientifically true picture, it may be less subjective (albeit more powerful) than the other traditional forms of journalistic coverage. The hidden camera may not reveal some sort of unadulterated, objective reality, but it may come closer to doing so than human reporters.

Two areas of scientific inquiry outside the legal arena are pertinent to the question under discussion: the Heisenberg Uncertainty Principle of quantum physics and the Hawthorne Principle of measuring worker performance.

HEISENBERG'S UNCERTAINTY PRINCIPLE

Is there any way to prove or disprove by objective, hard scientific evidence the general presumption that publicity disturbs trials? What insights might other disciplines, such as quantum physics, offer toward answering this question?

In 1927, as a postdoctoral assistant to physicist Niels Bohr in Copenhagen, Werner Karl Heisenberg formulated a theory of matrix mechanics (a form of quantum physics). From it evolved what has come to be known as the uncertainty principle. The young physicist-theorist, later a Nobel Prize winner, developed the idea that physical theories "should only be concerned with things that can actually be observed by experiments."[15] By drawing from the principles of quantum mechanics and its explanations of the interactions between matter and energy, Heisenberg came to a new understanding about the physical world: we cannot determine certain facts with exactitude because the observer affects the observed.[16]

Put in its most simple terms, Heisenberg's theory of uncertainty established that at a subatomic level, at least, one cannot observe a phenomenon without changing it. Thus, there is an uncertainty that limits our powers of exact knowledge.[17] To observe is to disturb. For example, "even the meagerest attempt to observe an atom is so disruptive to the atom that it is not even possible to picture what an atom looks like."[18] More specifically, it is the measurement of the variables in a quantum mechanical system (such as movement and position of an atom) that are disrupted during observation. In addition, the more precise the measurement of one variable, the greater the disruption of the others. "In the most extreme case, absolute precision of one variable would involve absolute imprecision regarding the other."[19] On an atomic scale, in other words, the process by which we observe the state of a mechanical system permits us to obtain information about that system, but at the same time allows fluctuation to enter.

Does this microscopic scientific principle of uncertainty apply to a macroscopic societal process like a trial? Does the camera modify the reality of a trial by displaying it?

Historically, scientists have developed theories about the nature of macro-observation. Galileo, for example, explored the difference between passive and active observation. The former involves situations where the presence of the observer has no effect on the nature or outcome of what is observed. An example is the setting of the sun, which results from the earth's rotation; it occurs regardless of its being observed. Galileo introduced the notion that there may be active observation that does not disrupt nature in explaining it.

Classical physics is rooted in the search for objective reality, both of the physical universe and of human behavior. Isaac Newton demonstrated that active observation was simply an extension of passive observation, and thus that instruments of science detected but did not alter the world they explored.

If any measurement of a system disturbs that system unpredictably, as Heisenberg proved, is there no way to observe without contaminating the observed? Heisenberg noted that if one agreed with a form of objective measurement—a ruler measures distance; a clock measures time—the mystery of time and space vanishes. What happens, he asked, when a concept has no generally accepted measurement of its operational definition? He dealt with atoms and microscopes and light waves. We deal in this book with the concept of justice and the workings of the trial system. Applied to human affairs, Heisenberg's revelations may be viewed as a metaphor. As one scholar of science told me, "Human activities are not at the atomic level and they involve entities with mind and will and emotions unlike atoms."[20]

Several years after Heisenberg's Principle was enunciated, another physicist advanced a profound idea about quantum mechanics. Erwin Schrödinger, an early twentieth-century Austrian scientist, proposed a hypothetical situation involving a mythical cat, to make a point about the difference between everyday perceptions of principles of physics and the insights of quantum mechanics, which are based on principles of probabilities. Suppose, Schrödinger suggested, that a live cat and a phial of poison were put in a closed, otherwise empty room. Suppose also that the poison was positioned so that there was a 50–50 chance that its container would open and the cat would be poisoned. Without looking inside, ordinary rules of chance would suggest that there is an equal chance the cat is dead or alive. But by rules of pure quantum mechanics, neither possibility is real unless it is observed to be so—the cat is in an indeterminate state until an observer sees what is in the room. Schrödinger's notion is that there is no fundamental reality in the world unless and until the world is observed.[21]

Schrödinger's and Heisenberg's insights are often compared;[22] the former focused on states of things as the source of change, while the latter focused on the variation of observables.[23] Dare one enter these deep and, to many, alien, waters, to speculate whether there are lessons to be applied from Heisenberg's Principle to the issue of cameras in courts? Not scientifically, because these principles do not apply to human systems. But the ideas lend credence to the supposition that the addition of television to courts affects the judicial process. Of course, even metaphorically, it does not suggest whether those effects would be positive or negative.

THE HAWTHORNE PRINCIPLE

One area of social science research concerning worker performance also suggests interesting insights to the question about the impact of observation.

Between 1924 and 1932, seven studies of worker productivity were conducted at the Western Electric Company's Hawthorne Plant near Chicago. These studies attempted to assess whether worker productivity increased when certain variable employment conditions were changed—such things as illumination, morale, milieu, supervision, rest pauses, duration of work, group influences, and method of payment. At the conclusion of the experiment, improvements in worker performance were noted. However, because certain increases could not be attributed to the control variables, the thesis was propounded that some other influences effected the improvement.

Labeled the Hawthorne Principle, this thesis stated that the mere awareness of their role in the experiment resulted in the workers' improved output over a period of time.[24] The study concluded that the experiment itself had produced an unwanted or at least unplanned effect. From the widely noted study, the theory evolved that unexplained results in experiments on human beings may be attributed simply to the fact that they were observed in an experiment and as a result experienced something they would not have otherwise experienced.

This study is often cited—as is the Heisenberg principle of uncertainty in quantum physics—for the proposition that a thing observed is a thing changed. That conclusion has been questioned by reputable social scientists.[25] One critic has postulated that "something other than what the experimenters explicitly introduced made workers' productivity increase."[26] But what was this extraneous variable? He speculated that conditioning through reinforcements such as information feedback and financial reward, as well as improved skills, might well have led to the workers' progressive increases in performance. In the language of behavior modification, "the consequences of subjects' performance affect what subjects do." Another author, studying the application of the Hawthorne Principle to criminal justice research, argued that the principle is misunderstood.[27] By providing feedback and removing obstacles to improved performance, standards are improved. Contrary to some interpretations of the Hawthorne experiment, he argued, mere interest in employees' well-being is not enough.

—

Does applying the Hawthorne Principle to the question of televised trials suggest that observation would change the process for the better? Do people behave better when they are being watched? Usually, we do. In trials, lawyers and judges are likely to be less idiosyncratic if their behavior is observed publicly. Certainly, in other situations people are inclined to behave better when they are being observed than when they are not. Without control groups, however, it is impossible to match the behavior of trial participants in televised and nontelevised trials. And it is impossible to create exactly comparable groups, even if one had the inclination and resources to try.

Relatively little legal research exists measuring whether and how press publicity affects trials. Some law and judicial journals and dissertations have explored the questions considered here; none are conclusive, though some are suggestive. For example, while most people presume that extensive press coverage of a case destroys the ability of the jurors to decide the case fairly, little empirical data supports this conclusion. If judges are presumed to be able to withstand the human effects of crime news, why not juries?

Is the journalism of criminal trials a reflection, rather than the creator, of community attitudes? Do juries reflect community attitudes? Are jurors swayed more by press comments than by their own past experiences and predispositions—their gender or race, for example? If the press is just one of the multitude of forces interacting on the collective psyche of the jury, why control this one and ignore the others? The influence of the press over juries is psychological and, though speculations abound, little has been done to examine it analytically. As one law journal reported: "The initial attitudes of the community and the circulation of the publication are relevant facts. But at the center of the analysis lie difficult sociological questions—to what extent do newspapers create community attitudes?—and psychological questions—to what extent do community attitudes affect the mind of the juror? The courts will have to rely on speculation from common experience to reach conclusions, until more reliable and specific studies are made than exist at the present time."[28]

Some studies have looked at the effect of the communications media on community mores. One sociologist studied crime reporting in a group of metropolitan newspapers throughout the country, concluding that crime news was noticeably embellished.[29] Such embel-

lishment sells papers and attracts a wider audience on radio
(presumably more so on television). Therefore, the advertisers who
support the communications media get their products before a larger
segment of the public when sensational crimes are featured.
Strangely, another authority noted that after the Hauptmann trial,
during which one paper's circulation increased five hundred thousand, newspapers actually lost money.[30] Seemingly, a lower caliber
of reader was attracted to the papers by the crime news. Those readers were not interested in the advertisements. Consequently, advertisers, finding the newspapers of little use in selling their wares,
discontinued their advertisements.

In *Radio and the Printed Page*,[31] Paul Lazarsfeld pointed out that
radio had a strong commercial effect, but no profound social impact.
According to him, radio broadcasters tend to be conservative in social matters. Thus, it would appear that the communications media
would have little influence on the prosecutorially disposed mass audiences of the large urban centers in which most criminal trials take
place. Then, too, adverse publicity may have the reverse effect from
that intended. The crowd, instead of judging harshly, may sympa-
thize with an accused because he is the underdog.

Readers tend to read only that with which they agree and do not
seek conflicting opinions, one researcher concluded.[32] News that
gives immediate psychological satisfaction, such as crime reports, is
of the greatest interest to the young and less educated. Probably most
jurors read papers whose reporting comes closest to their own preconceived attitudes, another indication that the press caters to preformed ideas rather than setting new standards of belief. A striking
illustration of the ways in which newspapers reinforce preformed
ideas was reported in a study of local newspapers at the time of one
notorious case in Baltimore.[33] Four city papers reported the killing
of a white woman by a black man. Three papers, which targeted
primarily white readers, favored a conviction. By contrast, the fourth,
an African-American paper, stressed the favorable background of the
accused. The same divisions of opinion along racial lines were glar-
ingly evident during the notorious O. J. Simpson trial. A University
of Southern California sociology professor who studied the effects of

media coverage among different races in the Simpson case concluded that it "had little effect on people's views over the course of the trial."[34] What people perceived merely confirmed what they already thought.

Many variables influence the effect of mass media on the public. Erwin Hovland observed that such variables as the order in which points are presented, who says what, as well as what is said, the prestige of the medium, and the interest in the topic all figure prominently.[35] Although social science has cast some light on the problem of public opinion and fair trials, it has not yet, and may never, provide a definitive answer to the question of the media's influence on trials. Until the psychological issues are resolved, provisional and imperfect remedies such as continuances, change of venue, and sequestration must suffice.

The Supreme Court said as much in reviewing a California capital murder case.[36] In *Stroble v. California,* one of the grounds of appeal was that inflammatory newspaper coverage of the defendant's arrest and confession of brutally killing a six-year-old girl deprived him of a fair trial six weeks later. However hysterical the widespread publicity was, the Supreme Court ruled, defense counsel never sought a change of venue. Without firm evidence of a prejudiced jury, the Court refused to presume that the publicity had impeded a fair trial. Justices Hugo Black and William Douglas dissented, urging that "Precisely because the feeling of the outside world cannot, with the utmost care, be kept wholly outside the courtroom every endeavor must be taken in a civilized trial to keep it outside." The dissenters despaired at the lack of scientific evidence to assess the impact of pretrial publicity upon a jury: "Science with all its advances has not given us instruments for determining when the impact of such newspaper exploitation has spent itself or whether the powerful impression bound to be made by such inflaming articles as here preceded the trial can be dissipated in the mind of the average juror by the tame and often pedestrian proceedings in court."[37]

Early social science research, based on newspaper and radio coverage, is of limited application to television. Many think that the pervasiveness of television creates a difference of kind, not merely of degree, from the impacts of radio and the printed page. Most research directly dealing with the effect of cameras in courts concludes that their presence does not adversely affect court proceedings, though few studies can be considered scientifically conclusive. While courts aspire to remain as open an institution as democracy demands, they hesitate to adopt changes based on substandard science. Much social science research varies largely in quality, and the risk of basing a legal rule on flawed research is obvious. Courts should place confidence in social science research if it "(a) has survived the critical review of the scientific community, (b) has used valid research methods, (c) is generalizable to the legal question at issue, and (d) is supported by a body of other [related] research." The critical question regarding social science is "how much success a scientific claim must have before courts will rely on it."[38]

Research into the effects of cameras in courtrooms has consisted largely of three types: surveys, case studies, and experiments. The most common research to date has been based on surveys using evaluative procedures such as after-the-fact interviews and questionnaires of trial participants. The problem of determining the effect of press comments on jurors is compounded by the practical difficulties of research in this area. Courts have been extremely protective of jurors' rights of privacy. Although jurors may subsequently disclose what went on in their minds during the trial and their deliberations, these later statements may be misleading or inaccurate since jurors cannot be observed in the actual process of deliberation.

Survey research provides information regarding individuals' attitudes toward a particular situation, but "a survey of public opinion cannot establish causal inference . . . we cannot prove that TV causes prejudice simply because people believe it does."[39] Furthermore, a report of what some people think is anecdotal is not necessarily factual. As one commentator noted, "A survey of judges and lawyers on their opinion of the validity of the Pythagorean Theorem would not change its true nature."[40]

An early example of survey research was conducted during Florida's year-long experiment with television in selected courtrooms in 1977–1978.[41] Researchers interviewed 121 trial participants at the conclusion of five criminal trials. Of the jurors, 39 percent found the cameras distracting, and 20 percent of these said cameras made them tense. In addition, 24.5 percent of the jurors thought that the cameras interfered with the conduct of the trial. Interestingly, 70.5 percent of them thought televising the trial was in the best interest of the public. The survey authors concluded that the question of subtle psychological effects of cameras in the courtroom, based on witness testimony and jury decision-making, remained unanswered.

In 1987, two researchers investigated people's beliefs about whether courtroom cameras would cause subtle psychological effects on participants in rape trials.[42] The researchers interviewed a random sample of male and female residents in the Minneapolis-St. Paul metropolitan area and found that more than 90 percent believed that the rape victim's trauma would increase as the result of televising the trial. Nearly 70 percent believed cameras would disrupt the trial process. Of the residents participating, 68 percent of respondents believed televising rape trials would reduce the reporting of rapes, while 42 percent believed doing so would raise awareness of rape issues and 35 percent thought televising the rape trials would encourage more rapes. The researchers reasoned that the participants' answers were more negative regarding the effects of television in the courtroom than the effects outside the courtroom. They attributed this to the fact that people are more capable of imagining television camera effects inside the courtroom.

In 1990, an informal survey of federal district court judges found that the majority of the sitting judges who responded supported a continued absolute ban on television in the federal courts.[43] While 62 percent opposed any media coverage of pretrial proceedings and 50 percent opposed coverage of trial proceedings, nearly 65 percent opposed any use of television in the courtroom. Only 13 percent strongly favored television coverage. The researchers also detected a sincere concern among judges that televised coverage of a courtroom might affect jurors' abilities to perform their duties. As one judge put it:

> Ordinarily, the problem which results when jurors talk with others about a case despite admonitions not to do so may not be too great. First, the temptation of the outsider to force the conversation is not too high when he knows little or nothing to begin with, so the ad-

monition may not be too often ignored. Second, both parties are likely to accept the premise that the opinion of the one who is there is probably more valid. When both are "there," however, the equation changes dramatically, and it is much harder for the one who must reach the actual verdict to defend his or her opinion. It is, therefore, much more subject to undue influence.

A 1991 survey conducted in New York State supported this suspicion.[44] When five hundred randomly chosen voters were asked over the telephone "how likely they would be to testify in court if they were a victim of crime and learned that the trial would be videotaped for broadcast on the evening news," virtually half (48 percent) were less willing to testify. Fewer respondents (43 percent) said they would be as willing to testify. Only 10 percent of those surveyed responded that they would be more willing to testify. The researchers concluded that "for every person who would be more willing to testify when cameras are in the courtroom, five people would be less willing to come forward and testify . . . or four out of ten potential victims . . . will be less willing to testify in a criminal case."

As noted earlier, Court TV's 1992 informal survey focusing on judges' reactions to cameras in the courtroom concluded that the cameras did not impede the judicial process; indeed, 60 percent of the judges thought Court TV's camera "helped convey the events of the trial in a way that contributed to public understanding of the legal system."[45] And the Federal Judicial Center's questionnaires and telephone interviews of judges and attorneys regarding cameras in the courtroom (during the period from July 1, 1991, to June 30, 1993) concluded that judges' attitudes toward electronic media improved over time. Both judges and attorneys reported witnessing little effect of cameras on trial participants. On the basis of this study, the research project staff recommended the authorization of the use of cameras nationwide in civil proceedings, subject to certain guidelines. This study had limitations: only perceived effects on courtroom participants were measured; only civil proceedings were covered; the sample was voluntary, not random; and most judges had prior experience with media coverage in their courtroom.[46]

The second type of research involves the case study. This is an examination of the impact of television on a single trial. The problem with this mode of analysis, from the perspective of policy-makers, is its lack of generalizability. Simply because one trial was or was not conducted fairly with camera coverage does not necessarily mean that other trials with other participants would lead to the same results. One doctoral dissertation concluded that "traditional speculation as to possible disruption to the judicial process by courtroom cameras appears to be unwarranted."[47] That study focused on the news coverage of four criminal trials in Florida's Eighth Judicial District and used participant observation (a researcher sitting in a courtroom watching proceedings), content analysis (analyzing trial coverage in local media), and juror exit polls (questionnaires answered by jurors). Among other things, participants were asked whether broadcast journalists following the guidelines disrupted the trial process. Generally, they answered that they did not feel distracted by courtroom cameras, nor did they have unfavorable feelings about them. The author admitted the limits of his study, which only included a handful of trials in a single jurisdiction and, therefore, must be replicated to have any validity. But he advanced his conclusion that "The empirical study does support the theoretical evidence presented by the handful of earlier experimental studies . . . that the mere presence of cameras does not lead to disruption of the judicial process."

Criticism of the survey and case study approaches include "the lack of well planned, comprehensive survey instruments, the failure to devise studies which would isolate and control the influence of a specific variable, the absence of strict control group comparisons, unstructured data collection methods, and superficial reporting of results." Furthermore, the data collected in these studies is purely anecdotal; it gives individual attitudes and perceptions of what happened, rather than attempting to demonstrate what might have actually occurred.[48]

A 1990 doctoral dissertation attempted to respond to this criticism in conducting a case study of the four-month murder trial of Joel Steinberg, the first major New York case in which televised coverage was seen on a daily basis, including gavel-to-gavel coverage of a leading witness's testimony.[49] The crime, child and wife beating, was gruesome, and the battered wife was the key witness. The study used the case as a forum to explore the question of whether the presence of a television camera affects the performance of court members and, ultimately, the nature of the process itself. The researcher believed his case study could "take into account the subtleties of human interaction and can uncover types of behavior and perceptions that otherwise may be difficult to ascertain or even recognize through traditional research methods." He used a qualitative research approach in which unobtrusive observation, in-depth interviews, and follow-up interviews were used not to seek the truth or morality of the case, but rather an understanding of peoples' perspectives.

In this study, as in the state surveys described in chapter 3, many participants reevaluated their previously held beliefs about cameras in the courtroom, finding that their experiences were different than their earlier beliefs. More importantly, the researcher discovered that "many participants appeared to 'live up' to the expectations that they believed the medium had of them, and it was that peculiar interaction that played a part in their performance during the trial." In other words, the way the particular participant defined the medium had a direct effect of her or his performance. One witness, who saw television in terms of entertainment, shielded her two daughters from any television coverage for fear it would be harmful. The prosecution viewed the cameras as a self-promotion tool of the television stations and avoided watching nightly accounts of the trial altogether. The defense attorneys admitted to using the daily news conferences as a medium to attempt to influence the jury and watched daily broadcasts to gauge their progress in manipulating public opinion. They even admitted changing their legal strategy after seeing how a major witness's testimony appeared in the news reports. The judge, who perceived the camera as a tool for self-evaluation, said he changed his behavior after seeing a news report depicting his anger at a defense attorney.

The researcher concluded that his case study revealed a complex environment in which participants often interacted with the medium based upon their previously held perceptions about how their role should unfold within this new environment. In certain cases this in-

The Scopes Trial. Clarence Darrow vs. William Jennings Bryan, debating the teaching of evolution, drew such large crowds that the trial was moved outdoors, due to the suffocating heat in the courtroom. (Courtesy of UPI/Corbis-Bettmann)

Bedlam in the courtroom during the trial of Bruno Hauptmann in New Jersey, January 7, 1935, which resulted in a fifty-year ban on broadcasting trials. Hauptmann was charged with the kidnaping and murder of Charles Lindbergh's son. Lindbergh can be seen, seated in the second row, near the extreme left, while Hauptmann is on the extreme right. (Courtesy of AP/Wide World Photos)

The scene in the press room (located in the prison garage) after Bruno Hauptmann's electrocution. Newsmen type their accounts of the execution and wire their narratives to a waiting world. (Courtesy of AP/Wide World Photos)

Dr. Sam Sheppard returning to the courtroom after recess in his first degree murder trial in November of 1954 on charges of beating his wife, Marilyn, to death. (Courtesy of AP/Wide World Photos)

Convicted ten years earlier to life in jail, Sheppard signs papers for his freedom under a $10,000 bond after his release from an Ohio penitentiary. The former osteopath was freed by a Dayton judge who believed he did not receive a fair trial due to prejudicial media coverage. The Supreme Court had ruled that, when cameras in courts create a carnival atmosphere, judges must take control of conduct in their presence, or risk the reversal of convictions. (Courtesy of AP/Wide World Photos)

Before the Estes and Chandler cases, a few states did experiment with photographed trials. After Chandler, most states—forty-eight as of 1997—permitted some broadcasting of trials. This 1955 bomb-murder trial of Henry Washburn in Waco, Texas, was reportedly the first murder trial televised in the United States. (Courtesy of Library of Congress)

The Estes trial. (Courtesy of the National Archives)

Cameras photographing a hearing to exclude cameras. In the early days of television, attempts to broadcast trials were criticized by most lawyers and judges, nearly resulting in a Supreme Court ban. These images depict the activities of still and motion picture photographers at a preliminary hearing to exclude cameras from the courtroom. (Courtesy of National Archives)

O. J. and Overkill Journalism. The cameras outside the home of O. J. Simpson during the double-murder trial of the football and television celebrity O. J. Simpson. Cameras were so conspicuous and plentiful outside the courtroom that the area across the street from the courthouse became known informally as Camp O. J. Coverage of such notorious trials can create havoc at the scene and inflame communities. (Courtesy of AP/Wide World Photos; photograph by Michael Caulfield)

The Trial of Timothy McVeigh. Even when cameras are banned inside courtrooms, their presence during celebrated trials is nonetheless ubiquitous and influential. Here, Stephen Jones, lead defense lawyer for Oklahoma City bomber Timothy McVeigh, is besieged by the media as he arrives at the federal courthouse. (Courtesy of AP/Wide World Photos; photograph by Ed Andrieski)

On Trial in Washington. New technology can eliminate physical disruption and interference by cameras. In the Supreme Court of Washington State, all arguments are televised, with little prejudicial effect on participants. (Courtesy of TVW; photograph by Michael Peters)

teraction fostered the pursuit of personal agendas; in others it enhanced a sense of public duty. Still others regarded it as an impediment to the traditional functions of the court, believing it altered the deliberative processes of law.

In contrast, one eight-year study of television in the courtrooms of eleven states, which included case studies, surveys, and experiments, concluded that "camera coverage of trials (even sensational criminal cases) does not necessarily influence the majority of trial participants to behave in ways that are noticeably different from behavior in nontelevised trials. This is not to say that many trial participants do not have mixed or negative attitudes toward camera coverage, only that the bulk of empirical research conducted to date shows little correlation between the presence of cameras at trials and perceived prejudicial behavior on the part of jurors, witnesses, judges, or attorneys."[50]

This study also noted a correlation between positive attitudes toward cameras and increased experience with camera coverage. Many participants reported that the presence of cameras in the courtroom was more likely to affect their neighbor rather than themselves, perhaps because "there may be a general tendency to see others as more easily manipulated and misled than oneself. . . . While acknowledging that a message is quite powerful, they may claim a superior level of resistance to its effects." In other words, television may have had a bad image, but it seemed to foster positive experiences.

The third device for studying the interaction of cameras and participants in the courtroom is experimental research. This technique is rare because of its expense and complexity. One commentator has stated, "Social scientists measure the intelligence of monkeys more effectively than courts have attempted to ascertain the effects of television in the courtroom."[51] In an experiment, the "investigator can systematically manipulate or alter an element of reality and then analyze the results that follow."[52] Additionally, "to test hypotheses, the experimenter deliberately introduces changes into the environment of subjects and observes or measures the effects of the changes. Because greater control is exercised over the conditions of observation than in any other research strategy, experiments more effectively eliminate the possibility of extraneous variables offering alternative interpretations of research findings. For this reason, experimental studies have long been regarded as the optimal way to test causal hypotheses."[53] The five essential characteristics of a good experimental design are unbiased observation, quantifiable descriptions, a high level of precision, an objective test of a hypothesis, and an overall efficiency of design (minimum cost for maximum results).[54]

A valid field study is said to be one in which a researcher observes real-life conditions and deliberately manipulates one or more variables. Before an experimental simulation can be carried out, "it is first necessary to identify the [prejudicial] factors operating in the trial environment before cameras are introduced."[55] Prejudice occurs if the presence of cameras "distorts the courtroom atmosphere in such a way that the jury is 'persuaded' to reach a verdict it would not have reached otherwise."[56] The obvious problem with this approach in the trial context is that real-life courtroom trials cannot be manipulated as experimental research environments. As one commentator has pointed out, "Any manipulation of standard trial procedures or selection of trial participants . . . would be constitutionally reprehensible."[57] As a result, researchers interested in experimenting with the effects of cameras in the courtroom are forced to rely on simulations. Critics contend that this limitation is fatal to the results produced because "the simulated trial lacks the very substance that is the subject of these communication processes . . . actors are incapable of conveying 'subtle information . . . relating to the issues that figure prominently in a real trial—guilt, innocence, fault, credibility, veracity, objectivity, accuracy, and persuasiveness.' "[58]

Others, however, are more hospitable to the idea that simulated trials might provide revealing insights.

> We think it highly improbable that such unique behaviors exist unless trial participants experience some mysterious type of communication metamorphosis when they testify at trial, a metamorphosis that significantly alters their behavior when compared to "testimony" provided in non-legalistic contexts such as interpersonal relationships. . . . [T]here may be changes in communication behaviors attributable to the increased stress of the courtroom, but these would constitute

an indictment of education generally and law school education specifically. The educational process relies extensively on the use of simulations to teach. . . . "Mock trials" are an integral part of most law school curricula and provide developing legal practitioners with experience that supposedly generalizes to the actual courtroom environment.[59]

During the pretrial period, potential jurors may be prejudiced by pretrial publicity, which may be filtered out in the jury selection and voir dire. One informal probability study suggests that we have an exaggerated notion of the frequency of the pretrial press prejudice problem. Using national crime statistics and conservative assumptions regarding juror behavior, the survey asserted that such bias would rarely occur.[60] The researcher posited that the conditions necessary for press coverage to prejudice jurors are threefold. First, there must be a jury trial, which occurs in only 10 percent of cases. Second, the case must be covered prejudicially by the press, which occurs 5 percent of the time. Third, the jurors must acquire and retain throughout the trial a prejudice from the press reports, which occurs only 2 percent of the time. By multiplying the three percentages, the researcher predicted that press-induced bias of jurors would occur only in one in every ten thousand cases. On this basis, the researcher concluded that "media reporting of felonies and arrests rarely affects a defendant's right to a fair trial."

Those who fear the impact of introducing cameras into courtrooms must remember that even without cameras, trials are not pristine events. During the trial itself, prejudices may arise through juror characteristics (some jurors may be more authoritative or prejudiced than others), defendant characteristics (whether the defendant is credible or sympathetic), the adversary process (the search is not always for the truth), the presentation of evidence (the number and order of arguments), attorney characteristics (prestige, age, appearance, and forcefulness), the subtle behavior of trial judges (their "editorial" smiles, frowns, head-shaking), and judicial instructions. Finally, during deliberation after the evidence is presented, prejudice may occur in many invisible forms: racism, sexism, and socio-economic differences in the relationship among jurors. For this reason, critics may conclude, as one author did, that "whether cameras are present or not, a courtroom is certainly not an impartial forum for the presentation of evidence. . . . It is an environment full of subtle, and sometimes obvious, prejudices, and the fact that cameras may be present will not necessarily alter the criteria used by jurors in reaching the verdict."[61]

The first relevant example of experimental research simulation was carried out in Wisconsin in 1976. The experiment sought to determine whether individuals are affected by the awareness that they are being televised.[62] Subjects were shown a brief film and were later asked questions about its content. Three groups were used. The first group of subjects answered the questions while a visible camera was in the room and they were told it was operating. The second group of subjects answered the questions after they were told a camera was operating behind a one-way mirror. The third group of subjects answered the questions in a room with no camera and only a researcher taking notes.

The results of the first group were most striking: they got the most answers correct, gave the longest answers, used the most number of words in answering, and waited the least amount of time to answer. The project director, James L. Hoyt, who heads the broadcast news sequence in the School of Journalism and Mass Communication at the University of Wisconsin, concluded that "the assumption that when faced by a television camera, persons' memories may fail . . . was not supported" because no significant difference was found in the respondent's verbal behavior when faced with a visible or hidden cameras.

Hoyt explained that "[p]eople apparently feel more compelled to speak more and to pause less when they are conspicuously aware they are being televised." Hoyt thought the key question was whether the lengthy answers by these subjects were full and correct: "The longer answers do not contain additional incorrect information. What they do contain is significantly more correct information directly relevant to the questions." He concluded, "[t]hese data indicate that far from being a danger and a potential hindrance to a fair trial, in this context television cameras can, in fact, lead to a fairer trial.

Because the witnesses could be expected to generate more complete and more correct information in response to the questions from the various attorneys, both sides should benefit from the increased information on which the court's decision could be reached."

Unfortunately, for several administrative reasons the Hoyt study has been deemed as only exploratory and inconclusive.[63] In the group working with no camera, the subjects did not have to answer questions in the presence of conventional media coverage, for example a print journalist or sketch artist. This ultimately meant that the "study did not adequately approximate the reality of a trial which is covered by conventional means." As a result, "no statement concerning the effects of electronic media coverage relative to conventional media coverage should be made."[64]

The second major simulation was conducted in California between 1980 and 1981.[65] This eighteen-month study was based on interviews with participants, evaluator observations, and general attitudinal surveys of judges, lawyers, and jurors. The experiment lacked the randomization of subjects that occurs in true experiments, but it followed an experimental approach through the use of field research evaluators. These evaluators "were able to see for themselves if witnesses were nervous, if prosecutors 'played up to the camera,' if jurors were distracted, and if judges were unable to keep order." The primary purpose of the study was to focus on the potential negative effects of extended media coverage on the proceedings by focusing on two questions: "Whether the presence and operation of broadcast, recording, or photographic equipment in a courtroom was a significant distraction to trial participants, disrupted proceedings, or impaired judicial dignity and decorum, and whether trial participants changed their behavior because of being televised in a way that interfered with the fair and efficient administration of justice."

Of the judges and attorneys interviewed, more than 80 percent perceived no loss of courtroom dignity and decorum because of the presence of the media. Most of the judges either concluded that media presence had virtually no effect on the proceeding or perceived a positive effect; few (only 8 percent) saw an overall negative effect. Judges were evenly divided regarding their experiences with media presence, with only 7 percent of all respondents viewing their experience negatively. The jurors' responses were more evenly split. One-third of those polled concluded that media presence had virtually no effect on the proceeding, while another third perceived a positive effect. The remaining third was split between perceiving some negative effect and seeing an overall negative experience. When asked their preference regarding the presence of electronic media, 23 percent of judges, 38 percent of attorneys, 24 percent of witnesses, and 20 percent of jurors preferred not to have cameras present. But, when asked if they would have any reluctance to participate again in a trial with cameras present, 89 percent of judges, 81 percent of attorneys, 86 percent of witnesses, and 87 percent of jurors stated they would not. The study concluded that "electronic media coverage rarely changes the behavior of proceeding participants in a significantly detrimental fashion."

A 1981 study investigating the effects of television cameras on the content of witness testimony supported the conclusion of the California study.[66] Using an actual courtroom setting, testimony from two groups (totaling fifty-eight college students) was gathered during a simulated trial in which only one group was televised. This testimony was then analyzed to determine its content, average word frequency, total length, and ratio of trivial words compared to the total number of words used. The researchers found that those individuals who were naturally apprehensive because of the courtroom setting tended to repeat more words, thereby giving longer testimony. The researchers ultimately concluded that "the presence of the camera, when considered as a single factor, had little or no effect on the verbal behavior of witnesses as far as possible effects can be measured statistically." It is questionable what insight to an actual trial can be drawn from this relatively unstressful courtroom situation, upon such an atypical group of pseudo-witnesses. But such is the nature of this kind of academic study.

A 1982 study looked at the extent to which the negative beliefs of jurors may be linked to television coverage about a case garnered from cameras outside the courtroom.[67] This research explored the possible effects of community pressure on trial jurors' ability to act independently when their identity is known to the public. In this experiment, 145 undergraduate subjects from Texas A&M University were split into two groups. Both groups read identical news stories and watched identical videotaped excerpts of a trial. While answering a questionnaire in which they were asked to render a verdict, one group was informed that they were being televised. Results indicated that 60 percent of the televised experimental group found the defendant guilty, compared to only 42 percent of the nontelevised group. The researcher concluded that "the data from this study, although certainly not conclusive, did suggest that televised trials could have an effect on jurors whose identity is available to the community."

The fifth major simulated experiment testing the effects of cameras in the courtroom was conducted in 1983.[68] It was designed to test the contention that TV cameras distract jurors, thereby reducing their reliance on evidence in the decision-making process. This view is known as the distraction hypothesis: "prejudice is believed to arise in jurors either directly because jurors are distracted, thereby reducing their knowledge of the evidence, or indirectly by altering the behavior of the other trial participants and the attitudes of the surrounding community." This researcher hypothesized that "the camera would impair recall in the initial stages, but that subjects would gradually adapt to its presence, redirect their attention to the environment, and show an improvement in their subsequent performance." He speculated that this trend would occur because "over the extended life of a televised trial, one might expect an habituation effect . . . a 'response decrease as a result of repeated stimulation.' " In addition, the researcher hypothesized that individual jurors would differ in sensitivity to the presence of TV cameras because of what he called the "Public Self Consciousness" theory. Under this theory, an individual's concern about his or her appearance, behavior, and self-presentation to others is "the dispositional analog to the state of self-awareness that is induced by an audience or a camera." Jurors with higher public self-consciousness levels were expected to be more adversely affected by the cameras' presence.

The experiment separated fifty-one subjects into two main groups of mock jurors. Each was shown a videotape of a civil negligence case and later was asked to answer factual questions. While answering, the subjects were separated into a physical distraction group in which a video camera was present but not operating, and an unobtrusive camera group where there was no camera present but subjects were told it was behind a ceiling vent. The results of the study indicated that "the presence of a camera did not systematically affect mock jurors' verdicts or evaluations of the individual witnesses or the trial as a whole. It did impair recall performance (presumably as a function of inattention), but this effect was limited in two important ways." First, the subjects' post-trial recall of important information was not significantly affected by the cameras, presumably because they adapted to their presence. Second, the camera impaired the recall of those subjects with low, rather than high, public self-consciousness levels, presumably because those with high public self-consciousness levels are more focused on themselves, rather than on the task at hand. The researcher concluded that "the presence of TV cameras does not irrevocably impair jurors' functioning[,] . . . the presence of TV cameras would not alter the outcome of jury deliberation," and ultimately "the disruptive effect of a camera on jurors is short-lived and has no bearing on verdicts or evaluations of testimony."

A 1985 doctoral dissertation investigated whether photographic coverage of trials would negatively affect audience members, potential jurors, and witnesses.[69] A total of 109 subjects, ranging in age from eighteen to sixty-five years, were randomly assigned to four groups. Each group watched a videotaped news recording covering the same fictitious trial, but each group's news broadcast was slightly different: one contained actual video coverage of the trial, one a sketch and voice-over, another a talking head news reporter, and one a non-courtroom news segment.

The subjects filled out a questionnaire that helped the researchers determine recall of material, attitudes toward the justice system, willingness to testify in a criminal trial or serve on a jury, and perceptions of defendants' guilt. The researchers found that the presence of cameras in the courtroom and the viewing of a videotape had no effect on a subject's willingness to testify in a criminal case or to serve on a jury, or on their perceptions of defendants' guilt. Again, the research resulted in a finding that "cameras in the courtroom enhance viewers' information about the trial but [reveal] no attitude changes that would imperil justice."

An extensive experiment was conducted in 1990 by three University of Minnesota professors.[70] The study, conducted in a laboratory setting, dealt only with a criminal case. In the experiment, control groups were used to establish the causal inferences of the type of media. Two media control groups were used. A total of 178 undergraduate students taking introductory psychology courses at the university were randomly split into three separate groups: electronic media coverage (EMC), in which a video camera was present; a conventional media coverage (CMC) group, in which a journalist was present; and a no media control group (Control), in which no media representative or equipment was present. All the subjects viewed a five-minute color videotape of a simulated armed robbery and were then split into three groups to serve as either jurors or witnesses in simulated trials. A few days later, the students testified as witnesses to the crime in front of a jury of peers.

Two major results were reached. First, while the presence of the camera did have some perceived psychological effect on witness behavior and there was greater nervousness among the EMC witnesses, the actual witness performance was not affected. The authors concluded that "such findings do not seem to support the concerns of those in the media who believe that cameras would be a distracting influence and make it more difficult to get the truth out of witnesses, whose powers of observation, recollection and communication are already limited in the emotional stress of the courtroom."

Second, the study found that perceived witness nervousness did not adversely affect the jurors' perceptions of the quality of those witnesses's testimony. In all three categories, jurors perceived witness testimony as believable. The study found that those who were exposed to electronic media had fewer negative attitudes than those who were not.

Again, the study found a large gap between what individuals believe is happening and what the empirical evidence suggests really is happening: "while people may *believe* that EMC is associated with a host of disruptive effects on judgment, memory, and decision making, the weight of empirical evidence from the present research does not provide support for such concerns." The researchers suggested that their study refuted the late Justice Tom Clark's concern, expressed in *Estes v. Texas*, that the impact of cameras is "simply incalculable . . . memories may falter, as with anyone speaking publicly, and accuracy of statement may be severely undermined."

In a 1991 dissertation, another researcher investigated whether the presence of a camera would affect the course of a trial—in this instance, the recall of testimony in a simulated rape trial.[71] At Colorado State University, 108 undergraduates in introductory psychology courses were selected from a larger group of 238 students who had completed a pre-screening test designed to scale their public self-consciousness level. The subjects were randomly assigned into three experimental groups to watch videotaped reenactments of a rape trial based on the transcript of an actual trial. The first group viewed the tape with no camera present. The second group did the same, with two cameras directed at them. The third group viewed the tape with two cameras directed away from them. Each group had an even match of subjects with high and low public self-consciousness levels.

The results indicated no statistically significant difference between groups in their recall ability. However, the group on whom the camera consistently focused had the lowest recall levels of any of the experimental groups. The researcher reported that his results were generally in line with the 1983 study discussed previously, which found that cameras had a short-lived disruptive effect on the juror's evaluation of testimony. He believed that "the temperamental characteristic of self-consciousness accounts for most of the variance in recall as opposed to the situational variable of camera presence." He did conclude, however, that his findings provide "cautious evidence that camera presence does serve to inhibit recall of trial testimony to some small degree, especially if the subject already harbors the tendency to become easily self-conscious anyway."

—

However limited these studies may be, they represent the only scientific attempts to measure the impact of cameras in courts. Taken together, they suggest that common lay assumptions about the likely impact of television on trials are off the mark.

Where do we go from this body of inconclusive evidence? Upon whom should the burden of proof lie? Should critics of television have the burden of demonstrating the sound basis of their fears before freedom of the press is impinged? Or should proponents of television be required to justify the presence of cameras to be sure that the fairness of trials is not jeopardized? Is an objective answer to the question even possible?

Although scientific evidence is accumulating that tends to disprove the fears that television inevitably prejudices participants, it is unlikely that satisfactory conclusive answers can come from such research. As one group of researchers concluded: "Scientifically valid evidence never will be available. Nor can any universal conclusions comfortably be embraced; the positive or negative effect of cameras certainly depends much more on the nature of the proceedings and the participants unique to each case than it does on the cameras themselves."[72]

Support for television in the courtroom must come from somewhere other than the common presumptions that are made about its presence. It would be helpful if there were scientific avenues to a clear-cut conclusion. But, ultimately, the conclusions lie in subjective value judgments that defy scientific proof. As one knowledgeable observer of the federal Judicial Center survey suggested: "Merely demonstrating the absence of a consistently malevolent effect on the proceedings does not make the case for opening the federal judiciary to such significant change and the administrative and organizational workload that would invariably accompany it. The answer lies, of course, in the enormous benefit that society and the federal system itself would realize in the long run by such a change in the position."[73]

Chapter 5

THE CRUCIBLE

C O U R T   T V

The very words *Court TV* sound anomalous. Courts and television? One is quiet, decorous, serious; the other loud, garish, frivolous. How could they be spoken of together? How could so illogical a mix of institutions—one of law, the other of communications—have evolved into such a fascinating chapter in the sociology of law? In the decade after the *Chandler* decision in 1981, most states conducted studies that led to the opening of courts to television under specific guidelines. By 1990, the cable industry had evolved and, drawing on this new opportunity, one cable network devoted itself to televising trials on a regular basis. The first six years of that network, Court TV, including gavel-to-gavel coverage of six hundred trials (about two-thirds criminal and one-third civil) in forty states, provides an extensive market test for an idea whose time appears to have arrived.

A good idea has many fathers, a venerable adage instructs. But the unconventional notion that a cable television channel dedicated to gavel-to-gavel coverage of actual trials would prosper could be said to have had a conventional father *and* mother. However, the offspring, Court TV, has been raised and nurtured—to complete the metaphor—by its father. Even he would agree, however, that the general idea of cameras in the courts was not the idea of any one person, but "is the story of the electronic media's longstanding and avid interest in covering judicial proceedings" and "the explosive growth of cable television."[1] Court TV's extensive experiment with cameras in courts provides the best available evidence for measuring the success of televised trials.[2]

THE FATHER

Court TV is an example of what can happen when a smart, aggressive entrepreneur combines a good idea and ripe timing. Steven Brill is a Yale-trained lawyer who specializes in the journalism of law. First a writer, then a publisher of law reports, legal newspapers, and a magazine, Brill expanded his timely vision to television in 1990 and became the chief executive of the Courtroom Television Network, the successful phenomenon known as Court TV. It is a twenty-four-hour, seven-day-a-week cable news channel that reports on the legal and judicial system in the United States and abroad. In its formative years, it was run by a private company, American Lawyer Media— of which Brill is a minority owner, though the major influence.

Brill's career as an impresario of popular legal journalism has been prescient and fast-paced. His first inspiration came when he was a student at Yale Law School.

> One day I was standing in front of the placement office at the Yale Law School, . . . I had a job . . . and on the bulletin board, there were all these letters from all these law firms saying they wanted to recruit at Yale Law School, and they all said they offered prospective applicants an unusual amount of responsibility for an unusually diverse group of unusually interesting and unusually important clients and an unusual amount of practice areas and they were looking for unusual standards of integrity and unusual standards of academic achievement. And I decided if they are all looking for something that unusual, it can't be that unusual. . . . And it struck me that there had

to be differences among these law firms—they all couldn't be exactly alike—and that's when I got the notion that I should write about law firms.

Soon after he graduated from law school, Brill wrote a magazine article about two law firms. That article led to the idea of doing a regular column about lawyers in a nonlegal magazine. Clay Felker, whom Brill reported to at *New York Magazine*, had taken over *Esquire*. Brill started a column in *Esquire* about lawyers. "The premise was that while . . . lawyers had this certain kind of anonymity, that is to say that lawyers shouldn't be tarred with or identified with his or her client, . . . but it didn't mean that lawyers should be completely anonymous or were irrelevant. . . . In any major legal battle or legal juncture, who the lawyers were, who the judges were really mattered. . . . It also helped tell the business story."

When the column did well, Brill thought, "Why don't I turn it into a magazine? I said to Clay, I'd like to talk to your financial backers, which was a company called Associated Newspapers based in London." Felker arranged for Brill to meet with Veer Holmsberg, Lord Rothsmere, at the Pierre Hotel in New York. The meeting was brief, from 11:00 to 11:45 on a Saturday morning, and successful. Brill's career was no longer as a journalist; he was now a businessman. Brill and Associated Newspapers created a partnership, The American Lawyer, and Brill hired a small staff of editors, who worked in cramped quarters in *Esquire*'s offices.

Brill prepared a four-page memo, stream-of-consciousness style, detailing the kind of stories he intended to use in the new magazine. By the next American Bar Association Convention, Brill was in the lobby of the Hilton Hotel personally handing out copies of his creation, the *American Lawyer*, to surprised lawyers. Subscriptions rose gradually to their present level of eleven thousand, mostly lawyers and others in the legal profession.

Brill had only just begun. He initiated a venture, first with Simon and Schuster, then with Little, Brown, to develop book projects. In 1985, *American Lawyer* expanded by buying local legal newspapers (several purchases were made in one day so that word would not get out and the prices go up). Legal newspapers in Atlanta, Connecticut, New Jersey, and other places across the country were cobbled on to Brill's media organization and remade. Venerable, dull, and barely profitable, these papers had been little more than tear-sheet-styled bulletin boards for legal notices of court calendars, local will probates, and bankruptcies. Brill added editorials and features, classified and display advertising, and spun off newsletters. Subscriptions rose markedly, as did costs. The original venture was becoming a small empire with a readership now totaling about one hundred thousand subscribers. In fact, there are many more readers because law firms may buy only one copy, but it is read by many lawyers and paralegals.

By 1989, Brill was well known as a legal publisher. Print journalism no longer seemed challenging; always ambitious, he was ready for a jump to a new medium. In June 1988, Brill was riding in a taxi in New York City listening to a radio account of a sensational trial, when he had an epiphany.[3] He had already demonstrated that newspapers devoted exclusively to law news could be profitable. Commercial television had proved the public's fascination with fictional courtroom drama; why not take the leap from *Perry Mason* and *LA Law* to the real thing? He had the network of journalistic and business connections to jump-start his idea.

"I got this idea that the way to bring the legal system to nonlawyers is to show it to them, the way jurors see when they are jurors." The networks would not be the right place for such a scheme because in Brill's mind it couldn't be done with individual programs. "I wanted to show the whole trial . . . the real guts of it had to be the motion of showing gavel-to-gavel or long-form coverage of trials." In a conversation in his Manhattan office, Brill described his initial vision for televised trials.

What's dramatic isn't the sound bite of what the *Post* says whatever the news is. It's when you get up and say "Good morning, Mr. Boesky, how are you, sir?" It's the leading up to it—that's what makes a trial, and that's what makes the trial for a jury. It's the whole thing, it's not the taking out the ten best quotes. And that's why it wouldn't have worked in print as a magazine article or any trial I have ever read as a magazine article. I was never able to make it as dramatic as the trial. I thought I wrote pretty good stuff, but I never thought I did justice, because you never get the rhythm and cadence of the trial, the way you do through show and tell. So it was really as a dramatic and as a truth telling device that I had the notion that you have to do long-form trials. Now if you do a long-form trial, then you can also do other stuff. . . . There is nothing wrong with CBS doing a five-minute report on a trial, if we're doing the whole thing, because then at least there is a frame of reference if someone really wants to see the whole trial. I'm not for news purposes denigrating sound bites of trials; what I'm saying is, the real appeal was a network that does it.

The timing for his idea was perfect. Before the era of cable, it would have been impossible.

In October 1988, he went to see Steve Ross, the head of Time-Warner, for financial backing. "I said, 'Listen, I've got an idea for a cable channel and it's a combination of C-SPAN and soap operas.' He said, 'Oh! You mean cameras in the courts during trials. You've got it.' " This was the second time Brill raised money for a business idea. This meeting took twelve minutes. Warner and Court TV were "a natural fit," Brill discovered: one had the cable systems, the other the programming. Warner soon bought out Associated Newspapers, Brill's *American Lawyer* partner.

Putting together the business network took a little longer, but Brill pushed ahead. "I said to Steve, if we're going to do this, we need, (a) the infrastructure for our publications and the credibility to find these trials all over the country, and (b) I'm not going to walk away from my publications to do this anyway. I don't want to walk away from my partners to start this new venture, because they are heavily invested in this current venture. So you and I, meaning Warner and me, have to buy out Associated and me. We will have to replace that partnership with this one. And I got Associated to do that, although they stayed in for 10 percent. They are a partner in America Lawyer Media."

Brill and his close advisors in the partnership (his wife, Cynthia Brill, is general counsel to American Lawyer Media, which manages the network; Bob Pittman was president of Time-Warner Enterprises) began working on budgets and brainstormed about possible risks. It looked to them like it would work. Once the project started, Brill's persistence overcame potential obstacles. Brill's approach to the limits of TV resembled the fabled child looking at the emperor's clothes.

> I was told you could never have a studio in this building, because the ceilings aren't high enough; you can't do television unless you have high ceilings for the lighting. And your beams are not far enough apart—so what do the beams have to do with it?—you don't have the maneuverability of the cameras. . . . I have a video camera, I take pictures in my house of my kids, I don't know how high my ceilings are and . . . if the beams are alright. But . . . I was actually closer to reality than they were, because . . . the television technical experts are people who grew up in the networks . . . in a time when camera technology was such that you really did have to have very high ceilings and beams. And I came from the current perspective. Listen, I don't care what you tell me about studio, because the people you will be seeing on television are from a courtroom, and I know I don't have control over the width of the beams or the height of the ceiling, and I know I'm going to put a camera in there, and I know I'm going to put it on television. So your job is to figure out how we're going to do it. So don't tell me that we can't do it in the studio. Because I don't need the studio to look all that much better than I need the courtroom to look, and I know I'm going to do the courtroom. And it turns out, lo and behold, that you don't need the ceilings to be that high and you don't need the beams that are that wide. You don't need it anymore because lighting technology has changed, and camera technology has changed, and audio technology has changed. But if you're using experts, this channel would have taken—we probably spent $800,000 at the beginning on all our equipment—and . . . the other two channels launched before us, namely cable channels, probably spent $8 million. So not knowing that stuff actually helps.

Brill pushed and probed, refusing to play by prevailing rules. "I would ask all kind of questions. Why do you need that? Who says you need to send three people? . . . CBS news would come and interview me, and they'd have three people standing around. They would have a real smart guy with a clipboard writing all the questions to ask, and then they would have a real dumb guy who looked good to ask all the questions. And the first thing you see is that if you can only hire a smart person that looks good, you can cut out one of those people right there. And you know what, if he doesn't look so good, who gives a . . . I'd rather have the smart person."

As his idea began to develop, Brill sought expertise to complement his administrative flair. The first person Brill turned to when his planning moved from the business end to production was Fred Graham, a former *New York Times* and CBS legal correspondent. Again, serendipity found Brill. A few years earlier, Graham had left CBS and returned to his original home, Nashville, Tennessee, as a local television anchor. Graham didn't enjoy that work and, not knowing what Brill was hatching, he wrote to Brill inquiring whether he could write a column for distribution in Brill's print network.

Graham had been developing an idea of his own to host a one-hour show about the legal system using as its centerpiece excerpts of televised trials around the country that raised interesting issues of wide public appeal. It was going nowhere. "I was trying to get back into legal journalism, and I called Steve—I probably hadn't talked to him in two or three years. . . . I was going to suggest that I write a column for the *American Lawyer* magazine, and I was going to put that together with maybe some other freelance things I'd be doing. . . . And he said to me, 'Fred, I've been thinking about calling you. . . . I'm talking with Steve Ross at Time-Warner about this idea I have . . . you know there are cameras in so many courts now, that you could . . . create an entire television network and just use the reality of what really happens in court.' I said, 'Yes, Steve, I've thought that, too. But,' I said, 'you misspoke there, You meant network television program, not network.' He said, 'No, I mean network.' I said, 'This is really something! I had thought about the same thing a few years before, but in terms of an hour program, based on real television.' "

Graham had been thinking about the same idea as Brill—using televised trials to enlighten the general public about the legal system. But Graham was thinking small. "My idea was what is now Court TV, but . . . to do it for PBS. I didn't have the vision to see that the new technology was going to make it possible for them to make so many channels available that you could do it twenty-four hours. I was thinking in terms of a one-hour program, maybe once a week. Obviously, he had thought through something that was much more visionary."

About six weeks later, Brill told Graham to forget the column, "this thing is going to fly." Brill knew all about legal journalism in print, and Time-Warner was in the media business. They needed someone who had done legal reporting on television, and that someone was Graham. "So I was the first employee of Court TV."

Graham began commuting to New York City from Nashville as a consultant to Brill, just a few days a week; soon he was working for Brill full-time. While both of them saw the potential in a cable channel devoted to courts and trials, they also anticipated the potential problems. One syndicated half-hour show based on taped trials had failed. It had a 2.5 Nielsen rating; the prevailing wisdom was that a rating of 3.5 was required for success. That put it about a million households short. And C-Span, the closest comparable channel devoted entirely to political news, had a rating of about 1.0.

They began to tinker with how to make the concept work. At first, Graham operated out of a small studio on his Nashville property. He had seen the intensive coverage of certain trials, such as the Claus von Bulow murder case in Rhode Island, and the Pulitzer divorce case in Florida. But Graham knew that there was a vast difference between covering an ongoing trial and justifying television station programming twenty-four hours a day. Graham recalls, "There was a lot more inventing of a new form than people now realize. . . . We didn't have any idea about taping things at that time, and nobody knew how many trials there are at any given time around the country in courts that are open to television, how many are there that you want to put on television."

Graham kept a log of the hypothetical trial coverage they were hoping to present and learned that continuing coverage of many cases being tried simultaneously was extremely complicated. Then, Graham remembered how CBS had handled a comparable production problem when he worked with Walter Cronkite covering national political conventions. Cronkite would converse with his reporters in remote locations so that he was not just a talking head. Instead of talking right into the camera, "I concocted the idea of always having a lawyer who handles the same kind of cases just sitting there. . . . That has not substantially changed, . . . there are a lot of really smart people who practice law and this is a way of using the talents of those people. . . . We ended up with a format that was based pretty much on what I had experienced at CBS and convention coverage."

As they experimented with ideas for making trial coverage consistently engaging, Graham learned that not everything could be transplanted from network television to this new, highly focused concept for cable. "We had a thing called the golf whisper—you know, like at golf tournaments where a person is lining up his shot and they're whispering over it. . . . Nothing is duller than a guy looking at a golf ball. And we thought there would be times like that in trials. I asked a technician to devise a device that I could use to turn down the sound in the courtroom, so I could explain what was happening if it got too obscure. And that was the golf whisper." But in this instance, Graham had guessed wrong. "We have a call-in line. Immediately we were deluged with calls from people who said, 'We are as smart as you are; I can hear what's going on. Shut up!' " The golf whisper is long gone, because the thing that Graham and his colleagues learned (and a market research report confirmed) was that people *can* get it. "We just waited until the judge finally gavelled the thing to a close and then we tried to sort it out. We would not attempt to do it now while people are talking."

Using Brill's extensive network of legal newspapers and his and Graham's personal contacts with reporters around the country, they called around to find out what interesting trials were in process. To test their idea, on a certain day they hired reporters and picked six or seven trials around the country. Graham recalled, "What we wanted to do was to have a test of what is going on at any given moment. We thought it would be like the NFL, where they pick games from around the country, or like a rain day in baseball, where you get rained on in New York and you put the St. Louis game on.

So I sent reporters to be the camera, to sit for a day. . . . What we would do is pick the one that was the lead trial . . . and when the trial would start, the reporter would call me, and report briefly what happened. I kept a log of this, and in my mind a new Court TV camera just went on in that courtroom. And then, as soon as there was a mid-morning break and I was hearing from the others, I would say we would now be going to another trial. It was an effort to get an idea how many cases there are."

Graham and Brill decided they needed input from someone with television production experience. Late in 1989, a former CBS colleague of Graham's recommended Joe Russin, a veteran freelance producer, and Brill brought him into the planning as a consultant.

Russin remembers that Brill insisted on one fundamental point: Coverage must be live. The integrity of the process required this feature. Russin described Roone Arledge's success with *Monday Night Football* and suggested adopting what he considered the central idea of that success. "Arledge's concept was not to take the football game to the television viewer at home as if he was on the fifty-yard line. The idea was to make it better than being there. My thought was to adapt Arledge's lesson and not strive simply to put the viewer in the courtroom, but to show the trial, and to make it better than being there by adding expert commentaries and analysis."

The planners had questions and concerns about how it would work. Actual trials had unpredictable stops and starts, much dead time, and different time zones. How would producers be able to maintain smooth programming if they relied on live trials? Their experiment followed two murder trials, one involving a socialite in New York City, and the other a Tennessee crash that killed school bus passengers. Brill got access to the set for *Inside the NFL* at the HBO studios. Graham anchored the coverage. Experts were used for commentaries. They simulated three hours a day coverage, with a reporter supplying on-the-scene comments. After several tests, the group agreed: It worked.

Budget discussions followed. The classic battle ensued among the planners, artists, and financiers. Brill thought that $13 to $15 million a year would be a reasonable goal. Russin thought the proper equipment, linkups, and reporters to do a variety of shows along with covering trials would cost more. Time-Warner's advisors pushed for economies. The future was not clear.

THE MOTHER

What Brill did not realize at the time was that he already had a competitor. Cablevision Systems Corporation was already in the cable business and had successfully launched thirteen networks, including American Movie Classics, Bravo and Sports Channel America. Unbeknownst to Brill, one of its subsidiaries, Rainbow Programming Holdings, was planning its fourteenth network—In Court—to provide live coverage of trials around the country. NBC was helping develop the planned network and would be a partner. Its plan was to cover all varieties of cases and feature legal expert commentators to provide analysis. The actor E. G. Marshall (known to many for his role in *The Defenders*) was to be the anchor, and Harvard law professor Arthur Miller was on board as the on-air instructor. A legal advice call-in show, an end-of-week recap of best trials, coverage of bar association meetings, and courtroom movies and television classics for fillers were planned.

In Court would attempt to get the jump on its competition by offering cable operators a nominal charge for taking other Rainbow offerings. It had two years of experience successfully airing live coverage of local trials in Long Island on a citywide, twenty-four-hour news station, News 12, and a substantial number of viewers had tuned in to watch local trial coverage. Its plan was to begin with fourteen hours of programming a day, starting at 5:00 A.M., and to become a twenty-four-hour operation in a year.

Sharon Patrick, the CEO of Rainbow, has also had a fast-paced career. A graduate of Stanford and Harvard Business School, at forty she had experience with government service at the Department of Health, Education, and Welfare and international management consulting at McKinsey and Company and had been in the cable industry for five years. She began In Court with a $300 million budget, a thousand-member workforce, and a diverse audience that was watching programs as varied as elections, hockey, and film classics.

Patrick had a huge head start on Brill. She knew about putting networks on satellites and wooing the then four thousand cable operators who in 1990 were already servicing 60 percent of American homes. She ran one of about fifty programming services in the country, all of which vied for thirty-five slots on cable casts. Patrick predicted that In Court would be "designed to meet the industry's current needs, which are to improve daytime service, without pressuring prime-time channel constraints." She retained Videoware Corporation, a direct marketing company, to help develop the project.

Cable operators were conservative about launching new networks. As the National Association of Female Executives noted in November 1990, "If the industry is not completely sold on the idea that viewers need one channel devoted to court proceedings, there's little hope it will support two."[4]

Patrick viewed In Court as "fundamentally a news service." She recognized that, as a pioneer, "the network has to handle the trial coverage in a highly responsible fashion." She knew about what the industry called "reality programming"—shows such as *COPS* that had a reputation for sensationalism. In Court's programs would be controversial "in a good sense," Patrick promised, but not sensationalistic. They would not cover, for example, the Central Park jogger murder by a roving gang of "wilding" youngsters because of the age of the defendants and the gory nature of the attack. To avoid the inevitable tedium of all trials, Patrick's plan was to switch to other trials or to commentary by specialists. Her expected advertisers would be the same marketers who advertise daytime soap operas, she predicted, because the people watching would be the same. But, she insisted, however targeted her subject may have been, the show was to be news. The planning research showed her that "a noticeable segment of cable subscribers" would watch In Court.

THE MARRIAGE

At the start, Patrick had the advantage of her experiences with cable, while Brill had his contacts in the legal system. But Brill possessed a singular passion about his mission, along with a focused drive to come from behind to develop the first cable network dedicated to trials. In Court had taken out ads in cable trade magazines. Court TV was soliciting cable operators with the demo tape Brill's team had prepared, and introducing its program to ad agencies they hoped would buy time on the channel. In August 1990, Brill wrote in *American Lawyer* that "television airwaves already filled with fictional law . . . are increasingly going to get a whole lot of the real thing." To those who feared the effects of television on the trial system, Brill replied that if "the tube can do more damage than most ink . . . it can also do more good."

While the two planned channels were competing in 1990 to sign up local cable systems, the *Los Angeles Times* reported that cable system operators, concerned that the market could not sustain two all-day channels, were urging the competitors to merge.[5] The press watched the rivalry build. The *Chicago Tribune* wondered "whether the public is ready for cable's new, heavy double dose of the living law."[6] The *Wall Street Journal* warned in a headline, "Two TV Court Channels Planned as Critics Ask If One's Too Many"[7] and wondered whether cable operators would "bump even moderately successful entertainment fare for an untested information channel." The *ABA Journal* intoned, "the real jury to watch may be the viewers."[8] Something—or someone—had to give.

By May 1990, talk of a merger was reported.[9] In October 1990, the trade press speculated that the two planned networks would merge, as had two comedy services, one owned by MTV and the other by Time-Warner, before one was perceived as having gained the foothold. It was clear that the lack of channel capacity would doom both ventures if they launched their networks at the same time. Brill went to see Tom Rogers, In Court's NBC connection, and persuaded him that Court TV was the more serious news channel. Since the marketplace would not sustain both competitors, Brill was able to persuade Rogers and his colleagues to fold their operation into Court TV. One key to Brill's success was locking in broad distribution. Tele-Communications, Incorporated (TCI), was the key because it controlled a quarter of the country's cable subscribers. TCI brought enough MSOs (multi-system owners) to the venture to make attracting a sufficient number of cable buyers possible. When Brill was able to bring in TCI as a partner, along with Time-Warner and NBC, he had the final piece to his puzzle. The deal was announced by the CEOs of Time-Warner (J. Richard Munro) and Cablevision (Charles Dolan).[10]

After a series of meetings between the key players in Brill's and Patrick's organizations, the competitors agreed to join forces, combine their advertising and subscribers, and let Brill run the joint operation.

On November 21, 1990, the Associated Press announced that Time-Warner and Cablevision would form a partnership. Brill would be the chief executive of the joint cable venture which would be launched the following July. Cablevision and its programming partner NBC would each own 10 percent of the new Courtroom Television Network. (Eventually, NBC bought out Cablevision's interest in the new venture.) A Time-Warner and *American Lawyer* partnership owned 80 percent, but Liberty Media, which bought the carriage agreement with TCI that completed the package would share in that 80 percent. Time-Warner cable operators had about 6.4 million household subscribers; Cablevision had about 1.6 million; and TCI had 8.5 million.[11] Of the universe of about 54 million, experts said it would take 7 to 10 million subscribers to start a new network. Another report stated that 30 million subscribers was the benchmark for national advertising.[12]

By July 1991, Court TV was able to launch its new venture with 4 million cable subscribers. Subscribers pay 40 percent of cable network revenue; with 60 percent coming from advertising.[13] The former competitors were now partners, and they presented a united front. Brill told one interviewer, "This allows us to get there quicker and with more confidence." Patrick said, "It makes all the sense in the world. I think this is really going to be a player on the cable landscape." One industry expert predicted, "It's America's ultimate ongoing theatre."[14]

Now, Brill and his organization shifted into high gear. For key staff appointments, Brill went to reporters he'd worked with and trusted. Steve Johnson, who had been editor of the *Fulton County Daily Report* in Atlanta, one of the legal newspapers in Brill's press conglomerate, became Brill's top aide and the executive producer of Court TV's first five hundred trials and fifteen hundred hearings (parole and sentencing proceedings, for example). How much interesting material would they find in ordinary cases, Brill asked? He had been fascinated by a New York City trial going on at the time involving a man who had abused his wife and killed their young daughter. But that case, along with another one they considered as their launch—the rape of the Central Park jogger by roaming violent youngsters—was sensationalized and gory and might confirm skeptics' fears that television would gravitate to and exclusively cover the proverbial "sex, drugs, and rock and roll."

Johnson's personal experiences and field research among colleagues who covered the legal scene suggested that an abundance of ordinary cases raised intriguing issues that would interest the public. While the channel would be aimed at "people, not lawyers," Fred Graham told inquirers, there would be a "legal ghetto" on weekends, with shows "basically by lawyers for lawyers." They would start by concentrating on the thirteen states that were liberal about letting in cameras—and especially New York, California, Massachusetts, Nevada, and Florida.

Brill was sure of his venture and continued developing his strategy and a business plan. He would appropriate some of his better employees from the legal press he controlled. They would feed stories to Graham, who had signed on to work as the network's chief anchor. Cynthia McFadden, then at PBS, now at ABC, was recruited as another experienced anchor.

Brill faced a skeptical legal hierarchy that had lived with a total ban of cameras in courts for decades, a blasé public that thought Court TV would be a bore, and others who thought it would be a blasphemous commercialization of a serious process that should be kept out of the world of entertainment. Industry doubters wondered whether middlebrow viewers, interested primarily in celebrities in trouble and lurid trials, would spend evenings watching "a lawsuit challenging the nutritional claims of oatmeal."[15] Brill enlisted his own publications and took advantage of every public invitation to proselytize, lobby, and cheerlead for his idea. "Video cameras," he wrote in *American Lawyer,* "are about to make the legal process as accessible and visible in the 1980's as it was in the 1890's when the courthouse was our favorite town theatre."[16]

Admitting that many viewers would be drawn exclusively to sensational and prurient cases, Brill aspired nonetheless to make the courtroom camera the medium of record. He publicly deplored the vagaries of existing courtroom information, which derived "from tabloid headlines, Hollywood docudramas, and the spins of lawyers and blow-dried eleven o'clock anchors."[17] Brill conceded that Court TV would be competing with soap operas, sitcoms, cop shows, docudramas, and tabloid reenactments. But he was adamant that the programming not be "tabloid." He was optimistic that "the real thing is better," more dramatic, rewarding, and entertaining. "Our hope is to become the authoritative source for legal news and commentary in this country and around the world."[18]

The less glamorous, but organizationally necessary, work of creating administrative ground rules followed. The organization had to have an extensive, explicit handbook of regulations prescribing appropriate conduct for its employees. The handbook includes obvious and ordinary regulations concerning administrative subjects such as vacations, sick leave, performance ratings, and insurance. It also details the ethical standards Brill expected of all employees, such as how to deal with sources (tell about a source's weakness), and the independence between editorial and advertising personnel (do not let advertising considerations influence coverage of any story). It is impressively rigorous in its requirements for fairness (when someone's reputation is impugned, try to get their comment in response), openness (be candid about corrections), propriety (block out profanities), and professionalism (never buy information from sources).

Choice of coverage, obviously, is a critical element of the company's work. One producer told me that an application for television coverage sometimes encourages settlements. The selection and coverage of trials follow a calculated, hierarchal game plan. The executive producer of Court TV runs the meetings, but Brill rules the roost. Discussion is free-form and informal. All staffers know, however, that Brill has veto power and the clear single hand on all decision-making. In practice, however, he rarely has to disagree with his staff because the governing policies on the selection of cases are generally accepted.

The editorial and production staff at Court TV headquarters chooses cases to cover based on various criteria: the public interest in the case, the newsworthiness of the issue and parties, the quality of the story, its educational value, and its probable duration. With more than a million trials in the United States each year to choose from, the material for Court TV is plentiful.[19]

Recommendations are received from a network of hundreds of trackers in the field (mostly *American Lawyer* editors and reporters) who are linked by computer to Court TV's New York headquarters. There, staff members write up an analysis for the producers and management identifying potential cases to cover. The analysis, usually running a few pages, is circulated to top company decision-makers, who meet every Wednesday to discuss projects. The summaries of potential cases—about a dozen a week—are succinct and matter-of-fact: "The highest court in Massachusetts will decide whether a rape counselor must turn her records over to the lawyer representing the man accused of raping her client." "Woman who allegedly killed husband claiming battered wife syndrome as defense." They include the name of the case, the predicted length of the trial, the place, judge, lawyers, contact phone numbers, and a several-page case description noting the significant facts, the key questions raised, the lawyers' views of the issues, the judge's view on cameras in the court (i.e., "Judge X denied us camera access the last time we applied to his court. However, this is not a high profile trial, and he may let us in."), and on occasion the tracker's opinion about two questions always on the producers' minds ("This case will not become a battle of the medical experts. Nor will it be overly graphic and gory.").

The trackers' reports usually do not editorialize or make recommendations. They include practical insights that only on-the-scene observers would know ("So far, the city has been unreceptive to talks of settlement, and the plaintiff's lawyer indicates that it is 'unlikely' that the case will settle; due to its length [five weeks] and the number of underage witnesses, it doesn't seem like something we would do."). They include details that are of critical interest to television producers ("All the parties involved are Haitian immigrants, but do not have heavy accents."). The trackers sometimes can provide inside information they have secured from their contacts ("a rumor has surfaced that one of them will testify.").

Sometimes recommendations are made by sources outside Court TV, including people involved in upcoming trials. Jeff Ballabon, senior vice president for corporate affairs, recalls that an Ohio Supreme Court case was not on Court TV's agenda but was added after local officials called to suggest that the issue—the constitutionality of state-financed education—was important. "We saw that exceptionally important issues were at stake. We sent a camera crew to cover it. We also made tapes of the program available to schools and institutions across the state." The judge in the Dow-Corning breast implant case asked Court TV to air his explanation of the settlement so that women in the class of potential beneficiaries would know of it. "We thought it would be a public service to convey this information in a passive way so we were not perceived as taking a side that this was a good settlement," Ballabon stated. The judge was televised explaining the settlement. Lawyers who opposed the settlement were given the opportunity to argue against it. Women who called in were provided with tapes of the show.

Were those cynics who doubt the educational value of televised trials to scan the list of cases covered by Court TV, they might reconsider their position. A perusal of the approximately six hundred cases aired by Court TV during its first six years discloses a diverse fare, filled with inherent drama, some complexity of issues, and much of the violence and contentiousness of life. The large majority were criminal trials, but a significant minority of the cases were civil. There is a sampling of celebrity trials (the Woody Allen-Mia Farrow divorce; the Jerry Garcia estate dispute; Bernard Goetz's libel suit against William Kunstler and the publisher of his biography; Martin Luther King Jr.'s heirs' dispute with Boston University over ownership of the late civil rights leader's papers; several prosecutions of Dr. Jack Kevorkian for allegedly assisting patients' suicides; the sentencing of Joseph Buttafuoco for statutory rape of his wife's attacker; the parole hearings of Charles Manson, Sirhan Sirhan, and James Earl Ray; Art Buchwald's suit against Paramount Pictures for appropriating his movie idea; Random House's unsuccessful suit against Joan Collins for not producing a publishable book), cases involving charges against professional athletes, and claims against actors and actresses; however, these high-visibility cases involving notorious parties compose a tiny fraction of the cases aired.

Cases were reported from all over the United States, though larger numbers arose in states hospitable to courtroom cameras: Florida, Georgia, California, Massachusetts, Michigan, and New York. Whether criminal or civil cases, the issues presented often were of broad general interest: a hospital's duty to its patients; the applicability of capital punishment; workplace discrimination of various forms (race, sex, age); the Bosnian war crimes trials; trade secrets; religious training of a child of divorced parents; the savings-and-loan security fraud trial of Charles Keating; smokers' suits against cigarette companies; spousal murders; affirmative action in awarding municipal contracts; a school condom-dispersal program; strike-breaking; child custody; vehicular homicide; a trademark dispute between Hertz and Avis; a surrogate mothering contract dispute; International Court of Justice litigation from the Hague; claims of copyright infringements of songs, movie ideas, and celebrity photographs; price-fixing by Ivy League universities; a settlement of a class action against General Motors; a challenge to a government ban on selling "adult" materials (*Penthouse* magazine) at military bases.

Among the televised cases were several whose coverage made the parties notorious: Bernard Goetz, Jeffrey Dahmer, Lorena Bobbitt, Jesse Timmendequas, William Kennedy Smith, Rodney King, and the Menendez brothers. In addition, there were cases whose oddity no doubt contributed to their general interest: schoolgirls who sued for the right to play fast-pitch rather than slow-pitch softball; two surfers who attacked a spectator at a surfing championship; an animal rights advocate's suit to prevent deer hunting, which harmed the bald eagle population; a TV reporter who conducted pit bull fights; a manslaughter trial for shooting a man mistaken for a deer; an economics teacher who extorted money from students for enhanced grades; a boxer who offered his opponent a bribe to lose their fight; a woman charged with killing her fetus by getting drunk.

Court TV also covered generic proceedings: a crime victim rights constitutional amendment hearing; the operations of a municipal court; attorney disciplinary proceedings; mental status hearings; clemency hearings; police brutality cases; parole and sentencing proceedings.

These interesting and edifying trials will continue as long as there is life, law, and a trial system. Alexis de Tocqueville noted long ago that "scarcely any political question arises in the United States that is not resolved, sooner or later, into a judicial question." While televised trials are edifying and revealing of the trial system, they do accent the violent and bizarre. But, in doing so, how different are they from standard network fare, many movies, or the news of the day?

Predictions that Court TV would be a combination of C-SPAN and soap operas proved correct. As one observer wrote, "Court TV offers a mixture of shocking back-page blood-and-guts trials and sober opinion-page explorations of liability, rights, and legal principles."[20] On any given day, one can watch Senate confirmation hearings of a proposed Supreme Court justice; excerpts and analysis of past (Nuremberg) and present (Yugoslavia) war crime trials; the soap opera-like, tearful testimony of Lorena Bobbitt explaining why she emasculated her sleeping husband; or the profound drama of a death-row convict pleading that he has found God and should be spared the ultimate punishment.

For all his brashness and toughness, Brill is as passionate about the integrity of Court TV as he is interested in its win-lose business side. This is evident in all his proselytizing in media and before professional, political, and judicial organizations, and in the hands-on way he runs his organization. In his mind, the defining moment in Court TV's history so far has been when the camera in the O. J. Simpson case accidentally showed a fleeting glimpse of a juror. Brill's staff notified the judge, and Brill went on camera to apologize. Brill has insisted on this kind of candor; indeed, each year the company commemorates "integrity day," in which one employee is given an award for exemplary acts of corporate honor.

Within six years, by January 1997, Court TV had televised about six hundred trials, and, according to Brill, was firmly in the black financially,[21] a year earlier than he had predicted. Because cable licensing fees go up each year, Brill says he expects profits to keep rising. As of mid-1996, of the approximately 100 million homes with television, 67 million were wired for cable, and Court TV had 26 million subscribers.

How Court TV balances its goals of commerce and journalistic integrity is a key consideration. Court TV receives its Nielsen ratings regularly, but select few staff members know what they disclose. As Ballabon reports, "We are a business. We do advertising sales and advertisers need to know who is watching. The cable operators want to know how many people tune in, and the demographics. . . . There are people at the network who know, but . . . it is an extremely small group." Brill is emphatic that the subject of ratings not be discussed by the editorial staff at its planning meetings. Ballabon attests, "You'll never hear anybody raise the question and issue of ratings at that meeting because that's not the criterion on which we will decide whether or not that's a good case."

Not everyone agrees with Court TV's inside report card. Carl Stern is an attorney and journalism professor who for over three decades was NBC's national legal correspondent, covering countless major trials, the Supreme Court, and the Justice Department. Stern has reservations about the public-service aspect of Court TV's programming. Long an advocate for televised trials, Stern now is offended by the frequent replays of sensational moments in notorious trials—such as the testimony of the alleged rape victim in the William Kennedy Smith case in Florida—in order to raise ratings and sell products.

"My heart just sinks sometimes when I see Court TV," says Stern. "I labored through many a bar meeting in the 1970s, trying to persuade judges and lawyers that televised trials would not be just another medium for selling beer and deodorants. I was wrong. Trials have turned out to be a commodity, a product sold and exploited for commercial value, and one in which most of the performers don't have to be paid. Court TV even seems to be marketing re-sale rights, selling trial videos to other shows, and to viewers who wish to order by phone using their VISA cards!"[22]

Stern faults Court TV for misappropriating sensational cases that have only prurient aspects. "How many times does Court TV intend to play the tape of the New England schoolteacher who was convicted of raping her fifteen-year-old student? When I saw it recently, for the umpteenth time, it ended with a 'bumper' tease to stay tuned for the next case which, if I heard correctly, involved a prostitute who sued her 'John.' I did not stay tuned.

"I realize there are some cases, like the Nuremberg trials, that deserve to be repeated on television until the end of time. But shouldn't human kindness and regard for letting parties and witnesses regain a modicum of privacy induce the Court TV to drop the sex stuff after the sixth or seventh airing?" Stern asks.

As a result of Court TV, Stern argues, citizens are never able to conclude the invasion of privacy that occurs in all trials, but at least used to end there. Now, he believes, Court TV shows the trial and resells packaged excerpts for money, not for public edification. Stern wonders whether his faith in courtroom cameras was misplaced. His rough judgment makes too sweeping a condemnation of the network's overall record, though it does raise a reasonable criticism of one of its excesses.

While Court TV's primary focus is trial coverage, the company has developed related spin-offs. As the archives of taped trials grew, along with the company's reputation, auxiliary revenue also accrued from spin-off programming, particularly the high-priced services for lawyers. Live courtroom coverage of actual trials are the heart and soul of Court TV's agenda. Monday to Friday, from 9 A.M. until 7:30 P.M., the program schedule is devoted to trial coverage. From 7:30 P.M. continuously until 9 A.M. the next weekday, Court TV has provided a variety of related programs, each with its own producer, anchor, and focus: *Supreme Court Watch, Trial Story, Justice Factory, On Appeal, Justice Today, Miller's Law, Washington Watch,* and its flagship daily program, *Prime Time Justice,* which wraps up the day's highlights each evening. *Supreme Court Watch*, hosted by Fred Graham, is broadcast from a studio in Washington, D.C., when the Supreme Court is in session. A half-hour weekly show, *On Appeal*, complements *Supreme Court Watch* by discussing important appeals around the country that have a major impact on the law. *Trial Story* produces documentaries (about a hundred so far) about important cases covered by Court TV, including excerpts, analysis, background and color. Issues such as custody, sexual harassment, hospital practices, and criminal procedures have been covered and are sold on videocassettes. A continuing legal education for-credit program is available. Weekends feature programs for teenagers and a variety of programs from the network's selections. For a typical schedule, see Figure 1.

Court TV produces a variety of educational programs in addition to its gavel-to-gavel trial coverage. *In Practice* is a series of continuing legal education seminars for practitioners that runs on weekends. *Class Action* is a weekly one-hour analysis of important issues raised in a particular trial, edited from cases in Court TV's archives. Court TV participates in annual mock trials held by competing high school students. It produces CD-ROM programs based on revealing trials. It televises monthly community forums on provocative subjects: domestic violence in Broward County, Florida; illegal immigration in Van Nuys, California; juvenile justice in Baton Rouge, Louisiana; parole reform in Hampton Beach, Virginia; and gangs in Albuquerque, New Mexico.

In April 1996, Court TV launched *Teen Court TV*, a weekend morning program that explores the justice system from the teenager's (12–18-year-olds) perspective. *Teen Court TV* includes three formats: a town hall, issue-focused, audience participation program on subjects such as drugs and competency; analysis by a host and guest of a trial that young people will find engaging; and an on-site, behind-the-scenes visit to actual locations such as a law school or a district attorney's office, presented in a magazine format that includes profiles, quizzes, and computerized variations.

The Court TV network also provides tangential programming through numerous interactive applications.

Figure 1. Court TV Programming Schedule, April 1997

HOURS	MON	TUES	WED	THURS	FRI	SAT	SUN	HOURS
9:00 AM						Washington Watch		9:00 AM
9:30 AM			Live Courtroom Trial Coverage — Morning Session			Supreme Court Watch/ On Appeal		9:30 AM
10:00 AM						What's the Verdict?		10:00 AM
10:30 AM								10:30 AM
11:00 AM						Your Turn		11:00 AM
11:30 AM								11:30 AM
12:00 PM						Justice Factory		12:00 PM
12:30 PM						Miller's Law		12:30 PM
1:00 PM			Justice Today			Trial Story	Prime Time Justice	1:00 PM
1:30 PM								1:30 PM
2:00 PM						Prime Time Justice	Cochran & Company	2:00 PM
2:30 PM			Live Courtroom Trial Coverage — Newsbreaks, Open Line, Daily Docket					2:30 PM
3:00 PM						Cochran & Company	Prime Time Justice	3:00 PM
3:30 PM								3:30 PM
4:00 PM						Trial Story	Cochran & Company	4:00 PM
4:30 PM								4:30 PM
5:00 PM						Prime Time Justice	Prime Time Justice	5:00 PM
5:30 PM			Live Courtroom Trial Coverage — Evening Session					5:30 PM
6:00 PM						Cochran & Company	Cochran & Company	6:00 PM
6:30 PM								6:30 PM
7:00 PM						Trial Story	Prime Time Justice	7:00 PM
7:30 PM	Supreme Court Watch/On Appeal	Justice Factory	Justice Factory	Miller's Law	Washington Watch			7:30 PM
8:00 PM			Prime Time Justice			Prime Time Justice	Cochran & Company	8:00 PM
8:30 PM								8:30 PM
9:00 PM			Cochran & Company			Cochran & Company	Prime Time Justice	9:00 PM
9:30 PM								9:30 PM
10:00 PM			Trial Story			Trial Story	Trial Story	10:00 PM
10:30 PM								10:30 PM
11:00 PM			Prime Time Justice			Prime Time Justice	Trial Story	11:00 PM

Segments may be preempted when necessary for live courtroom coverage

Prime Time Justice Complete hilights of the day's coverage	**In Practice** Continuing Legal Education (CLE) program for lawyers 6–9 AM Sat & Sun	**Teen Court TV** Programming for kids
Daily Docket The day's schedule of trials	**Newsbreak** Breaking legal news	**Open Line** Live call-in segment

Reprinted by permission of Court TV.

Back Channel is an online network that provides a wide range of information to subscribers about whatever trial is currently on Court TV. For additional information, viewers can access "Casefiles," which deliver quick, concise data on the case and explain the key issues and possible social repercussions resulting from it; "People," which offers brief bios on the major witnesses; and "Words," which offers subscribers an on-screen law dictionary for all legal terms used. Another feature, the "Armchair Lawyer," calls for subscriber input on the trial—anything from guessing the contents of a closing argument to predicting the verdict.

In the *Case Simulation Game*, users learn the facts of a real case and then prepare and argue a simulated trial. Players compete over the internet and await the computer's written decision declaring the winner and including a critique of both sides.

The *Court TV Law Center* is a website that enables surfers to obtain a wide range of legal information about commonly asked questions, access to a library of legal documents, and the ability to meet and chat with other users on legal issues and current events. Other applications include a lawyer check, where online users e-mail names of lawyers they are thinking of hiring and they check their references. Another feature, "CyberCourt," offers an online dispute resolution forum.

Multimedia Casemaker uses video from trials for educational use. This CD-ROM program was developed to educate students of the judicial system by giving them access to real cases. The *Casemaker* includes video footage, transcripts, and press articles from the case, as well as related information necessary for a student to understand, dissect, and analyze a case.

Video-on-Demand makes available one- to two-hour videocassette summaries of the network's most important trials. Each summary includes footage as well as interviews with participants in the case.

Cable in the Classroom provides in-depth coverage of important legal issues for classroom teaching purposes.

A versatile and potentially profitable spin-off project at Court TV is *Counsel Connect*. For a modest fee ($120 per year), this computer software service for attorneys, law librarians, and paralegals provides unlimited e-mail and internet access for users to share memos, briefs documents, news, advice, and recruitment, to plug into seminars, and conduct private conferences. In mid-1997, it had fifty thousand subscribers.

All of these programs except *Supreme Court Watch* are planned and broadcast from the company's offices on four floors of the plain-looking Manhattan building that houses Court TV's studios, archives, and production and business offices.

___

After a half-decade, Court TV has carved a unique niche. As one of its self-congratulatory ads claimed: "For world news, there's CNN. For Sports, there's ESPN. MTV is music television and C-SPAN is our eye on Congress . . . since 1991, legal journalism has had its own brand name: Court TV." More impressive is the judgment of its peers in the press. After the O. J. Simpson trial, the *Los Angeles Times*'s media critic, David Shaw, reported: "The most comprehensive Simpson coverage of all came, of course, on the stations that broadcast every word of trial testimony, and reporters and attorneys . . . expressed great admiration for that coverage and, in particular, for the gavel-to-gavel coverage of Court TV and CNN." "The most impressive people to me, probably, in television are the Court TV . . . reporters," *New York Times* reporter David Margolis said. "Court TV is wonderful, and the Court TV reporters are incredibly smart and energetic. They've done . . . terrific and very responsible work. . . . Every day they break stories. I think they've set a standard for everybody,"[23] Shaw observed.

Champions of Court TV claim that it "has brought the Sixth Amendment into the Twentieth Century with its extension of the public trial to the electronic nation. The C-SPAN of the judicial branch, it is providing a unique service that may be more about citizenship than commerce."[24] Arizona law professor David Harris believes that Court TV "does a better job of showing viewers what a trial really is. . . . Flash and excitement seldom show up on court TV." More than the derivative and incomplete version of trials that the print press presents, Harris argues, Court TV provides an "almost immediate version of the proceedings."[25]

Yale law professor John Langbein, a skeptic of the trial system, takes this argument a step further. The public has been educated to think that criminal trials were what they saw on *LA Law* and *Perry Mason*. Courtroom cameras show a more realistic picture of the justice system, he argues, and provide "ordinary citizens a view of the truth-disregarding and truth-defeating potential of late twentieth century American adversary procedure."[26] It is important for the public to know that "Money is the defining element of our modern American criminal justice system," one which is less an investigation into truth than "a staged battle of partisans committed to distortion."[27] What it is showing people is the way the system really works. The courtroom camera is more dignified, more tasteful, and more accurate than the unruly, tabloid-driven, out-of-court media coverage of trials.

Court TV's Jeff Ballabon bases his case on the difference between news and information. Most media report news that may be informative, but may also distort how the legal system operates, he argues, whereas Court TV "will choose cases for their information value over their news value." Journalism has been called the "first draft" of history, so speed and excitement are criteria for coverage, along with accuracy. It is left to historians to reflect about the truth and reality of past actions. Would not the televised trial be a better record of history than evanescent news reportage?

When the difference between news and information is blurred, distortion results. Because of the bizarre verdict that awarded a huge sum to a woman who spilled hot coffee on her lap, Ballabon argues, the public believes the trial system is a bonanza for imaginative lawyers and litigious plaintiffs. But Court TV also presented cases brought against swimming pool and inline skate manufacturers by sympathetic injured parties who got no money because they could not prove that their injuries were caused by anything more than their own negligence. "No one covered that, so far as I know, except Court TV," says Ballabon. Most reporters don't cover civil cases, particularly when there are defendant verdicts, he notes, and they contradict the hot coffee verdict that has prompted calls for law reform. His point: "We are there for both news and information in a way that most networks are not."

The long-form approach to issues of more than local or temporal interest provides a truer picture of the system and, Ballabon argues, presents "a higher journalistic ethic." The network needs viewers, so notoriety is a factor in deciding which cases get broadcast. Thus, a copyright infringement case involving claims against the celebrated film *Jurassic Park* drew an audience because of the famous movie, director, and author; but the Court TV audience was provided an analysis of both the "substantial similarity" legal test that governs claims of copying, and the way courts protect ideas. "Our mission is to tell about the legal system . . . with accuracy and dignity," says Ballabon. Jeffrey Toobin, a former prosecutor who covered the Simpson trial for the *New Yorker* and later wrote a book about the case,[28] expressed the same viewpoint: "Journalism in the real world is as much about what's interesting as it is about what's important."[29] Perhaps the highest compliment comes from the brilliant TV producer of legal drama (*Hill Street Blues* and *L.A. Law*, for example), Stephen Bochco. "I'm a real Court TV junkie," he says, "it's the best show on TV."[30]

Reporters continue traditional coverage of legal cases, providing synopses and analysis in print and on camera. The television networks and CNN show segments of high-profile trials. CNN also has broadcast extensive, if not gavel-to-gavel, coverage of several celebrated cases—Carol Burnett's libel claim against *National Enquirer* (1981), the Claus von Bulow murder trial (1982), the New Bedford gang rape case (1984), a libel case against *60 Minutes*, Zsa Zsa Gabor's assault of a policeman, actor William Hurt's palimony case, the McMartin nursery school child-abuse case charges, and others. PBS has provided gavel-to-gavel coverage of less notorious cases, as have individual courts in many states.[31]

In order to feed a curious public, "docudramas" of trials offer a bridge between dramatization and reporting. Another cable channel, E! Entertainment Television, covered the Simpson criminal case as Court TV did, gavel to gavel. When the cameras were banned in the civil case, E! switched to "infotainment." E! reenacted highlights of the Simpson civil trial daily in one-hour dramatizations using actors on a set. The actors used excerpts from the transcripts and notes of reporters on the scene describing the actual witnesses' and partici-pants' gestures and inflections. This re-creation was followed by expert analysis and interviews with commentators. E!'s program di-rector explained that viewers wanted it: "When there are no cameras allowed in the courtroom and they want to be inside, we think this is a fair and accurate way to take them inside."

In response, one critic replied succinctly, "Either it's real or it's not." Ballabon adds, "Re-enactment is worse than just having reports in the newspapers . . . because people think they are seeing reality." What they are seeing, he argues, is an "illusion of some sort of re-ality," without the actual demeanor, inflections, tone, and passion that goes on in court. The camera lets people see all this for them-selves.

Some alternatives to Court TV's approach have been suggested. A non-profit network, like the one in Washington State, or C-SPAN could broadcast all judicial proceedings, without all the commentary and spin-offs that Court TV uses. Harvard law professor Alan Der-showitz has proposed such a network—"J-Span," he called it—to be operated under the supervision of bar associations and law schools.[32] Offended by what he sees as the commercialism and sen-sationalism of Court TV, which intersperses its coverage with adver-tisements to "sell cereal, soup and dog food," as well as a perceived focus on salacious as opposed to educational cases, Dershowitz pro-poses that J-Span be guided by lawyers, judges, and lay people who would choose educational cases, not simply entertaining ones. David Harris has noted the administrative, economic, and ideological prob-lems surrounding such an idea, and has suggested an alternative, Community Court TV, which would tap into Court TV but widen its scope, localize its coverage, and present a more realistic picture of the system to the public.[33]

For the moment, however, Court TV offers the closest thing to the medium of record. How well and how long that is the case remains to be seen. Early in 1997, news reports disclosed that Brill had of-fered to buy out the network for $300 million. When Time-Warner refused, Brill opted to sell his interest, reportedly for between $20 and $40 million. The cable network was reportedly worth $450 million, with 30 million subscribers, and a profit of $3.5 million in 1996 and one of $12 million predicted for 1997. Insiders predicted that Time-Warner will spend more money on the network to boost its ratings and profits, a change from Brill's emphasis on programming standards.[34]

A veteran Court TV insider reports that things are changing fast in the post-Brill era. All television networks, including niche channels like Court TV, are suffering declining audiences. This means Court TV will be showing more sex and celebrity cases, he predicts, and paying more attention to ratings. Advertisers prefer changing audiences, so niche channels whose followings remain relatively static are a less desirable forum for commercial sponsors. Under Brill, few Court TV personnel were aware of ratings (the executive vice president had to find smuggled reports). Now, serious programming, such as the Yugoslavian war crime trials which had low ratings but high cerebral value, have less of a chance of coverage.

How much Court TV may change under different leadership and whether a new channel will emerge are questions that will be answered as the century ends.

Chapter 6

CONCLUSION

TV OR NOT TV

The recurring free press-fair trial debate did not involve television until late in the twentieth century. In the first half of the century, there was no television; later, in the early years of television, the new medium was forbidden in courts. Thus, the experiment with televised trials has been a short-lived one. During the time between the Supreme Court's opinion in the *Chandler* case in 1981 and the O. J. Simpson criminal trial in 1995, the actual use of cameras in courts changed dramatically, as did public opinion on the subject. For a decade after *Chandler*, states experimented actively, widely, and in most cases successfully with televised trials. The federal court system also experimented, though much less extensively and more cautiously. By the 1990s, with a cable network offering gavel-to-gavel coverage and other networks broadcasting excerpts of trials, the practice has become commonplace.

Then, the overdose of coverage of the Simpson case left many observers with an angry case of TV indigestion, cynical about the medium's values and legitimacy in a court of law. We are currently in the midst of another cycle of questioning the merits of publicized trials and the proper balance between our nation's commitment to a free press and to fair trials. As chapter 1 demonstrated, our nation's history is filled with cases where saturated publicity about various "trials of the century" are followed by morning-after handwringing in which the press and the bar scrutinize their own perceived excesses and resolve to act with more restraint in the future. Does the Simpson case—the latest and possibly most extreme example of this phenomenon—warrant reconsideration of our present practices with courts and television?

Reconsideration, perhaps; but not a change of direction. First, the problem must be viewed in its proper perspective. The pervasiveness of the free press-fair trial dilemma, which involves competing constitutional rights, is exaggerated, according to one venerated federal judge. News media interfere with fair trials "in only a precious few cases," the late Judge J. Skelly Wright told a federal bar group in 1965.[1] Less than 1 percent of the hundreds of thousands of criminal cases each year get even a line of press notice. In the federal system in which Wright presided, the large majority of defendants plead guilty; only about 8 percent have jury trials. Voir dire, challenges, postponements, and removals cure most of the problems caused by pretrial press coverage.

In Judge Wright's opinion, the extreme remedy of dismissing a relatively few cases "would be a small price to pay for the great benefits we all receive—the public generally and persons accused of crime in particular—from the disclosures made in the press with respect to the goings on in police stations, district attorneys' offices, and courthouses throughout the country." These government agencies perform sensitive functions and the public has the right to know how they are being performed. Wright quoted Lord Acton's aphorism—"Everything secret degenerates, even the administration of justice"—and coined one of his own: "A healthy democracy requires fresh air and light. Public officials . . . function best in a goldfish bowl."

Wright, a former prosecutor, asked with some sense of irony, Why is it that Canon 20 of the Code of Professional Ethics, which is "supposed to curb comments by lawyers about pending cases (including district attorneys)," is ignored, while Canon 35 of the Code of Judicial Ethics banning cameras in courts is rigidly enforced? Is this another example of the cynical observation that the only standard is the double standard?

Chief Justice Tom Moyer of Ohio, a recent president of the U.S. Conference of Chief Justices, also sees courtroom coverage as a way to build public confidence in the justice process. It is an opportunity, Moyer has said, "to educate the public about the nature of our work. Given the technological advances of video equipment and satellite communications, we now have the emergence of Court TV. It is a fact of our time. And it is an appropriate time to renew the debate about cameras in the courtroom." Moyer urges that the historical principle of open courtrooms in the full view of the public has followed a logical progression through to cameras in the courts. Televising trials, he argues, is "another opportunity, not an intrusion."[2]

Indeed, the trend—appropriately, I would argue—is toward more open government. For example, in recent years many states and the federal government have enacted "sunshine" laws requiring open meetings of quasi-judicial administrative proceedings on the theory that important public decisions should be made openly. The idea behind these laws, which applies with equal force to the value of televised judicial proceedings, is that the people should have the fullest possible knowledge of the government's decision-making process.[3] Deliberations of judges and juries require privacy, of course, but not trials and appellate proceedings.

When the subject of televising the proceedings of the House of Representatives was debated in congressional hearings in 1975, one legislator remarked:

> I do not believe, that the public confidence in our Government will ever be restored until the public has a clear idea of just what we are doing and how we are doing it. Trust must be based on understanding, and understanding must spring from a clear public perception of our intentions and our actions.
>
> The television camera, I believe, is a tool for providing that perception. I am familiar with the argument . . . that the camera can be used as much to distort as to reveal, but I would not reject broadcast coverage on that basis because ultimately I believe that the ability, honesty, integrity, and professionalism of the American media will

prevail. Such a trust is necessary if our conception of a free press is to survive. That is not to say that there will not be mistakes, that there will not be errors and injudicious editing which could result in a less than accurate portrayal of what transpires. . . . But I believe on balance this is a small price to pay and a small risk to be taken for the benefit which can be derived.[4]

Of course, now Congress's work is televised regularly, from the mundane filibusters before empty chambers to the sensational special hearings such as Watergate and the Anita Hill-Clarence Thomas hearings. To those who think these broadcasts do more to embarrass Congress than to reflect positively on it, one member commented: "It just seems to me that in the people's House of the Federal Legislature which we represent the time has come when the American people are entitled to all the information they can get."[5]

The late Supreme Court Justice Louis Brandeis remarked that "Sunlight is the best disinfectant." Former California Chief Justice Rose E. Bird expressed a similar sentiment: "The press is the light that shines on the interstices of our government and its bureaucracy . . . we must have a free press to inform us of any corruption or tyranny. Anything less is a threat to our most deeply held democratic principles." We are, legal scholar Lawrence Friedman has stated, "a public opinion society," one in which the legal culture is shaped by what people know and think about the law.[6] People can monitor and shape their government only if they are informed about its functioning, the famous jurist Jerome Frank wrote.[7]

Even critics of courtroom television have seen the value of this medium. Law professor and columnist Susan Estrich, who has been concerned about the mischievous potential of televised trials, called the notorious trial of Timothy McVeigh for the Oklahoma City bombing "a textbook example of a case of substantial public interest. . . . It would be far better to restore public faith in the justice system by letting people see more of it, not less, and to see it directly, not filtered by the press."[8] The *New York Times* editorialized that in such terrorism trials, what is good for the victims and survivors might be good as well for the wider public audience. Court TV was approached by groups that wanted it to broadcast the trial so that others could not charge the government with controlling and distorting the portrayal of the justice system in those cases. Self-restraint by lawyers and individual responsibility by journalists to act in the public interest rather than in their immediate parochial interests, Estrich concluded, as did Wright, would do more to dignify the trial process than would banning cameras.

In addition to exaggerating the frequency of the problem, the debate about the propriety of televised court proceedings is misguided on another fundamental level. On the legal or constitutional level, the dilemma is not due to a conflict between competing constitutional rights as much as to the need to accommodate between complementary rights. At its best, the free press assures fair trials. And in important instances, the assurance of a fair trial system has benefited the press as much as it has other individuals and institutions. The Supreme Court has ruled consistently that the First Amendment may not be shackled nor the press prevented from assuring the widest dissemination of information from diverse and antagonistic sources, even by the government itself.[9]

If the excesses of the press occasionally intrude on the fairness of a trial—either before the trial, as in *Shepherd v. Florida*, or during a trial, as in *Sheppard v. Maxwell*—the resulting conviction can be overturned. In the Florida case, it was decided that "prejudicial influences outside the courtroom, becoming all too typical of a highly publicized trial, were brought to bear on this jury with such force that the conclusion is inescapable that these defendants were prejudged as guilty and the trial was but a legal gesture to register a verdict already dictated by the press and the public opinion which it generated."[10] The late Justice Robert Jackson wrote in the *Shepherd* opinion that when newspapers in the exercise of their constitutional rights do deprive defendants of a fair trial, the resulting conviction does not meet our standard for the "civilized conception of due process of law."[11]

In the *Sheppard* case, the Supreme Court reversed a murder conviction because the carnival-like atmosphere created by the press in the trial courtroom itself warranted judicial monitoring. When a trial is not free from prejudice, passion, and excitement, the late Justice

Tom Clark ruled, and the press causes a miscarriage of justice rather than acting as a "handmaiden of effective judicial administration," the appellate courts must intervene and reverse the conviction because it does not conform with the due process of law requirements of the Fourteenth Amendment.[12] This is not a question of legal gimmickry, but of justice. Recent disclosures suggesting that Dr. Sheppard did not commit the crime demonstrate that the reversal of his conviction was not merely a case of judicial insistence on procedural formality.

Is the occasional reversal of a conviction too high a price to pay for a vigorous press? Reversal or inhibition of prosecution is the cure of choice in other situations—for example, when the publicity surrounding a congressional investigation might preclude a subsequent criminal trial—without the suggestion that there should be no congressional investigations. Such a result is the accepted price for maintaining the necessary powers of important institutions.[13] Courts reached this conclusion in the Watergate and Iran-Contra investigations, to name two notorious examples. Furthermore, as the televising of trials has become more refined in the years since *Estes*, fewer reversals of convictions based on intrusive and prejudicial coverage have been necessary.

Courts need not go so far as reversing cases to protect the fairness of trials. As the late Justice Tom Clark reminded in the *Estes* case, judges have the power to control much of the mischief that may interfere with the fairness of trials, short of barring cameras. For example, Judge Ito could have managed the Simpson case much better and avoided some of the problems later blamed on television. But it seems not all judges will exercise these available powers rather than placing the responsibility on television. In a murder case in Decatur, Georgia, in 1997, the trial judge declared a mistrial when a witness admitted she had watched Court TV when another witness testified. Despite the fact that he had ordered all witnesses not to watch or read any trial reports, the judge reportedly stated that he understood why the witness could not resist the temptation to watch the televised trial. The judge took no action against the witness who had disobeyed the court order. As one columnist stated:

Punishing television for being too popular, too easy to switch on, too hard to resist is a perverse sort of logic; it rests on the assumption that public trials are all right as long as they are not unduly public. The burden is on the court to see to it that jurors and witnesses abide by the rules, which are admittedly mighty hard to enforce. Nevertheless in this instance, it was Mrs. Rhame, not Court TV, who, as the defense lawyer put it, committed a "willful, intentional violation" of the rules.[14]

Television did not create the problem of trial publicity. Historically and recently, in trials where there was no television coverage—the Mike Tyson rape case, the Charles Manson murders, the Patty Hearst kidnapping, and many others—extensive press coverage did not result in any known prejudice at the trials. More importantly, no decisive evidence exists that heavy publicity before or during a trial necessarily leads to the oppressive and prejudicial result that occurred in the two governing (*Sheppard* and *Shepherd*) cases. Indeed, in some well-known recent examples, the exact opposite was true. The acquittal in the first Rodney King case came after incriminating videotapes of his beating were widely and repeatedly broadcast and most of the world presumed the policemen were guilty. And the O. J. Simpson acquittal was viewed by a vast, worldwide public as a nullification of the evidence broadcast before and during his trial. In numerous recent celebrated trials—the William Kennedy Smith rape trial, the Lorena Bobbitt case, and the McMartin nursery school child-abuse cases, to name a few—acquittals followed extraordinary publicity and widespread public presumptions of guilt that the juries did not share.

Crusading media exposé have led to the undoing of injustices in cases where a persistent press caused the judicial system to correct miscarriages of justice. And, if defendants can receive fair trials (translation: win acquittals) in highly publicized cases, so too can prosecutors (in their view, gain convictions) as we saw recently in the second Menendez brothers murder case and the second (federal) prosecution of the policemen in the Rodney King case. Those cases raise what one journalist aptly called a nagging issue "about the distance between legal evidence and real-life truth."[15] However, this issue is created not by cameras in courts, but by the rules of evidence that keep from juries information available to the public. The civil trial of O. J. Simpson, not televised, included evidence that the jury in the criminal case did not know about (though the audience of that televised trial did), and the civil jury held Simpson financially responsible for the acts he had been acquitted of committing in the criminal case.

Critics contend that it is troublesome when television portrays a different version of the facts of a case than the one the jury sees at trial. However, there is another perspective. The Simpson case, often cited by these critics, also provides an example of the reverse possibility. If the jury verdict in the Simpson criminal trial is at war with the widespread public perception of his guilt, a total miscarriage of justice may be avoided as a result of the widely seen television coverage of the trial. While, under the special rules that govern trials, Simpson's guilt was not proved beyond a reasonable doubt (or was proven, but was nullified by the jury), he will not avoid the verdict of the public and will face a more expansive, if informal, form of sanction in the community. Why should he not? Without television, it could be argued, a villain would have escaped all retribution; because of television, he will pay a price in the world outside the courtroom. To the argument that such an idea condones a pernicious evasion of due process of law, the response is that the adversary process and the marketplace provide different avenues to truth. Each is appropriate in its own arena. History provides many examples of cases where it could be said that community sanctions prevented perversions of justice. The Rodney King case, countless civil rights civil disobedience cases, the Medgar Evers retrial, and the Scottsboro rape case each were salutary examples of cases where the public's media-created perception of justice arguably assuaged courtroom miscarriages of justice.

The First Amendment, it must be remembered, protects good journalism and bad, publicity that aids the trial process as much as some that interferes with it. Whether it is pretrial publicity that threatens to prejudice a later jury, or televised trial coverage that may add pressures but also may lead to new evidence in the search for truth, the Constitution applies without value judgments about the content of press coverage. As one former judge has written:

> It is all too easy to suggest that in criminal cases the press or radio is simply pandering to a low public taste for scandal for its own profit. In a democracy it is inappropriate for government officials to decide what is worth reading and hearing. Moreover, it cannot be determined in advance of the trial whether there is a public interest in the particular crime of which the accused is charged. The public concern frequently becomes manifest later if alert reporting indicates a link between crime and government administration. Therefore, a classification by subject matter of cases in which press coverage may be restricted would be unwise even if possible.[16]

Skeptics have shifted their criticism of cameras in courts through the years. Several decades ago, the most common objection raised against television in courts was that the cameras were obtrusive, noisy, and disruptive. Now that the technology is such that camera coverage of court proceedings is invisible and decorous, the argument against television has changed. Today the chief criticism—unprovable, though logical and widely held—is that the presence of cameras inevitably changes the behavior of the trial participants in negative ways. Are these subjective presumptions correct?

The legitimate concern that the participants at trials will be adversely effected cannot be proven; indeed, the best anecdotal evidence suggests otherwise. Experiments to date have generally satisfied even the skeptics. Court TV has broadcast hundreds of trials with no known prejudicial ramifications. Court TV's Jeff Ballabon points out, "No one who has watched us—the judges, the lawyers, the participants—has ever argued that we don't give an accurate description of the system. . . . We get the reverse . . . many of them say it's the most accurate portrayal of what goes on in the courtroom that they have ever seen." All the surveys of the impact of television on jurors, witnesses, lawyers, and judges described in chapter 4 concluded that these fears are exaggerated if not misplaced and that most trial participants are not adversely effected by the presence of cameras.

The notion that television cameras in courtrooms will unduly influence judges is at war with a fundamental precept of trial lore and evidentiary law. The rules of evidence are based upon the idea that judges are *not* influenced by outside pressures, as juries are thought to be—or, if influenced, they are able to disassociate themselves from such nonjudicial contaminations in making their rulings. Historically, judges were assumed not to be "sensitive to the winds of public opinion," in the words of the late Justice William O. Douglas, and "to be men of fortitude, able to thrive in a heady climate."[17] Aside from this evidentiary consideration is a psychological one: Will judges alter their behavior for egotistical reasons (to be celebrities) or political ones (to curry favor or get reelected)? This unprovable possibility exists, but it is to be weighed along with the equally likely possibility that judges are less apt to misbehave or act idiosyncratically on camera.

How do we measure television's impact on jurors—the key concern supporting demands for limitations, if not a ban? As noted in chapter 4, one analyst calculates that press-induced bias is likely to occur in only one of every ten thousand cases.[18] A recent study of the jury system adds further perspective.[19] Data gathered in 1990 disclosed that 1 percent of all civil cases in state courts are decided by juries; in the federal courts, the figure is 2 percent. Less than 5 percent of state criminal cases are tried by juries. Two-thirds of criminal cases in the state courts and 86 percent at the federal level result in guilty pleas. Likewise, there are convictions in two-thirds of the state jury trials and in 80 percent of the federal trials. And juries convict at a higher rate (84 percent compared to 62 percent) than judges (in cases where the right to a jury is waived). Indeed, a more appropriate question is whether televised trials present the public with a realistic picture of the criminal justice system, in view of the fact that the overwhelming majority of the action is handled off camera in negotiated pleas, private settlements, and off-the-record dispositions in judges' chambers.[20]

Running some uncertain, and possibly curable, risks in so few cases, the late Judge Wright suggested, is a small price to pay for having the press acting as a watchdog to the goings on in the criminal justice system.[21] The press provides the public with important information about what transpires on the streets or in the precincts, at "the gatehouses of justice," rather than at the trial itself, "the manor house,"[22] to borrow the metaphors of law professor Yale Kamisar. Actually, the courtroom camera pictures both "houses": it portrays the evidence of law enforcement's efficiencies and deficiencies that comes out at trials, and the judiciousness of the trials themselves, usually the more formal and mannered phase of the criminal justice system.

If this is so, why is the camera blamed for the scenes it portrays? In the Simpson case, public and professional disgust with the behavior of the lawyers, the case management of the judge, the action of the jurors, and the exploitation of the witnesses, as well as revulsion toward the excesses of all the media, resulted in the widespread condemnation of television. It was as if the public wished to smash the mirror because it did not like what it saw reflected there. Just as the eighteenth-century German physicist and satirist Christoph Lichtenberg compared books to mirrors—"if an ass peers into it, you can't expect an apostle to look out"—so too is television a medium of communication characterized by both the observer and the observed. "The nineteenth century dislike of Realism is the rage of Caliban seeing his own face in a glass," Oscar Wilde wrote in *The Picture of Dorian Gray*. We might ask a similar question about twentieth-century skepticism of televised trials. Much of the current criticism of televised trials amounts to killing the messenger while ignoring the message.

In the aftermath of the Simpson case, there was a perceptible retreat from television by some judges, and calls for curbs by some politicians and commentators. One media observer, comparing the televised criminal trial with the untelevised civil trial, concluded that "without the all-seeing television cameras, the courtroom's emotional temperature has subsided to a near-normal tone, very unlike the self-important, melodramatic tension of the first time."[23] Although cameras were banned from the courtroom, the media frenzy persisted outside. One report noted that "great white mushrooms of television-truck satellite dishes have sprouted and the lawn interviews drag on," and that the public fascination "just will not die."[24] The *New York Times* reported that "a surreal, festive air" persisted on the palm-lined street outside the courthouse.[25] A cable channel presented daily docudramas about the trial, while the conventional media continued to O.D. on O.J.

With regard to the behavior of the legal profession, some personal self-censuring and bar monitoring is called for. Before the era of televised trials, the late Fred Rodell of Yale Law School wrote perceptively and pungently about the legal profession's propensity for pomposity and mystification. Rodell argued that lawyers use jargon, mumbo-jumbo, paternalistic patter, and silly ritual to create a mystique of pseudo-seriousness. Not unlike the church, the legal profession—especially in its courts—inclines toward archaic costume (robes), grand rooms in imposing buildings, and tortured language. Judges enjoy the trappings of authoritarianism, University of Texas law professor David Anderson has commented more recently, "surrounding themselves with a level of decorum that a parent, preacher, mayor or university president can only envy."[26] Another law professor, David A. Harris, has written perceptively about what he calls "the cult of the robe," which, along with "esoteric judicial vocabulary," creates "the illusion of the infallibility of courts and judges."[27] In order for the popular culture to operate properly in a democratic society, he suggested, the court system must be legitimized by being more open and available to the public.

Antagonism toward the press may derive from the fact that it is the principal agent of defrocking previously venerated institutions. In Anderson's words, "the principal agent of demystification is television." He adds, "The demystification of courts could turn out to be the greatest political change of our time. . . . Never in the history of the world . . . have the courts held as much power as they hold in the United States today. . . . What is occurring in the last decade of the twentieth century is not a temporary crisis in the courts' management of publicity, but a fundamental shift in the public's relationship to the courts. People are no longer willing to let lawyers and judges spin out the mysteries of law in arcane obscurity. Having learned not to trust priests, Presidents, or generals, they are ill-inclined to trust judges."[28] A similar suggestion was made by a federal judge who favors public information about the judicial process: the aura of tradition and mystery surrounding judicial decision-making is attributable, he stated, to the myth of the judge as being detached and neutral, "which can only survive from afar where judges are not vulnerable to criticism and censure." The judicial code of silence, he claimed, is based on "a strange combination of arrogance and fear."[29]

The objection of some members of the legal profession to televised trials might well be based on their subconscious commitment to mystification. Most groups prefer to operate in the dark. Remember that the judges and lawyers who are resistant to televised trials are members of the very groups that would be exposed to more public scrutiny by these cameras, and thus would be more accountable for their own contributions to the vagaries of our justice system.

Courts are public institutions and do not belong exclusively to the judges and lawyers who run them. As one respected federal judge advocated, "We should open ourselves and our courts to the public, for it is such openness . . . that will ultimately make us better judges and that will assure the legitimacy of the judicial system in the eyes of the American people."[30]

Nonetheless, despite experiences that support televised trials and recommendations to allow it, the federal judiciary refuses to follow the trend. And the Supreme Court is the most adamant in its opposition. The two recent Chief Justices, Warren Burger and William Rehnquist, both have spoken against the practice, and in 1996 Justice David Souter told a congressional committee that there would be television in the Supreme Court "over my dead body," a sentiment shared by Justice Anthony Kennedy. It is hard to imagine who or what would be hurt by televised Supreme Court proceedings, except the Justices' notions about their own sanctity and privacy. The educative possibilities seem beyond argument.

The late Justice Burger stated that television was "the most destructive thing in the world" and vowed there would be "no cameras in the Supreme Court of the United States while I sit there." Alleging that he feared show business distractions, Burger denied MBS's request to provide radio coverage of oral arguments in the case questioning the constitutionality of the deficit-reduction law, hardly an example of yellow journalism, an issue of prurient public interest, or the conversion of serious discussion into frivolous entertainment. But shortly before retiring after seventeen years as Chief Justice, he told the American Society of Newspaper Editors that he might relent in his adamant opposition if he could be assured that selective excerpts of the oral arguments could be avoided. He feared distortions by the use of sensational snippets, he said. The suggestion was that if coverage were live and complete, opposition from the Court would ease.

Yet two years later, when C-SPAN offered to cover all Supreme Court oral arguments—the sexy ones and the dull ones—and to provide unedited and uninterrupted coverage, the Rehnquist Court declined. When Rehnquist testified at his televised Senate confirmation hearings for the chief justice post, he suggested that his Supreme Court would be the first to entertain sympathetically the prospect of media coverage. Asked his opinion of television coverage of the Supreme Court, candidate Rehnquist, then an Associate Justice, replied: "If I were convinced that coverage by television of the Supreme Court would not distort the way the Court works at present, I certainly would give it sympathetic consideration. But if it meant a whole lot of lights that would disturb the present relationship between lawyers and judges and arguing cases, I don't think I would be for it."[31]

Once confirmed, Rehnquist refused a request by ABC Radio to provide live coverage of an important abortion case argument, without consulting his colleagues. The same Chief Justice who has deplored the failure of educational institutions to teach students about the legal system and the Supreme Court threatened to sue a political science professor who published transcripts and accompanying cassettes of oral arguments before the Court in twenty-three interesting cases.[32] The transcripts of all oral arguments since 1995 are kept at the National Archives, just as the lawyers' written briefs are available at the Supreme Court. When his initial complaint engendered strong responses, Rehnquist backed off and the archives are now open for the public, as they should be. The book, *May It Please the Court* (the salutation with which all Supreme Court advocates begin their remarks), included excerpts of the oral arguments and analysis by the author of landmark cases of special interest to students, lawyers, and the general public—including *Roe v. Wade*, the Pentagon Papers, *Loving v. Virginia* (barring miscegenation), Solicitor General Robert Bork arguing the constitutionality of capital punishment, and Thurgood Marshall challenging segregation in Little Rock public schools. The tapes included the voices of revered Justices debating the issues and parrying with lawyers. Together they provided "a fascinating look at court culture and a practical introduction to appellate advocacy."[33] Despite the fact that these studies portrayed the seriousness of the Court, the talent of the lawyers, and the complexity of the issues, they did not "please" the Court, which had restricted the usage of these transcripts.

Interestingly, despite long-standing hostility by the federal judiciary, the Judicial Conference, and members of the Supreme Court toward the notion of television in courts, two journalists who cover the Supreme Court told me that they have been told in private conversations with a few justices that they favored the idea. Publicly, however, the atmosphere has been cold and negative, and none have spoken in favor of televised trials.

There is, as well, a bit of self-aggrandizement and self-interest among many press representatives who are critical of the need for television in the courts. When I debated this subject on a national radio show, I was challenged by the host: "Don't you trust journalists?" Of course I do, I replied, but I do not believe them more than my own eyes, to paraphrase Chico Marx's memorable line in *Duck Soup*. Old aphorisms like "seeing is believing" and "I want to see for myself" derive from a deep belief in the reliability of one's own sensory perceptions. And this preference is compounded by people's cynicism about press bias and their reluctance to believe what they read in the newspapers, viewing it as second-hand and thus distorted information. That wise and worldly novelist, the late Robertson Davies, a former journalist himself, was quoted as saying that while newspapers "like to represent themselves as wonderfully romantic and hitched in to world events, they really are an entertainment and manufacturing business. The news is what you can squeeze in before you have to go to press; it's not what's happening in the world."[34]

Many print journalists and even some television commentators believe, arrogantly, that the public needs them to describe or explain what transpires at trials. While some of these commentators undoubtedly have interesting insights to offer concerning the proceedings they observe, those commentaries are more editorials than reporting and are different from the valuable insights members of the public can gather from their own observations. Such commentaries, like those that follow a State of the Union address or presidential debate, are often superfluous and of little value. Having seen the real thing, we do not need a pundit to tell us what we just saw. Court TV's expert analyzers can provide interesting insights, but that is different from the actual presentation of the trial itself.

A classic example of print journalists' reactionary rejection of broadcasting as a lesser form of reporting was related by author Richard Reeves in his Library of Congress Goldman lecture, "Journalism New, Old or Dead."[35] Reeves told of one network television correspondent who was interviewing a senator, holding a microphone before the senator's face as he spoke. At one point, when the reporter thought the senator was saying something remarkable, he tucked the mike under one arm, pulled out his pen and pad, and started taking notes. There is an irony to the argument that savvy reporters see more than the camera. Because seating for the media in the courtroom was limited, most of the press coverage of the O. J. Simpson trial was based on what the reporters saw of the case over television.

Not every print journalist demeans the value of televised trials. One network legal correspondent told me that the advent of televised trials has meant that he had more opportunities to treat important legal issues on the air. Because there was wide exposure to the cases and the issues, he was able to demand the air time to cover them that he might not have had otherwise. The late Theo Wilson, the *New York Daily News*'s courtroom reporter for three decades, made the policy argument for televised trials:

> With judges refusing to allow the public to see trials on camera, we have retrogressed. The camera is the most honest tool of the criminal justice system, if it is allowed to show the public a trial, unadorned from gavel to gavel in the courtroom—without the TV

celebrities, without the brain-dead interviews, without the second guessing pundits.

As citizens, we have a right to see our system, warts and all, judge for ourselves. Nobody should have the power to deny us, the tax-payers, the right to watch what is happening in the courts we pay for or should be allowed to tell us that by watching a trial on a camera, in our homes, we are jeopardizing any other citizen's rights.[36]

Print reporters and critics within the legal profession fault television for presenting "snippets" of trials that are likely to distort and sensationalize judicial proceedings. Gavel-to-gavel trial coverage is the antithesis to snippets. Moreover, a quote in a news article is comparable to a sound bite on television—it may be accurate, but it is without context. More fundamentally, all press coverage other than gavel-to-gavel television or full print transcripts is no more than a snippet, the reporters' best take on what transpired, presented in the limited time and space available.

Leslie Maitland, a former legal reporter for the *New York Times*, recalls the agony of a conscientious print reporter operating within the constraints of a daily newspaper report.[37] Maitland covered the 1976 retrial of Rubin (Hurricane) Carter, a boxing star convicted of triple murders ten years earlier on questionable evidence. Indeed, it was the *Times*'s stories, along with the interest of celebrities—Bob Dylan, Muhammad Ali, and Candice Bergen—who thought Carter had been railroaded by an overzealous New Jersey district attorney and judge, which led to the retrial. Maitland related to me the difficulties she, like all reporters covering all trials, encountered writing her "snippets" (in a newspaper known for its careful coverage and having a stake in this particular case):

> To cope with the situation and meet a deadline of 7:00 P.M. for the first edition, my editors had me file an early version of the day's events at lunchtime so that we would have a piece that day regardless of how late the judge held court. At night when proceedings ended, I would file an updated version, again racing against the clock to get the afternoon highlights into the paper. When significant testimony came late in the day, I was often sick at heart to realize that readers

of our first edition—available that night on the city newsstands—
would miss it.

There is also, of course, always a concern for space or air time in
any media account. My plea for space to recount the day's developments would, of necessity, be balanced against other newsworthy
events and the number of pages that advertising revenues allowed.
When significant new testimony came late in the day after other stories had already been "budgeted" for space, it was difficult to argue
for a greater share. Including compelling testimony that came at 5:00
P.M., for instance, could therefore require cutting out something else
that had seemed crucial just that morning.

On December 21, for example, when both sides delivered their
summations, I was allotted 14 paragraphs or less than 1,000 words
to encapsulate six weeks of contradictory and complex testimony—
much of which had differed substantially from other sworn accounts
given by many of the same witnesses in other venues.

And even when reporters write to the space allotted, they cannot
be sure how much of what they file will actually wind up in print.
Editors, juggling demands of other late-breaking news events, may be
making cuts in stories that reporters will only learn about when they
read the next day's paper.

When space is a priority, moreover, one of the first things to go is
the sort of subtle observation of tone or mood or body language that
may signal something important. I can still remember, 20 years later,
how some of the jurors hid behind sunglasses and shut their eyes—
sleeping, it seemed—while John Artis was on the witness stand, proclaiming his innocence.

The judge, to cite another example, made no effort to disguise before the jury his disdain for the defendants' lawyers, and with the
prosecution and defense at war, the jury often looks to the judge for
Solomonic wisdom.

As a result of her experiences, Maitland has a melancholy reflection of the power of the press in assuring fair trials:

> When all was said and done, it was, of course, not the press, but
> the judge who wielded the conclusive power. All my stories outlining
> the conflicting, changing testimony of the witnesses could not prevent
> Carter and Artis from being sent back to prison. And while the press

could help win a second trial for the two men, it could not guarantee that that trial would be a fair one. It could only tell the world about the facts as they unfolded that led so tragically to a second subversion of justice in the courtroom.

Maitland also noted the subjective nature of the best reporter's coverage, in the best of situations.

> A reporter covering a trial performs a valuable service in sifting through the hours of often tedious testimony to pick out the most important information presented to the jury. But the decision as to which witness, testimony or evidence to focus on each day—and thus which headline to create—can sometimes be a subjective one, on which reporters covering a trial may differ.

Maitland is not alone in her judgment about the subjectivity of newspaper accounts of trials. A perceptive editor commented to me about this phenomenon in the context of the Simpson case. She happened to see the televised dramatic episode in the criminal trial when the defendant tried on the glove in front of the jury. The next day, she read three different accounts of that episode in responsible newspapers; each was different from the others, and all varied from her own observations of the televised version. Judge Wright wondered whether "the public image of justice is distorted because we judges have turned our backs to the news media and have allowed their writers to draw on their imaginations instead of reality, and to report only a tiny part, instead of the rich whole, of the face of justice."

In addition to the inevitable ideological predispositions of print journalists and the built-in limitations described by Maitland, the possibility also exists that human reporters are susceptible to being corrupted by outside interests. One well-known prosecutor told me about an investigation into a public scandal, where the reporter from a prestigious newspaper was influenced by the defense team to skew his coverage in favor of its side. One can bribe a reporter, but not a camera.

Some critics of televised trials think that at worst observation breeds contempt, and at best it leads to vulgarization. Some judges wince, for example, at the prospect of advertisements interrupting serious trials (though not at newspaper accounts, which also are surrounded by advertisements). Yet, we cannot deplore the vast wasteland of television fare and the decline of TV news, while prohibiting one major option which, if not completely educational, at least combines educational features with entertainment.

If television in courts is an entertainment as much as an educative vehicle, it is no more so than a State of the Union presidential speech to Congress, a political convention, C-SPAN coverage of a legislative hearing, or any other operation of government that is broadcast publicly. If participants alter their conduct due to the presence of cameras, that change may well be an improvement. And it may permit holding officials accountable, as well as providing a platform for their performances. If C-SPAN shows a representative acting like a fool, the folks back home may be better able to judge whether to reelect him or her.

The critical facts, it seems to me, are that government operates best in the open, and that television has expanded the concept of a public trial in ways that are, for better or worse, consistent with the modern technological state of public affairs. It can be edifying in new ways, as is the case in Washington, where all the state's Supreme Court arguments are broadcast successfully. It can also be awesome to some trial participants in highly charged cases, where outside pressures threaten the sanctity of the court proceedings and thrust private citizens into public attention as celebrities.

Some critics have voiced concern that the ubiquity of television expands the benign concept of a "public" trial to perverse and dangerous proportions. Comparisons have been made to the mass, public show trials of dictatorial regimes. Is the televised trial the natural progression of Justice Oliver Wendell Holmes's instruction a century ago that trials should take place under the public eye, and "every citizen should be able to satisfy himself with his own eyes as to the mode in which a public duty is performed?"[38] Or is it a perversion of Justice Holmes's promise that "The theory of our system is that the conclusions to be reached in a case will be induced only by evidence and argument in open court, and not by any outside influence, whether of private talk or public print."[39]

Court TV's champion, Steven Brill, argues that television makes trials accessible to a vast public without intrusion, and despite the entertainment aspect of the medium, "the audience will be at home and quiet and able to see and hear everything without disrupting or otherwise affecting the proceedings."[40] It is ironic that television creates a circus atmosphere, not in the courtroom where its presence is contested, but outside the courtroom where it is accepted. The obnoxious scenes of reporters and cameramen running after reluctant interviewees, and of phalanxes of reporters and paparazzi stalking private homes and courthouse environs, are what creates images of intrusive television coverage of notorious cases. But those scenes have nothing to do with cameras *in* the courts. As one former newspaper editor noted, "No camera ever let out an involuntary exclamation of horror, dismay or amusement on the utterance of a witness. No camera ever grimaced or coughed during testimony. No gallery of cameras ever burst into applause and had to be rapped into order by the court. No camera ever wept or laughed."[41]

As a practical matter, there really is no debate about whether there should be cameras in courts. Television is a fact of life to be reckoned with, not a newfangled procedure awaiting general acceptance in the world of public affairs. For better or worse, televised court proceedings are realities of judicial life. The remaining questions concern the appropriate limitations on its use—where, when, and how cameras can contribute to public interests without causing problems of constitutional import. The experiences in most states, on Court TV, and even in the limited federal experiments have been positive in the judgments of most participants and detached observers.

In our increasingly technological society, it seems unlikely that evolving constitutional notions about public trials and free press will be constrained by the undertow of old habits and the limitations of obsolete techniques. As public interests become more global and media options more sophisticated, televised trials are likely to become the rule rather than the exception. Former *New York Times* columnist Anna Quindlen called this phenomenon "teledemocracy." As one student of the subject concluded, "Once television has infiltrated a critical arena of American sociopolitical life, it seems to find a permanent home."[42] Fears that by allowing cameras into courts we will have struck a Faustian bargain and compromised the judicial process by succumbing too quickly to superficial claims for progress are not supported by our experiences to date. One judge speculated to a media and the law symposium that judicial acceptance of television may be generational. "Judges that are sixty or up almost have a visceral reaction against the idea of having cameras in the courtroom under any circumstances . . . younger judges are somewhat more receptive."[43]

As long ago as 1980, one informed commentator suggested that we were beyond the point of no return on the question of cameras in courts because, in his words, "Once televised trials attract a large national following, the process will be irresistible, cumulative, and probably irreversible."[44] A respected federal district court judge, Pierre N. Leval, speculated in 1984 that "It is a safe prediction that the eventual entry of the camera into the federal courtroom is inevitable."[45] His speculation is particularly surprising because this remark was made in a celebrated case (the Westmoreland libel claim against *Time* magazine) in which he denied CNN's request to televise judicial proceedings, despite his personal opinion that it would be in the public interest to permit it. Judge Leval thought at the time that he had no power to permit television in his courtroom as a result of the forbidding rules of the Judicial Conference.

The nontraditional features of the courtroom of the future are unobtrusive and easy to use. They can be seen at William and Mary Law School's experimental prototype, Courtroom 21, which was developed by the law school and the National Center for State Courts in Williamsburg, Virginia. As one expert advised: "Technology is changing litigation. And technological development can be expected to accelerate in the future."[46] As Marshall McLuhan wrote, "Societies have always been shaped more by the nature of the media by which men communicate than by the content of the communication."[47] Participation via television, he prophesied, would improve democracy by making the living room the voting booth. Why would that not also be true of the impact of television on the administration of justice? If the electronic revolution has made the human environment "a teaching machine," as McLuhan put it, one which maximizes the process of discovery and perception, why not view television in courts as an example of the positive value of new technology on the historic concept of public trials? If no messenger can reflect reality perfectly, why not rely on the recorder of events that transmits the on-the-scene reality to the faraway listener or observer as closely and fully as possible? Television is the most influential purveyor of information and the most profound influence on legal and popular culture.[48]

A standard manual for architects planning the design of future courts notes that courthouses are "experiencing dramatic changes in their use of electronic technology."[49] That prestigious and influential manual recommends that "serious thought should be given to the state of technology and the areas of technology that might become important" and advises planners to "provide conduits for television and computer cables so that automation can be easily installed."[50]

Television has been a versatile and common feature in recent courtroom design, not only for the purpose of broadcasting trials. For example, courts are using closed-circuit TV to record testimony in child sexual abuse cases, and remote two-way television to broadcast arraignments from remote sites. Indeed, the modern courtroom is designed to exploit new technological features that go beyond televising proceedings—electronic translators, recorders, computer graphics and animations, crime-scene simulators, video conferencing equipment for depositions and arraignments, monitors permitting jurors to review evidence, and electronic machines in lobbies for filing motions and looking up cases.

The new high-tech courtrooms have multiple cameras that are voice activated and aimed with controls. Computer-assisted transcripts are prepared in real time so that seconds after the court reporter types the transcript, it appears on monitors that are available to the judge, lawyers, and deaf jurors. A presiding judge can preview documents on his computer screen before jurors see them, or access online research and CD-ROMs. The lawyers' high-tech podium permits them to display evidence and access records and research. Jurors may monitor documents, evidence, live or prerecorded real-time transcriptions, and graphics from the jury box, as well as being aided by language translation and enhanced infrared listening equipment. In a future era of virtual reality, interactive media, and digital and fiber-optic technology, some courtroom action could be replaced by tele-conferencing. The presence of mere TV monitors to broadcast proceedings to distant audiences soon will be old stuff, and someday may be viewed as quaint.[51]

It is feasible, if not likely, that in the next century home viewers will be able to watch trials in real time or taped on their television sets or computers. A silent, invisible camera in the courtroom will transmit trials live over cable to television sets or send the same signals via internet fiber-optic telephone lines to computers. Text as well as images can be transmitted via interactive media in real time, or packaged. A twenty-first-century viewer at home or in an office will be able to tune in to a commercial cable network like Court TV or a statewide C-SPAN-like network with open audio access on the Internet, like TVW in Washington State, or go online on a computer to watch all or part of a distant trial, past or ongoing, in text or in images, for edification or entertainment.

These are the facts. The questions remaining are: How well will it be done and how much in the public interest? It is a dilatory digression to fret over speculative fears and unprovable arguments about what dangers inhere in the presence of cameras in courts. As one cultural commentator noted about the proper new role of the technology:

> Television is our most underappreciated medium, mostly portrayed in terms of stupefying children and inciting violence, the proverbial vast wasteland. But it is a phenomenal thing. A television set is easy to install and lasts for years. It brings the whole world into your house, using little power, it turns on every time you want it to, producing clear color pictures and good-quality sound. It costs one-fourth the price of a good computer. It can occupy and amuse children, show the Oklahoma City Federal Building minutes after a bomb explodes, and go around the world to wars, cultural events and volcanic eruptions. It shows great old movies, history, drama and, yes, lots of trash too. Far more popular, enduring and important than

most people acknowledge or realize, it is becoming one of our most interactive forms of communication. . . . There is no reason to make such simple-minded and divisive choices. Each culture complements the other.[52]

New technology can provide salutary answers to old problems. For example, television has provided a positive solution to one recent public policy problem. When the notorious Oklahoma City bombing trials of Timothy McVeigh and Terry Nichols were moved to Colorado, on a change of venue motion by the defendants who feared they couldn't get a fair trial in Oklahoma, the local families of victims who could not attend complained that they were prejudiced by not being able to attend. In response, Congress passed a law permitting federal trial courts to order closed-circuit televising of proceedings "for viewing by such persons the court determines have a compelling interest in doing so and are otherwise unable to do so by reasons of the inconvenience and expense caused by the change of venue."[53]

Wise as this step was, it has its limitations. No one else, except court and security personnel, was allowed to view these closed-court broadcasts. Objections were made by the public and the press. More than two thousand people claiming to be victims, as well as a group of small media outlets, vied for the 130 available seats in Oklahoma City to observe the trial on closed-circuit TV. How can sensible priorities be set? Why limit the observation of a trial that concerns a subject of national public interest to a finite group of immediate victims?

Though it was not what the law's authors had in mind, might there be other audiences in these cases and in other trials where a genuine public interest would warrant public viewing? For example, there was a compelling national public interest in observing the Jack Ruby trial for murdering presidential assassin Lee Harvey Oswald. In a trial concerning an oil contamination of coastal waters, might not environmental groups and commercial fishermen have a "compelling interest" in seeing the trial? As the lawyer who devised the strategy for the Florida rule that led to the *Chandler* case, Talbot D'Alemberte, has pointed out, broadcasting cases involving controversial issues such as police brutality allows citizens to make their own judgments and provides better community acceptance of trial results.[54]

A truly educational purpose could be served by the closed-circuit broadcast to students of just about any trial or appeal. Law schools would do well to teach courses in evidence, or any substantive course, by recourse to actual trials and appeals. A Georgetown law professor told me he uses the O. J. Simpson broadcast to teach a course on trial procedure, and New York University professor Burt Neuborne says he views his commentaries on Court TV "as a chance to teach constitutional law to a mass audience." Another law professor has called for increased use of C-SPAN by law schools, to move legal education out of its "Gutenberg mentality."[55] Since 1979, C-SPAN has broadcast about twenty thousand hours of programming, including briefings, conferences, symposia, and weekly legal programs, in addition to its gavel-to-gavel coverage of Congress, to about fifty million households. And its archive at Purdue University is available, free, to educators for classroom use. Televised government proceedings provide, television commentator Jeff Greenfield has said, "a blend of modern technology and a Jeffersonian faith in the people."[56]

The Simpson case is the latest example of the adage that bad cases make bad law, and thus should not be viewed as precedents. No case before it, and probably for long after, will match the pervasive and intense public interest that accompanied this 1995 double-murder prosecution in California. Pretrial publicity was pervasive, and the trial judge considered a press ban of the trial itself. When Court TV and associated press organizations objected, the trial judge relented and allowed a stationary camera that did not show the jury and to which press organizations had access on a pooled basis.

Though no proof ever emerged that the televising of those proceedings caused any demonstrable prejudice to anyone or any institution, many commentators complained that it did, and many people attributed the disquieting vagaries of that case to the presence of television. Columnist George Will complained that the presence of cameras in the courtroom converted the criminal justice system into a form of entertainment; he equated the public right to know with "voyeurism tarted up in rights talk." Were the jurors fearful of community attitudes? Were the lawyers playing to the unseen audience? Were witnesses distracted by their moments of notoriety? Or opportunistically cashing in on their fifteen minutes of fame?

Former Los Angeles District Attorney Ira Reiner claims that the media excesses of the Simpson case and other notorious (untelevised) trials like it derive not from courtroom television, but rather from courtrooms filled with reporters, camera crews crushing lawyers and witnesses, attorneys giving regular press conferences, and saturation coverage. "[I]f you pulled the plug on live television coverage of a high-profile trial, the courtroom seats still would be filled with journalists, the news still would be saturated with trial coverage and . . . the behavior of the participants still would be responsive to the attention." With a courtroom camera on, he believes, "all the participants are usually on their best behavior."[57]

Indeed, television coverage of the Simpson trial provided strong evidence of the traditionally claimed raison d'être of the "public" trial, as well as fueling the fears prompting cynicism about the process. One historic rationale for public trials is the idea that unknown witnesses may come forward and perjury will be disclosed. That was exactly what happened with the notorious testimony of Los Angeles policeman Mark Fuhrman about his past racist comments. A North Carolina researcher saw and heard his testimony on television and disclosed her devastating tapes of his prior inconsistent statements. Many observers concluded that the dramatic discrediting of Fuhrman's testimony created a fatal flaw in the prosecution's case that might otherwise have gone undetected.

Long after the Simpson criminal trial, Fred Goldman, father of one of the murder victims, and one with a genuine stake in the justice of the trial system, told critics of televised trials: "we wanted the truth to be shown. . . . Our suffering was increased by longstanding and substantive inadequacies in the criminal justice system and, yes, by the outside courtroom media sensationalism. The cameras inside the courtroom, however, played an important role in revealing those inadequacies and countering the media hype."[58]

Just as a transcript provides a written record of a trial, the video record of this trial is of both immediate and archival value. "TV exposure made us smarter about this trial and its possible social underpinnings," one TV critic concluded, it "seated you with the jury."[59] In addition, the video record will find future educational uses. University researchers have used the trial records for educational purposes to teach criminal law and procedure, and to demonstrate social accommodations to new technology. Serious scholars will be able to dissect the meaning and lessons of the case in ways that the first flush of biographies by partisans cannot.

On the other hand, those who feared the contaminating potential of television pointed to various examples of the behavior of the judge and lawyers as proof of their concern. Indeed, at one point in the trial, Judge Lance Ito told the lawyers he thought they were playing to the cameras (some critics, it might be added, thought the judge was, too) and threatened to "pull the plug." And, as already noted, some critics despaired of the danger that underlies the disparity between the evidence the jury was permitted to see and what the public knew from watching parts of the proceedings that were kept from the jury (such as Simpson's infamous and incriminating Bronco ride as a fugitive, which was not part of the prosecution's case). In the aftermath of the case, several concerned judges denied requests to televise other notorious cases, including Simpson's civil trial, fearing they would be overwhelmed by the distractions of the media.

Those who thought that televised trials would make an undignified circus of the trial process saw their worst fears realized. Those who argued that television provides an educative opportunity to demonstrate to the public the workings of the justice system—for better or worse—claimed this trial as Exhibit A. The conundrum continues.

One law professor suggested a compromise. If televised trials are inevitable, he recommended delaying transmission until thirty days after the final decision.[60] This would eliminate the hazard of juror intimidation, focus both jurors and judges on the merits of the case, reduce the temptation to judges and lawyers of playing to the public through the camera, lessen the need to sequester jurors, reduce public misperceptions about the evidence, and reduce the size and salacious interest of the audience. His first three reasons are plausible, but the latter three are neither logical nor persuasive.

A legal journal recommended a "Rule of Inverse Publicity" under which, in its words, "the greater the public interest in a particular trial, the less compelling the case for cameras in the court."[61] If the case is of broad public interest, this thinking goes, the print media will pounce on the case. Where a case involves important or novel issues that might escape notice because no celebrity defendants or flamboyant lawyers are involved, television is needed. This thinking is naive and unhelpful. A case like the Simpson trial had all the elements—issues, lawyers, and a celebrity defendant. The issues point makes the case for televising appellate arguments and decisions, but does not resolve the dilemma with trials.

In chapter 4, I explored whether the mere invisible presence of television does indeed prompt the participants to modify their ordinary behavior, and whether this is necessarily bad. Knowing they are being observed, might trial lawyers come to court better prepared and be better behaved? Might judges be less autocratic, less idiosyncratic? Might witnesses be more careful about testimony for fear of being caught in lies? Most people in most situations behave more properly when they are being observed. The evidence is not conclusive, though I believe it tilts toward better behavior, not worse, in widely observed trials.

Chapter 4 also explored whether television cameras would project "reality," or at least a less mediated reality than the print media or television narrators. How could it be otherwise? Postmodernist scholars argue that there is no objective reality, only competing versions of what reality is. But if that is so, how can one mediate any question about a particular reality? Court TV's Jeff Ballabon argues, "There is no perfect, all-seeing, omniscient universal point of view, and there will always be an editorial point of view," but the camera in the Court "is the most accurate way to convey information . . . more accurate than any other medium. . . . I don't think it's possible to achieve anything that is perfectly accurate . . . this is as good as we have in our technology."

The question about what constitutes reality at trials is complex. Because of the way the adversary system works—contending lawyers advancing their positions on the theory that "truth" will emerge—

the reality reported by all media is suspect from the start. In other words, all evidence is edited or mediated by the lawyers, whose focus in not reality but their version of it. Recapturing past events is an imperfect process at best, and the adversary system adds to the distortions.

TV producer Stephen Bochco has commented on the unique quality of televised trials. "It's the camera. The camera that just watches very dispassionately what goes on in the courtroom. And reveals so much more than what we've ever revealed before. . . . It's educated the public as to what goes on below the waterline. And there's a lot that goes on. And so I think people are more appreciative of the complex nature of the legal proceeding."[62] Indeed, one reporter expressed the opinion that "the conscientious reporter . . . sets aside personal views when reporting events, and tries to emulate the detachment of a camera lens."[63] "I am a camera with its shutter open, quite passive, recording, not thinking," author Christopher Isherwood wrote.[64] Janet Malcolm commented in another context about the unique perspective provided by cameras: "photography's special capacity for revealing hidden truths—truths the mind-ruled eye prefers not to see, but that the mindless camera is forced to record."[65]

Film scholar Bill Nichols's comparable view of cinéma vérité moviemaking is persuasive on this point.[66] He compared the fixed presence of the camera on scenes filmed completely (such as Frederick Wiseman's films) with the more common expository mode of observational filmmaking. In the latter form, "the techniques of exposition [that] turn the sounds and images of others into accomplices in someone else's argument," while the epiphanies of cinéma vérité originate "in the historical world rather than in the defamiliarizing strategies of an argument." His conclusion is that cinéma vérité provides a more vital form of learning, and a less mediated, more ideal form of observation.

This is not to say that documentary filmmaking presents pure fact in comparison with theatrical films, which are fiction (substitute gavel-to-gavel televised trials compared to newspaper or radio or television summaries of trials). All mass media present artifacts and interpretations. "Even the most neutral presentation of a locked-down security camera interprets a scene through camera height and direction, lens focal length, image resolution and size, and so on. That *any* presentation through media is an artifact, an interpreting construction, is unavoidable. On any location, simply the choices of where to place the camera, where to point the camera, what lenses to use, and what to include in the frame—all can be arbitrary and meaningless, or a series of production decisions based on subject, theme and treatment."[67]

Carey Goldberg, the *New York Times* reporter who covered the Simpson civil trial, wrote that "the very concept of reality seems frayed."[68] At the earlier criminal trial, she noted, television viewers "could define reality for themselves, watching every tic of a cheek and twist of a DNA strand in the courtroom." But at the untelevised sequel, the public never witnessed "the strange spectacle" and had to rely on descriptions by commentators. At the later civil trial, the commentators from the criminal trial had to rely on third-party observers' reports and thus could not be sure exactly what had happened. At the earlier televised trial, "we sat and watched it and formed our own opinions," one lawyer was quoted as saying. Goldberg wondered whether this quandary was the quintessential example of the "post-modernist idea that there is no objective reality . . . only words and a subjective point of view." The lack of cameras seemed to her to turn this trial into even more of an exercise in postmodernism, with its tenet that there is no way to get to the reality behind words, that humans are imprisoned in language and that there is no way to know who "the real O. J." is or what "really happened."

Because television expanded the public view of the trial, observers were able to project their individual meanings—their "spins and twirls," to use Goldberg's phrase—onto the Simpson screen, obscuring the line between interpretation and simple fact (and, she could have added, highlighting the line between traditional journalism and television coverage). "Journalists report on events that no one else has seen and struggle to convey what happened. But the criminal trial turned that tradition upside-down by allowing viewers to become direct witnesses, and millions of Americans got used to forming their own impressions." Another reporter commented of the Simpson criminal trial, "we were all watching a different movie in our heads. Just as psychiatric patients interpret Rorschach inkblots differently, we could see a variety of stories."[69]

Print journalists and television anchors, by their physical presence, probably disrupt trials more than inconspicuous stationary cameras, and by their pursuit of participants, they may have as much, if not more, impact on the trial participants than the cameras. "It is the overwhelming media coverage that is lavished on a small group of cases—not the live, unobtrusive camera—that can affect the behavior of the participants, and consequently the course of a trial," former prosecutor Ira Reiner argues. All the "crimes of the century" described in chapter 1 and the criticisms that followed them, occurred without television cameras. Could it be that television has helped resolve, rather than exacerbate, the free press-fair trial problem?

Another point of comparison is crucial. If the addition of television does change the events it portrays, even when this portrayal is troubling, the change may still be for the better. When television went to war, in Vietnam, for example, it became impossible for the public at home to ignore the implications of what it saw on the evening news broadcasts. When the world witnessed barbarism in Yugoslavia, carnage in Zaire, starvation in Somalia, natural emergencies in faraway places, those problems could not be ignored. The power of television to educate, expose, and prompt reform should not be overlooked. Those pictures made positive responses unavoidable. The same could be said about reforming the justice system; for that to happen, the general public must witness what transpires.

An attorney on the New York committee that considered the question of televised trials in 1993–94 concluded that there should be "a legal presumption favoring audio-visual access on a permanent basis."[70] Tethering the press to the legislature, he argued, is "unsound public policy." It is based on the false premise that television interferes with the trial process. Such a premise, he wrote, is "contemptuous of the autonomy of viewers," and is based on a "misplaced paternalism" that "improperly casts judges in the role of censors."

The debate over televised trials will continue only so long as the question is deemed to be an intramural matter for the courts. Should the question be decided on constitutional grounds—that is, that there is a constitutional right for cameras to be in courts—neither legislators nor judges will be the sole arbiters of the question on an ad hoc basis. In such a case, the question addressed (it would be addressed by a court) would not only be whether the administration of justice is served, but also whether the press and public is being as fully served as it might be. The institutional interests of the press are not identical with those of the courts. The question is, Upon whom should the responsibility fall to prove scientifically—if it is even possible to do so—that the presence of cameras in courts has a serious negative impact on the quality of justice dispensed by those courts?

Federal Appeals Court Judge Stephen Reinhardt has predicted that "some day, perhaps not far in the future, this question will be resolved on first amendment grounds." In his opinion, "The public has an overriding interest in knowing what is happening in its courtrooms and we, as judges, have no right to ban the medium which provides the public with the vast majority of its information."[71] He concludes: "Judicial openness, I believe, will provide a stronger foundation for our legitimacy. Under a truly democratic system, the public's confidence in our decisions should be based upon its knowledge rather than upon its ignorance, upon openness, not mystery. We are in a position of public trust; there is no justification for hiding from public scrutiny."

Years before Judge Reinhardt's pronouncement, the same idea was propounded by the venerable judge and legal scholar Jerome Frank. In *Courts on Trial*, Judge Frank mocked what he called "the cult of the robe," the accrual of power by symbols, language, and procedures that shroud courts in mystery. These devices ill serve democracy, Judge Frank warned, by maintaining the illusion of infallibility and hindering attempts at reform. "It is the essence of democracy that the citizens are entitled to know what all their public servants, judges included, are doing, and how well they are doing it. The best way to bring about the elimination of those shortcomings . . . is to have all our citizens informed as to how that system functions. It is a mistake . . . to try to establish . . . through ignorance, public esteem for its courts."[72]

The Florida judges who crafted the rule that led to the *Chandler* decision noted at the time that television in courts created risks. But risks are the price of a democracy, they reminded. "A democratic system of government is not the safest form of government, it is just the best man has devised to date, and it works best when its citizens are informed about its workings."[73]

On balance, it is preferable to preserve the constitutional right of the television medium to broadcast a trial unless that broadcast clearly results in an infringement of a recognized constitutional right. Given that, courtroom cameras should be made available as a matter of course, not as a matter of judicial or legislative grace—though any participant in the trial should be allowed to claim exceptions in the interest of justice in a unique situation, upon reasonable proof of a manifest danger. Extraordinary notoriety, as existed in the Simpson and Oklahoma City bombing cases, might be a factor to consider in assessing the likelihood that televising a trial would create a manifest danger. While in the former case hindsight might suggest that television exacerbated distractions at trial, in the latter case a strong argument could be made that there was a national interest in seeing those judicious proceedings. The party claiming the problem should have the responsibility of proving it. We would move from the position that the due process of law clause of the U.S. Constitution does not per se prohibit electronic media coverage of trials, to a more positive position—that the First Amendment mandates all media equal access to courts.

For television, finally, the First Amendment would not stop at the courthouse door, to use one Supreme Court justice's phrase.[74] There have been suggestions in post-*Estes* opinions that television may have a presumptive First Amendment right to access to courts,[75] and that "there can no longer be a meaningful distinction between the print press and the electronic media."[76] There is no "principled basis" to discriminate between different media when two decades of experience demonstrates that old fears about the intrinsically negative impact of television in courts are misplaced, one law review article concluded.[77] Television is commonly used in most public buildings and proceedings, and it is most people's primary source of information. It alone can provide the public with the immediacy and both the aural and visual approximation of the actual trial. Therefore, "there should be a presumption in favor of allowing such coverage in the absence of a compelling justification for preventing it." This thesis is corroborated by the fact that since 1981, when *Chandler* opened the way for cameras in courts, no verdict has been overturned on the basis of prejudice caused by television.

I expect that all the courtrooms of the future—state and federal, trial and appellate—will be equipped with cameras. I suggest that all trials should be available for broadcast—as is generally the case in most states. A publicly run, noncommercial channel, like the one in Washington state, would present all proceedings, pursuant to legal rules. Future viewers, on their sophisticated new home or office "instruments" (a new-breed computer screen or television set), could tune into any case anywhere, anytime. The archival record of all trials would be available to the public. The right to oppose the broadcast of any trial should be available to a defendant, witness, juror, or participating lawyer. The circumstances under which a judge could grant such a request could be set by the legislature or the court system itself, but all guidelines and limitations on the general presumptive constitutional right to publicize public proceedings would have to be determined ultimately by the Supreme Court. The visibility of the judicial system is in the public interest and in the overall interests of justice.

APPENDIX A

CAMERA COVERAGE IN THE STATES

TABLE A-1. TYPES OF COURTS THAT PERMIT COVERAGE

Coverage permitted	States	Total
Trial and Appellate Courts	Alabama, Alaska, Arizona, Arkansas, California, Colorado, Connecticut, Florida, Georgia, Hawaii, Idaho, Iowa, Kansas, Kentucky, Maine, Maryland,[1] Massachusetts, Michigan, Minnesota, Missouri, Montana, Nebraska,[2] Nevada, New Hampshire, New Jersey, New Mexico, New York, North Carolina, North Dakota, Ohio, Oklahoma, Oregon, Rhode Island, South Carolina, Tennessee, Texas,[3] Utah,[4] Vermont, Virginia, Washington, West Virginia, Wisconsin, Wyoming	43
Trial Courts Only	Pennsylvania	1
Appellate Courts Only	Delaware, Illinois, Louisiana	3
Total number of states allowing media coverage		47

Source: Copyright © 1996 by Radio and Television News Directors Association. Used by permission.

[1]As approved by the Court of Appeals, Maryland's experiment originally encompassed coverage of civil and criminal cases in trial and appellate courts. Subsequently, however, an act barring coverage of criminal trials was passed by the legislature and approved by the governor. The rule permitting appellate coverage was made permanent in 1982, and the experiment allowing civil trial coverage was continued until 1984 when the court adopted permanent rules permitting coverage.

[2]Nebraska permits extended media coverage of appellate proceedings and audio coverage only during the sentencing portion of criminal trial proceedings and open court non-jury civil trial proceedings in the district courts of the thirteenth and eighteenth judicial districts.

[3]Texas permits extended coverage in all civil cases (trial and appellate), but allows audio coverage only of criminal appellate proceedings.

[4]Utah's rules permit still photography of all courtroom proceedings and broadcasting, televising, or recording of appellate court proceedings.

TABLE A-2. PERMANENT VERSUS EXPERIMENTAL
COVERAGE

Coverage permitted	States	Total
Permanent	Alabama, Alaska, Arizona, Arkansas, California, Colorado, Connecticut, Florida, Georgia, Hawaii, Idaho, Illinois, Iowa, Kansas, Kentucky, Louisiana, Maine, Maryland, Massachusetts, Michigan, Minnesota, (appellate), Missouri, Montana, Nebraska, Nevada, New Hampshire, New Jersey, New Mexico, New York (appellate), North Carolina, North Dakota, Ohio, Oklahoma, Oregon, Rhode Island, South Carolina, Tennessee, Texas,[1] Utah,[2] Vermont, Virginia, Washington, West Virginia, Wisconsin, Wyoming	45
Experimental	Delaware, Idaho (trial), Minnesota (trial), Nebraska (certain trial), New York (trial), Pennsylvania	6

Source: Copyright © 1996 by Radio and Television News Directors Association. Used by permission.

Note: Since Idaho, Minnesota, Nebraska, and New York fall into both categories, the total number of states with permanent and/or experimental rules is really 47 rather than 51, the sum of the two categories. Forty states (Alaska, Arizona, Arkansas, California, Colorado, Connecticut, Florida, Hawaii, Idaho, Illinois [appellate], Iowa, Kansas, Louisiana, Maine, Maryland, Massachusetts, Michigan, Minnesota [appellate], Missouri, Montana, Nebraska, Nevada, New Jersey, New Mexico, New York [appellate], North Carolina, North Dakota, Ohio, Oklahoma, Oregon, Rhode Island, South Carolina, Tennessee, Utah, Vermont, Virginia, Washington, West Virginia, Wisconsin, and Wyoming [appellate]) have implemented permanent rules during or after a period of formal experimentation.

[1]See Table A-1, note 3.
[2]See Table A-1, note 4.

TABLE A-3. TYPES OF PROCEEDING FOR WHICH COVERAGE IS PERMISSIBLE

Overall rule	Type of proceeding coverable	States	Total
Trial Coverage Only	Civil and Criminal	None	0
	Criminal Only	None	0
	Civil Only	Pennsylvania[1]	1
Appellate Coverage Only	Civil and Criminal	Delaware, Illinois, Louisiana	3
	Criminal Only	None	0
	Civil Only	None	0
Trial and Appellate Coverage	Civil and Criminal	Alabama, Alaska, Arizona, Arkansas, California, Colorado, Connecticut, Florida, Georgia, Hawaii, Idaho, Iowa, Kansas, Kentucky, Maine, Maryland (appellate),[2] Massachusetts, Michigan, Minnesota, Missouri, Montana, Nebraska,[3] Nevada, New Hampshire, New Jersey, New Mexico, New York, North Carolina, North Dakota, Ohio, Oklahoma, Oregon, Rhode Island, South Carolina, Tennessee, Texas, Utah,[4] Vermont, Virginia, Washington, West Virginia, Wisconsin, Wyoming	43
	Criminal Only	None	0
	Civil Only	Maryland (trials),[5] Texas (trials)[6]	2

Source: Copyright © 1996 by Radio and Television News Directors Association. Used by permission.

Note: Maryland and Texas appear twice under trial and appellate coverage (see Table A-1, notes 1 and 3).

[1] Pennsylvania and Nebraska limit civil trial coverage to non-jury proceedings.

[2] See Table A-1, note 1.

[3] See note 1 above.

[4] See Table A-1, note 4.

[5] See Table A-1, note 1.

[6] See Table A-1, note 3.

Entity	States with prior consent as absolute precondition	States with prior notice as absolute precondition[1]	States with no prior consent or notice required
Court's Consent[2] (all cases)	Alabama, Alaska, Arizona, California (written approval), Colorado (approval noted in record), Connecticut, Georgia, Hawaii (trial), Idaho (trial), Iowa, Kentucky,[8] Maine, Maryland,[9] Michigan, Minnesota (trial), Missouri, Nevada (written approval),[10] New Hampshire, New Jersey, New York, North Dakota, Ohio (written approval), Oklahoma, Oregon (trial), Pennsylvania, South Carolina, Tennessee, Texas,[11] Washington, West Virginia, Wyoming (trial) (31 states)	Delaware, Illinois,[15] Kansas, Louisiana, Massachusetts, Minnesota (appellate), Montana, New Mexico, Utah (appellate),[16] Wisconsin (10 states)	Arkansas, Florida, Georgia (Supreme), Hawaii (appellate), Idaho, Nebraska, North Carolina, Oregon (appellate), Rhode Island, Utah (still photography), Vermont, Virginia, Wyoming (appellate) (13 states)
Defendant's Consent[3] (criminal trials)	Alabama, Arkansas, Minnesota, Oklahoma, Tennessee[12] (5 states)	Utah[17] (1 state)	Alaska, Arizona, California, Colorado, Connecticut, Florida, Georgia, Hawaii, Idaho, Iowa, Kansas, Kentucky, Maine, Massachusetts, Michigan, Missouri, Montana, Nebraska, Nevada, New Hampshire, New Jersey, New York, New Mexico, New York, North Carolina, North Dakota, Ohio, Oregon, Rhode Island, South Carolina, Tennessee,[25] Vermont, Virginia, Washington, West Virginia, Wisconsin, Wyoming (36 states)

Prosecutor's Consent[4] (criminal trials)	None	Alabama, Arkansas, Minnesota (3 states)	Alaska, Arizona, California, Colorado, Connecticut, Florida, Georgia, Hawaii, Idaho, Iowa, Kansas, Kentucky, Maine, Massachusetts, Michigan, Missouri, Montana, Nebraska, Nevada, New Hampshire, New Jersey, New Mexico, New York, North Carolina, North Dakota, Ohio, Oklahoma, Oregon, Rhode Island, South Carolina, Tennessee, Utah,[26] Vermont, Virginia, Washington, West Virginia, Wisconsin, Wyoming (38 states)
Party's Consent[5] (civil cases and criminal appeals)	Oklahoma,[18] Pennsylvania, (appellate coverage not permitted), Utah[19] (3 states)	Alabama, Arkansas, Maryland (civil cases),[13] Minnesota (trials), Texas (5 states)	Alaska, Arizona, California, Colorado, Connecticut, Delaware, Florida, Georgia, Hawaii, Idaho, Illinois, Iowa,[27] Kansas, Kentucky, Louisiana, Maine, Massachusetts, Michigan, Minnesota (appellate), Missouri, Montana, Nebraska, Nevada, New Hampshire, New Jersey, New Mexico, New York,[28] North Carolina, North Dakota, Ohio, Oregon, Rhode Island, South Carolina, Tennessee,[29] Utah (appellate),[30] Vermont, Virginia, Washington, West Virginia, Wisconsin, Wyoming (41 states)

Table A-4 (Continued)

Entity	States with prior consent as absolute precondition	States with prior notice as absolute precondition[1]	States with no prior consent or notice required
Counsel's Consent[6] (civil trials and all appeals)	Alabama, Arkansas, Maryland (civil trials), New York,[14] Texas (5 states)	None	Alaska, Arizona, California, Colorado, Connecticut, Delaware, Florida, Georgia, Hawaii, Idaho, Illinois, Iowa, Kansas, Kentucky, Louisiana, Maine, Maryland (appellate), Massachusetts, Michigan, Missouri, Minnesota, Montana, Nebraska, Nevada, New Hampshire, New Jersey, New Mexico, New York, North Carolina, North Dakota, Ohio, Oklahoma, Oregon, Pennsylvania, Rhode Island, South Carolina, Tennessee,[31] Utah,[32] Vermont, Virginia, Washington, West Virginia, Wisconsin, Wyoming (44 states)

| Witness's Consent[7] (civil and criminal trials) | None | Alabama, Alaska (victims of sexual offenses), Arkansas, Iowa (victims in sexual abuse cases only),[20] Kansas,[21] Maryland (victims only),[22] Minnesota, Missouri, New York,[23] North Dakota (sex offense victims only), Ohio, Oklahoma, Oregon, Pennsylvania, Rhode Island, Texas (civil), Utah[24] (17 states) | Arizona, California, Colorado, Connecticut, Florida, Georgia, Hawaii, Idaho, Iowa,[33] Kentucky, Maine, Maryland (all witnesses except victims),[34] Massachusetts, Michigan,[35] Montana, Nebraska, Nevada, New Hampshire, New Jersey, New Mexico,[36] North Carolina, South Carolina, Tennessee, Vermont, Virginia, Washington, West Virginia, Wisconsin,[37] Wyoming[38] (29 states) |

Source: Copyright © 1996 by Radio and Television News Directors Association. Used by permission.

Note: In this table, the term absolute precondition means that the particular entity's consent or acquiescence must be obtained for any coverage to occur. Limited condition, unless otherwise stated, means that if consent is not obtained or objection is made, that particular entity (e.g., jurors) may not be covered but the remainder of the proceeding may be. In states where consent is not required or a limited condition is not imposed, coverage of the proceeding or the entity is not contingent upon consent.

[1] States with prior notice as an absolute precondition for coverage require that the court receive notice of an intent to cover a proceeding prior to its commencement. Explicit consent is not required.

[2] A total of 47 states (all states allowing trial and/or appellate coverage) are classified under the three consent categories for this entity description. Georgia, Hawaii, Idaho, Minnesota, Oregon, Utah, and Wyoming appear twice here, since their court consent requirements for appellate proceedings are different from those for trials. Although judges have ultimate control over their courtrooms and will make the final determination as to whether to allow coverage of a proceeding, some states, as shown here, have rules which require either the court's explicit permission or prior notice of intent to cover.

[3] A total of 41 states (those allowing trial and appeals coverage of criminal proceedings [41 states] and those allowing only trial coverage of criminal cases [0 states] are classified under the three consent categories for this entity description. Tennessee appears twice. Maryland and Pennsylvania do not allow coverage of criminal trial proceedings. Prior to passage of legislation forbidding coverage of criminal trials, Maryland permitted coverage only if the defendant consented.

[4] A total of 41 states are classified under the three consent categories for this entity description. See note 3 above.

[5] A total of 47 states (all states allowing trial and/or appellate coverage) are classified under the three consent categories for this entity description. Minnesota and Utah fall into two of the three categories, as noted. Special consent rules relating to domestic relations and other sensitive matters are dealt with in Table A-7.

[6] A total of 47 states (all states allowing trial and/or appellate coverage) are classified under the three consent categories for this entity description. As used here, the term *counsel* excludes only prosecutors in criminal trials. Prosecutors are covered in a separate category. Maryland and New York fall into two of the three categories, as noted.

[7] A total of 44 states (those allowing trial *and* appeals coverage [43 states] and those allowing trial coverage only [1 state]) are classified under the three consent categories for this entity description. Iowa and Maryland, as noted, fall into two of the three categories described herein.

[8] Under Kentucky's rules, requests to cover a proceeding must be made to the court. While there are no specific provisions in the rules governing the court's response, permission must be obtained for coverage to occur.

[9] Maryland's rules require that a request for coverage be submitted. Although the court's consent is not specifically required, the judge must approve the type and location of the equipment to be used prior to the commencement of the proceeding to be covered.

[10] Nevada's rules do not state specifically when approval is to be obtained.

[11] See Table A-1, note 3.

[12] In Tennessee juvenile court proceedings, consent for coverage must be obtained from the accused in criminal cases and the parties in civil cases.

[13] In Maryland, a party may move for termination or limitation of coverage in criminal appellate cases. Consents of governmental entities or officials who are parties are not required.

[14] Counsel's consent is required in jury trials in progress.

[15] Illinois's rules also refer to the notice as a "request." The judge or presiding authority, upon receiving written notice, may decide to prohibit coverage prior to the commencement of a proceeding.

[16] See Table A-1, note 4.

[17] See Table A-1, note 4.

[18] It is not entirely clear what would occur in Oklahoma if a criminal defendant objects to coverage of his appeal. Taken literally, the rules of this state would seem to permit coverage of the proceedings but preclude coverage of the defendant in those circumstances. Since many defendants do not attend their appeal proceedings, the point may be a relatively minor one.

[19] See Table A-1, note 4.

[20] In Iowa, a victim/witness in a sexual abuse case must consent to coverage of his or her testimony. The objections of certain types of witnesses to coverage of their testimony enjoy a presumption of validity. These include victims/witnesses in other forcible felony prosecutions, police informants, undercover agents, and relocated witnesses.

[21] In Kansas, a judge may forbid coverage of a witness if he or she objects; however, when a police informant, undercover agent, relocated witness, juvenile witness or victim/witness objects to being covered, the judge is required to forbid coverage of that person. In addition, when a participant in a proceeding involving divorce, trade secrets, or a motion to suppress evidence objects to coverage, coverage of that participant is forbidden.

22See Table A-1, note 1.

23In New York, sex crime victims must request coverage and undercover peace and police officers must give written consent for coverage.

24See Table A-1, note 4.

25See note 12 above.

26See Table A-1, note 4.

27In Iowa, consents of parties are not required except in "juvenile," dissolution, adoption, child custody, or trade secrets cases."

28In New York, consents of parties are not required except in arraignment and suppression hearings.

29See note 12 above.

30See Table A-1, note 4.

31See note 12 above.

32See Table A-1, note 4.

33See note 22 above.

34See Table A-1, note 1.

35In Michigan and New Mexico, the judge has sole and plenary discretion to exclude coverage of certain witnesses, including, but not limited to, victims of sex crimes and their families, police informants, undercover agents, relocated witnesses, and juveniles.

36See note 35 above.

37In Wisconsin and Wyoming, the objections of certain types of witnesses to coverage of their testimony enjoy a presumption of validity. These include victims of crimes, confidential informants and undercover agents.

38See note 37 above.

TABLE A-5. COVERAGE OF JURORS

States where coverage is prohibited	States where coverage is limited[1]	States where coverage is not limited by rule
Alaska, Arkansas, California, Hawaii, Idaho, Maine, Michigan, Minnesota, Missouri, New Mexico, New York, North Carolina, North Dakota, Ohio, Oregon, Tennessee, Utah, Virginia (18 states)	Alabama, Arizona, Colorado, Connecticut, Georgia, Iowa, Kansas, Massachusetts, Nevada, New Hampshire,[2] New Jersey, Oklahoma,[3] Rhode Island, South Carolina, Vermont, Wisconsin, Wyoming (17 states)	Florida, Kentucky, Maryland,[4] Montana, Washington, West Virginia (6 states)

Source: Copyright © 1996 by Radio and Television News Directors Association. Used by permission.

Note: A total of 41 of 43 states (those allowing trial and appeals coverage (43 states) and those allowing trial coverage in jury cases (0 states) are classified under the three coverage categories for this entity description. Pennsylvania and Nebraska do not permit any coverage of jury proceedings. Texas is excluded.

[1] Unless otherwise indicated, states in this category prohibit close-up or identifiable coverage of the jury but allow coverage if the jury is part of the background of another shot.

[2] In New Hampshire, prior approval of the Presiding Justice is required to cover the jury in criminal cases.

[3] In Oklahoma, coverage of an objecting juror is not permitted.

[4] See Table A-1, note 1.

TABLE A-6. TIME REQUIREMENTS FOR ADVANCE NOTICE OR REQUESTS TO COVER COURTROOM PROCEEDINGS

States where no advance notice or permission is required	States where no time is specified	States requiring notice/request one day in advance	States notice/requiring between two and seven days in advance	States requiring notice/request more than seven days in advance
Arkansas, Florida, Hawaii (appellate), Idaho, Nebraska, North Carolina, Oregon (appellate), Rhode Island, Vermont, Virginia, Wyoming (appellate) (11 states)	Alabama, Arizona,* Delaware, Georgia (trial), Hawaii* (trial), Idaho (trial), Kentucky, Maine, Massachusetts,* Montana, New Hampshire, New Jersey,* New York (appellate), Ohio, Oregon (trial), Oklahoma, Pennsylvania, South Carolina, Texas, Washington, West Virginia (21 states)	Alaska,† Arizona (Supreme), Colorado,† Minnesota,† New Mexico,† Ohio (Supreme), Wyoming (trial) (7 states)	California (5 days), Connecticut (3 days—trial), Georgia (7 days—appellate), Illinois (5 days), Kansas† (7 days), Maryland† (5 days), Michigan† (3 days), Missouri (5 days), Nevada† (3 days), New York† (7 days —trial), North Dakota (3 days—appellate, 7 days—trial), Tennessee† (2 days), Utah (2 days), Wisconsin† (3 days) (14 states)	Connecticut (13 days—appellate), Iowa† (14 days), Louisiana (20 days) (3 states)

Source: Copyright © 1996 by Radio and Television News Directors Association. Used by permission.

Note: Since Arizona, Connecticut, Georgia, Hawaii, Idaho, New York, Ohio, Oregon, and Wyoming fall into more than one category, the total number of states allowing extended media coverage is 47 rather than 56.

* In these states, the requests or notice are to be made a "reasonable time" in advance of the proceedings.

† In these states, the time requirement may be waived at the discretion of the judge.

TABLE A-7. COVERAGE EXEMPTIONS FOR SPECIFIC TYPES OF CASES AND CATEGORIES OF WITNESSES

The rules of a number of states (e.g., Connecticut, Nevada, and Oklahoma) make clear the fact that coverage is not permitted when access is otherwise restricted by law. Moreover, although the courts in all states that permit coverage retain the authority to preclude coverage on a case-by-case basis, the following states have rules explicitly prohibiting or limiting coverage in particular types of cases or prohibiting coverage of certain witnesses in a covered proceeding.

Type of case/witness	States
Adoption	Alaska,[1] Arizona, Arkansas,[2] Connecticut,[3] Idaho, Iowa,[4] Maine, Maryland,[5] Missouri, North Carolina, Oregon, Rhode Island, Virginia (13 states)
Child Custody	Alaska,[6] Arkansas (guardianship),[7] Connecticut,[8] Idaho, Iowa,[9] Maine, Maryland,[10] Minnesota, Missouri, New Jersey,[11] North Carolina, Oregon, Rhode Island (if child is a participant),[12] Pennsylvania, Virginia (15 states)
Divorce	Alaska,[13] Arkansas,[14] Connecticut,[15] Iowa,[16] Maine, Maryland,[17] Minnesota, Missouri, New Jersey,[18] North Carolina,[19] Oregon, Pennsylvania, Virginia, Wisconsin[20] (14 states)
Juvenile Proceedings	Alabama, Alaska, Arizona, Arkansas,[21] Georgia, Idaho, Iowa,[22] Maine, Maryland,[23] Minnesota, Missouri, New Jersey,[24] North Carolina, Oregon, Rhode Island,[25] Tennessee,[26] Virginia, Wisconsin[27] (18 states)
Motions to Suppress	Hawaii,[28] Maryland,[29] Massachusetts, Minnesota, New York,[30] North Carolina, Rhode Island,[31] Virginia, Wisconsin,[32] Wyoming[33] (10 states)

Type of case/witness	States
Police Informants	Arkansas,[34] Maryland,[35] Michigan,[36] Minnesota, New Mexico,[37] North Carolina, Virginia, Wisconsin,[38] Wyoming[39] (9 states)
Relocated Witnesses	Maryland,[40] Michigan,[41] Minnesota, New Mexico,[42] North Carolina, Wisconsin[43] (6 states)
Sex Crimes	Arkansas (victims),[44] Connecticut,[45] Hawaii,[46] Maine, Michigan,[47] Minnesota, New Jersey,[48] New Mexico (victims and their families),[49] New York, North Carolina (victims and their families), North Dakota (victims, witnesses), Oregon, Virginia (victims and their families), Wisconsin[50] (14 states)
Trade Secrets	Connecticut,[51] Hawaii,[52] Iowa,[53] Maine, Maryland,[54] Minnesota, New Jersey,[55] North Carolina, Oregon, Virginia, Wisconsin[56] (11 states)
Undercover Agents	Arkansas,[57] Hawaii,[58] Maryland,[59] Michigan,[60] Minnesota, New Mexico,[61] New York, North Carolina, Virginia, Wisconsin,[62] Wyoming[63] (11 states)
Orphans' Court	Connecticut,[64] Maryland,[65] Rhode Island (if child is participant)[66] (3 states)
In Camera Proceedings	Arkansas,[67] Colorado, Hawaii, North Carolina, Virginia (5 states)
Proceedings before Clerks of Court	North Carolina (1 state)
Proceedings before Magistrates	North Carolina (1 state)
Probable Cause Proceedings	Massachusetts, North Carolina (2 states)
Minor Witnesses	Hawaii,[68] Maryland, North Carolina, Virginia (4 states)

TABLE A-7. CONTINUED

Type of case/witness	States
Motions to Dismiss	Massachusetts, Minnesota, Rhode Island[69] (3 states)
Voir Dire Hearings	Colorado, Connecticut, Hawaii, Iowa, Massachusetts, Minnesota, New Mexico, New York, North Carolina, Oregon, Rhode Island (11 states)
Motions for Judgment of Acquittal or Directed Verdict	Minnesota, Rhode Island (2 states)
Motions *In Limine*	Minnesota, Rhode Island (2 states)
Witnesses in Jeopardy of Serious Bodily Injury	Hawaii[70] (1 state)
Hearings on Admissibility of Evidence	Minnesota (1 state)
Domestic Disputes	New Jersey (Municipal),[71] Oregon (2 states)
Arraignments	New York[72] (1 state)
Grand Jury Proceedings	Idaho (1 state)

Source: Copyright © 1996 by Radio and Television News Directors Association. Used by permission.

[1] "Family matter" proceedings may be covered on a case-by-case basis with the consent of all parties in Alaska.

[2] Arkansas prohibits coverage of minors without parental or guardian consent. It totally prohibits coverage of juvenile, adoption, guardianship, or domestic relations proceedings.

[3] Generally, the Connecticut Supreme Court will not permit coverage of these proceedings. The Connecticut Superior Court forbids coverage of these proceedings and, in addition, prohibits coverage of proceedings held in the jury's absence and sentencing hearings in criminal cases in which the trial was not covered.

[4] In these types of cases, Iowa permits coverage if consents of the parties (including the parent or guardian of a minor) are obtained. In all other cases, Iowa requires no consents of the parties.

[5] Maryland provides that the objections of participants are presumed to have validity in cases involving police informants, minors, undercover agents, relocated witnesses, evidentiary suppression hearings, trade secrets, divorce, and custody. Maryland's rules for coverage do not apply to its Orphans' Courts. See Table A-1, note 1.

[6] See note 1 above.

[7] See note 2 above.

[8] See note 3 above.

[9] See note 4 above.

[10] See note 5 above.

[11] New Jersey absolutely precludes coverage of these proceedings and, additionally, in cases where coverage would cause a substantial increase in the threat of harm to any participant or otherwise interfere with a fair trial.

[12] Rhode Island prohibits coverage in any matters in Family Court in which juveniles are significant participants.

[13] See note 1 above.

[14] See note 2 above.

[15] See note 3 above.

[16] See note 4 above.

[17] See note 5 above.

[18] New Jersey prohibits coverage of cases involving divorce or "matrimonial disputes." See note 11 above.

[19] North Carolina forbids coverage of temporary and permanent alimony proceedings as well as divorce proceedings.

[20] Wisconsin requires that objections of participants to coverage in these cases shall be presumed to have validity. Wisconsin's rule extends to the victims of crimes, including sexual crimes.

[21] See note 2 above.

[22] See note 4 above.

[23] See note 5 above.

[24] See note 11 above.

[25] Rhode Island explicitly forbids coverage in these cases. See note 12 above.

[26] In Tennessee, consents of parties are required for coverage to occur.

[27] See note 20 above.

[28] Under Hawaii's rules, a trial judge will grant requests for coverage unless good cause is found to prohibit coverage. A presumption of good cause exists if the proceeding is for the purpose of determining the admissibility of evidence, testimony regarding trade secrets or from undercover agents is being received, children witnesses are testifying, complaining witnesses in sexual offense cases are testifying in a criminal trial, or a witness would be put in substantial jeopardy of serious bodily injury.

[29] See note 5 above. By statute, Maryland's experiment has been precluded from encompassing coverage of criminal trial proceedings.

[30] In New York, consents of parties are required for coverage to occur.

[31] Rhode Island also forbids coverage of hearings to determine competence or relevance of evidence.

[32] See note 20 above.

[33] Wyoming requires that objections of participants to coverage in these cases shall be presumed to have validity. The rule also extends to the victims of crimes.

[34] See note 2 above.

[35] See note 29 above.

[36] See Table A-4, note 35.

[37] See Table A-4, note 35.

[38] See Table A-4, note 20.

[39] See note 33 above.

[40] See note 29 above.

[41] See Table A-4, note 35.

[42] See Table A-4, note 35.

[43] See Table A-4, note 20.

[44] See note 2 above.

[45] See note 3 above.

[46] See note 28 above.

[47] See Table A-4, note 35.
[48] See note 11 above.
[49] See Table A-4, note 35.
[50] See Table A-4, note 20.
[51] See note 3 above.
[52] See note 28 above.
[53] See note 4 above.
[54] See note 5 above.
[55] See note 11 above.
[56] See note 20 above.
[57] See note 2 above.
[58] See note 28 above.
[59] See note 5 above.
[60] See Table A-4, note 35.
[61] See Table A-4, note 35.
[62] See note 20 above.
[63] See note 33 above.
[64] See note 3 above.
[65] See note 5 above.
[66] See note 12 above.
[67] Coverage of *in camera* proceedings in Arkansas is prohibited unless the court explicitly consents.
[68] See note 28 above.
[69] Coverage of motions to dismiss for legal inadequacy of the indictment, information, or complaint (criminal or civil) is not permitted in Rhode Island.
[70] See note 28 above.
[71] See note 11 above.
[72] See note 30 above.

APPENDIX B

SUMMARY OF STATE CAMERA
COVERAGE RULES BY THE
RADIO-TELEVISION NEWS
DIRECTORS ASSOCIATION

The following is a four-tier listing of states arranged in the order of the estimated utility of their rules in permitting extended media coverage of courtroom proceedings revised as of January 1, 1996.

The first tier includes those states that appear to allow the most substantial coverage. These states employ a variety of rule formulations and the scope and amount of coverage varies. Florida has a unique "qualitative difference test" that a participant must meet in order to justify camera exclusion. Twelve other states recognize an especially broad discretion in the presiding judge to permit or exclude audiovisual coverage. Other states in this tier have rules that specifically restrict coverage, such as by prohibiting coverage of or requiring consent of sex crime victims, informants, or undercover agents or by providing that objections by these and several other types of witnesses to coverage of their testimony enjoy a presumption of validity. This tier also includes states that deny coverage of certain types of proceedings not deemed essential for wide coverage, such as preliminary hearings, family law, and trade secrets proceedings.

The second tier includes states that have restrictions prohibiting coverage of especially important types of cases or of all or large categories of witnesses who object to coverage of their testimony.

The third tier includes states that allow appellate coverage only, states that have restrictive trial coverage rules (e.g., requiring consent of the parties in all cases or requiring the consent of the defendant in criminal cases), and a state with judges that routinely deny coverage under a rule recognizing their broad discretion so that little or no trial coverage actually occurs.

The fourth tier lists those jurisdictions that prohibit trial and appellate coverage entirely and are not counted among the forty-seven states that permit some form of camera coverage.

Tier I: States That Allow Most Coverage

Alaska—requires sex offense victim consent
Arizona—coverage of juvenile/adoption proceedings prohibited
California—broad discretion in presiding judge
Colorado—broad discretion in presiding judge
Connecticut—coverage of trade secret and "family" cases prohibited
Florida—"qualitative difference" test
Georgia—broad discretion in presiding judge
Idaho—broad discretion in presiding judge
Iowa—need victim/witness consent in sexual abuse cases
Kentucky—broad discretion in presiding judge
Massachusetts—coverage of certain proceedings prohibited
Michigan—judge may prohibit coverage of certain witnesses
Montana—broad discretion in presiding judge
Nevada—broad discretion in presiding judge
New Hampshire—broad discretion in presiding judge
New Mexico—judge may prohibit coverage of certain witnesses
North Carolina—coverage of certain cases/witnesses prohibited
North Dakota—broad discretion in presiding judge
Rhode Island—coverage of certain proceedings prohibited/broad discretion
   in presiding judge
South Carolina—broad discretion in presiding judge
Tennessee—broad discretion in presiding judge/coverage of minors is re-
   stricted
Washington—broad discretion in presiding judge
West Virginia—broad discretion in presiding judge
Wisconsin—broad discretion in presiding judge
Wyoming—broad discretion in presiding judge

TIER II: STATES THAT HAVE RESTRICTIONS PROHIBITING COVERAGE OF IMPORTANT TYPES OF CASES, OR OF ALL OR LARGE CATEGORIES OF WITNESSES WHO OBJECT TO COVERAGE OF THEIR TESTIMONY

Hawaii—coverage of certain cases and witnesses prohibited

Kansas—many types of witnesses may object

Missouri—many types of witnesses may object

New Jersey—coverage of sexual penetration cases prohibited

New York—numerous restrictions on coverage of witnesses

Ohio—victim/witness has right to object to coverage

Oregon—witnesses' discretion to object to coverage of certain cases

Texas—no rules for criminal trial coverage, but such coverage allowed increasingly on a case-by-case basis

Virginia—coverage of sex offense cases prohibited

TIER III: STATES THAT ALLOW APPELLATE COVERAGE ONLY OR HAVE SUCH RESTRICTIVE TRIAL COVERAGE RULES AS TO ESSENTIALLY PREVENT COVERAGE

Alabama—consent of all parties/attorneys required

Arkansas—coverage ceases with objection by party/attorney

Delaware—appellate coverage only

Illinois—appellate coverage only

Louisiana—appellate coverage only

Maine—appellate coverage, civil trials, arraignments, sentencings, and other non-testimonial proceedings in criminal matters

Maryland—appellate coverage/civil trial only

Minnesota—appellate coverage/trial—consent of all parties required

Nebraska—appellate coverage/audio trial coverage only

Oklahoma—consent of criminal defendant required

Pennsylvania—any witness who objects will not be covered, civil trials only without a jury

Utah—appellate coverage/trial coverage, still photography only

Vermont—broad discretion in presiding judge

TIER IV: JURISDICTIONS THAT PROHIBIT TRIAL AND APPELLATE COVERAGE ENTIRELY

District of Columbia
Mississippi
South Dakota

NOTES

NOTES TO THE INTRODUCTION

1. William O. Douglas, *The Public Trial and the Free Press*, 46 A.B.A. J. 840, at 840, 842 (1960).

2. Jerome Barron, *Inside Story*, PBS, February 1982.

3. *In re Petition of Post-Newsweek Stations, Florida*, 370 Southern 2d 764, at 776 (1979).

4. Gerry Spence, quoted in "Simpson Case Backlash Keeps Cameras out of Other Courtrooms," *New York Times*, September 17, 1995, 35.

5. J. Skelly Wright, *A Judge's View: The News Media and Criminal Justice*, 50 A.B.A. J. 1125, at 1126, 1127 (1964).

6. Ibid., 1127, 1128.

7. *Cowley v. Pulsifer*, 137 Massachusetts 392, at 394 (1884).

8. *Press Enterprise Co. v. Superior Court of California, Riverside County*, 478 U.S. 1, at 18 (1986).

9. *Gomez v. U.S.* and *Chavez-Tesina v. U.S.*, 490 U.S. 858, at 875 (1989).

10. ,Stephen Gillers quoted in Paul Marcotte, *Courts on Cable* 76 A.B.A. J. 19 (April 1990).

11. Sir John MacDonnell, *Historical Trials* 234 (Rothman, 1983).

12. Meg Greenfield, "In Defense of Sensationalism: The Media and the O.J. Simpson Case," editorial, *Washington Post* and *Newsweek*, September 19, 1994.

NOTES TO CHAPTER 1

1. *The Associated Press and Los Angeles Herald Examiner, Hearst Corporation v. U.S. District Court, Central District of California*, 705 F.2d 1143 (1983), concurring opinion of Judge Poole.

2. Correspondence with author.

3. *Irvin v. Dowd*, 366 U.S. 717, at 730 (1961).

4. Michael Belknap, *American Political Trials* 22 (Greenwood Press, 1981).

5. James Alexander, *A Brief Narrative of the Case and Trial of John Peter Zenger* (Stanley Katz, ed., Harvard University Press, 1972); Vincent Buranelli, *The Trial of Peter Zenger* (New York University Press, 1957).

6. Carl Calmer, *For the Rights of Men*, 7 (Books for Libraries Press, 1947); Livingston Rutherford, *John Peter Zenger: His Press, His Trial and a Bibliography of Zenger Imprints* (Dodd, Mead, 1904).

7. Rutherford, *John Peter Zenger* 61.

8. Samuel Engle Burr, Jr., *Napoleon's Dossier on Aaron Burr* (Naylor Co., 1969); Walter F. McCaleb, *New Light on Aaron Burr* (Texas Quarterly, 1963); Philip Vail, *The Great American Rascal* (Hawthorn Books, 1973); Milton Lomask, *Aaron Burr: The Conspiracy and Years of Exile, 1805–1836* (Farrar, Straus and Giroux, 1982).

9. Lomask, *Aaron Burr* 230.

10. Leonard Steinhorn, *Man on Trial: The Unwritten Law and Victorian American Male Sexual Honor* (1978).

11. Quoted in *Baltimore Sun*, April 29, 1859.

12. Milton Rugoff, *The Beechers: An American Family in the Nineteenth Century* (Harper and Row, 1981).

13. Robert Shaplen, *Free Love and Heavenly Sinners* 216–217 (Knopf, 1954).

14. Ibid., 225, 253.

15. David Garrard Lowe, *Stanford White's New York* 324–325 (Doubleday, 1992).

16. Paul R. Baker, *Stanney: The Gilded Life of Stanford White* 387 (Free Press, 1989).

17. Lowe, *Stanford White's New York* 324–325.

18. Baker, *Stanney*, chaps. 21, 22, and 24.

19. Another turn-of-the-century case that captured the extraordinary attention of the press was described in Martin L. Friedland, *The Death of Old Man Rice, A True Story of Criminal Justice in America* (New York University Press, 1994). This trial by newspaper, as it was called by the author, concerned a controversial will forgery and murder case, in which Texas multimillionaire William Marsh Rice, founder of Rice University, was the victim and one of his attorneys was the alleged offender.

20. Irving Stone, *Clarence Darrow for the Defense* (Doubleday, Doran & Co., 1941).

21. Ibid., 436, 437.

22. Ludovic Kennedy, *The Airman and the Carpenter: The Lindbergh Kidnaping and the Framing of Richard Hauptmann* (Viking, 1985).

23. *The Lindbergh Baby Kidnapping: The Crime That Won't Go Away*, the History Channel, 1997.

24. Kennedy, *The Airman and the Carpenter* 259.

25. *Sheppard v. Maxwell*, 384 U.S. 333 (1966).

26. U.S. Bureau of the Census, *Statistical Abstract of the U.S., 1995: The National Data Book*, 115th ed. at 571.

27. *Estes v. Texas*, 381 U.S. 532 (1965).

28. The *Los Angeles Times* was acknowledged by many observers to be the print medium of record, publishing over fifteen hundred Simpson stories in sixteen months. Its coverage, especially by David Shaw, who commented extensively and perceptively about the media, was noteworthy. Much of Shaw's commentary has informed this author.

29. "The Simpson Verdicts: Valuable Lessons of TV in Courtroom," *Los Angeles Times*, October 5, 1996, A7.

30. Ira Reiner, "Cameras Keep Justice System in Focus," *National Law Journal*, October 23, 1995, A23.

31. *Abrams v. U.S.*, 250 U.S. 616, at 630 (1919); and see *Maryland v. Baltimore Radio Show, Inc.*, 338 U.S. 912, at 920 n. 29.

32. *Maryland v. Baltimore Radio Show, Inc.*, 338 U.S. 912 (1950).

33. *Bridges v. California* and *Times Mirror Co. v. Supreme Court of California*, 314 U.S. 252 (1941).

34. *Press Enterprise Co. v. Superior Court of California, Riverside County*, 478 U.S. 1, at 7 (1986).

NOTES TO CHAPTER 2

1. *Gitlow v. U.S.*, 268 U.S. 652 (1925).

2. See Fredrick Siebert, Theodore Peterson, and Wilbur Schramm, *Four Theories of the Press*, ch. 1 (University of Illinois Press, 1956).

3. Ibid., ch. 2.

4. William Blackstone, 4 *Commentaries* 151–152.

5. Letter to Eldridge Gerry, January 26, 1799, 7 *Writings of Thomas Jefferson* 328 (Ford ed., 1894).

6. See generally Siebert, Peterson, and Schramm, *Four Theories of the Press*.

7. See Hugo Black, *The Bill of Rights*, 35 N.Y.U. L. Rev. 865 (1960).

8. Zechariah Chafee, *Government and Mass Communications* 6 (University of Chicago Press, 1947).

9. Ronald L. Goldfarb, *The Contempt Power*, ch. 2 (Columbia University Press, 1963; Anchor Books, 1971).

10. Lois Forer, *A Free Press and a Fair Trial*, 39 A.B.A. J. 800, at 843 (1953); Walter Nelles and Carol Weiss King, *Contempt by Publication*, 28 Columbia L. Rev. 401 (1928).

11. Ironically, the actual situation for defendants in England is not so different, despite the stricter contempt rules, because until recently pretrial—as opposed to trial coverage—publicity was permitted. In any event, convicting a contemptuous press agency does nothing for a defendant who has been hurt by press misconduct.

12. ABA Committee on Professional Ethics and Grievances, Formal Opinion 67, March 1932.

13. Special Committee of the Bar Association of the City of New York, *Radio, Television, and the Administration of Justice* (Columbia University Press, 1965). See the selective bibliography on pp. 319–321.

14. ABA Committee on Professional Ethics and Grievances, Opinion 212 (1941), 500–501 (1967).

15. 77 ABA Report 607 (1952). See also Report of Post-Newsweek Stations, Florida, Inc., to Supreme Court of Florida, Case #46,835 in its Petition to adopt the new Florida Rule for a good history of the prevailing rules.

16. Informal Opinion No. 490 interpreting Canon 35. Opinions of the Committee on Professional Ethics, 1967 edition, published by the American Bar Association and the American Bar Foundation.

17. For full history of Canon 35, see Appendix to Justice Harlan's Opinion in *Estes v. Texas*, 381 U.S. 532, at 596–601 (1965).

18. See *Kavanaugh v. Courtroom Television Network*, 91 Civ. 7959 (RPP), Declaration of Steven Brill, March 3, 1992, at 15, citing decisions in New Mexico, Pennsylvania, Georgia, and Florida.

19. 2 *ABA Standards for Criminal Justice*, 2d ed., 1986 Supp., commentary at 8:30.

20. Susanna Barber, *News Cameras in the Courtroom: A Free Press-Fair Trial Debate* (Ablex, 1987).

21. Memorandum dated February 13, 1997.

22. Correspondence with the author.

23. *Patterson v. Colorado*, 205 U.S. 454, at 462 (1907).

24. *Stroble v. California*, 343 U.S. 181 (1952).

25. Harold Sullivan, *Contempt by Publication* 178 (Yale University Press, 1940).

26. *Cockrell v. Dobbs*, 381 S.W. 2d 756 (S.C. Arkansas, 1964).

27. *State v. Thompson*, 123 N.W. 2d 378 (S.C. Minnesota, 1963).

28. *Irvin v. Dowd*, 366 U.S. 717, at 722, 723 (1961).

29. *Community Hostility and the Right to an Impartial Jury*, 60 Columbia L. R. 349, 368 (1960). In *Delaney v. U.S.*, 199 F.2d 107 (1st Cir. 1952) a verdict was reversed for failure to grant a continuance under what were considered appropriate circumstances. A prior legislative hearing regarding the same matter had saturated the community with comments about the case.

30. *Application of Roy M. Cohn*, 332 F.2d 976 (2d Cir. 1964).

31. *U.S. v. Dennis*, 183 F.2d 201 (2d Cir. 1950).

32. *Reynolds v. U.S.*, 98 U.S. 145 (1898).

33. *Maryland v. Baltimore Radio Show Inc.*, 338 U.S. 912 (1950).

34. Dale Broder, *Voir Dire Examinations: An Empirical Study*, 38 So. Calif. L. Rev. 503 (1965).

35. *Maryland v. Baltimore Radio Show, Inc.*, 338 U.S. 912 (1950).

36. *U.S. v. Leviton*, 193 F.2d 848, at 857 (2d Cir. 1951).

37. *Editor and Publisher*, August 14, 1965, quoting Federal Judge William J. Neelon.

38. Ronald L. Goldfarb, *Public Information, Criminal Trials, and the Cause Célèbre*, NYU L. Rev. 810 (1961).

39. *Shepherd v. Florida*, 341 U.S. 50 (1951).

40. *Rideau v. Louisiana*, 373 U.S. 723 (1963).

41. *Sheppard v. Maxwell*, 384 U.S. 333 (1966).

42. *State v. Van Duyne*, 43 N.J. 369, 204 A.2d 841 (1964).

43. A discussion of this subject appeared in Alfred Friendly and Ronald L. Goldfarb, *Legal Restraints on Crime News* 14–16 (Freedom of Information Center Report No. 185, August 1967).

44. *Palko v. Connecticut*, 302 U.S. 319 (1937); *Schneider v. State*, 308 U.S. 147 (1939).

45. Jeremy Bentham, 1 *The Rationale of Judicial Evidence* 585 (Garland, 1978).

46. Edward Jenks, *The Book of English Law* 91 (Ohio University Press, 1937).

47. Sir Frederick Pollock, *The Expansion of the Common Law* 42 (Stevens and Sons, 1904).

48. *In re Oliver*, 333 U.S. 257, at 266 (1948).

49. Sir Thomas Smith, *De Republica Anglorum*, bk 2, ch. 15, at 79, 101, 111 (Alston ed., Cambridge University Press, 1972).

50. Sir Matthew Hale, *The History of the Common Law of England* 343–345 (Runnington ed., Henry Butterworth, 6th ed., 1820).

51. Blackstone, 3 *Commentaries* 375.

52. Max Radin, *The Right to a Public Trial*, 6 Temple L.Q. 388 (1932).

53. Ibid.

54. Francis X. Busch, 1 *Law and Tactics in Jury Trials* 2–15 (encyclopedic ed., Bobbs-Merrill, 1959); Charles T. Coleman, *Historical Sketch of Trial by Jury*, 40 Can. L.T. 732 (1920).

55. See generally William S. Holdsworth, 1 *A History of English Law* 312–327, 332–336 (7th rev. ed., 1956); Smith, *De Republica Anglorum*; 1 *Journals of the Continental Congress, 1774–1789* (Ford ed., 1904).

56. Sir John Vaughan 135, Bushell's case, 124 Eng. Rep. 1006 (C.P. 1677).

57. *Trial of John Lilburne*, 4 How. St. Tr. 1270, 1274 (1649), cited in *In re Oliver* at 266.

58. *Earl of Shaftesbury's Trial*, 8 How. St. Tr. 759, at 771–774 (1681), cited in Philip B. Kurland and Ralph Lerner, eds., 5 *The Founder's Constitution* 247 (University of Chicago Press, 1987).

59. Radin, *The Right to a Public Trial* 384.

60. The Supreme Court has also stated: "In light of this history, it is most doubtful that the tradition of publicity was ever associated with the rights of the accused. The practice of conducting the trial in public was established as a feature of English justice long before the defendant was afforded even the most rudimentary rights." *Gannett Co. Inc. v. DePasquale*, 443 U.S. 442 (1979).

61. Joel Prentiss Bishop, 2 *New Criminal Procedure, or New Commentaries on the Law of Pleadings and Evidence and the Practice in Criminal Cases* 768 (T. H. Flood, 1913).

62. Thomas M. Cooley, *A Treatise on Constitutional Limitations* 312 (Little, Brown, 1972).

63. 1 *Journals of the Continental Congress* at 69.

64. *In re Oliver*, 333 U.S. 257, at 266 (1948).

65. E.g., *State v. Copp*, 15 N.H. 212 (1844); *E.W. Scripps Co. v. Fulton*, 100 Ohio App. 157, 125 N.E.2d 896 (1955).

66. Herman Ames, *The Proposed Amendments to the Constitution of the United States during the First Century of Its History* 183 (B. Franklin, 1970).

67. During the first session of the First Congress, on June 8, 1789, Mad-

ison stated that he had a set of amendments that he wanted to introduce. He had "strong hopes [that the Amendments] will meet with the unanimous approbation of this House, after the fullest discussion and most serious regard." Ibid. (citing 1 *Annals of Congress* 424–450).

68. 1 *Annals of Congress* 756.

69. The House of Representatives adopted seventeen proposals; the Senate rejected two and consolidated the number to twelve. These twelve were later accepted by the House; ten were subsequently ratified by the states. See generally Ames, *The Proposed Amendments* at 184–185.

70. The Senate debates were not reported at that time. Bernard Schwartz, 5 *The Roots of the Bill of Rights* 984 (Chelsea House, 1980).

71. Wesley Frank Craven, *New Jersey and the English Colonization of North America* 64–65 (Van Nostrand, 1964).

72. William Penn is often cited as the author of the Concessions (see Edwin P. Tanner, *The Province of New Jersey 1664–1738* 113 [Columbia University Press, 1908]; and Richard L. Perry, ed., *Sources of Our Liberties* 182 [American Bar Foundation, 1978], although other historians hold otherwise ("But there is just as good reason for attributing the authorship to Edward Byllinge, . . . who seems to have made comparable proposals for the government of England in a pamphlet published as far back as 1659." [Craven, *New Jersey and the English Colonization of North America* 69–70]).

73. The Pennsylvania Declaration of Rights of 1776 (cited in Schwartz, *Roots of the Bill of Rights* 265).

74. *In re Oliver*, 333 U.S. 257, at 270 (1948).

75. *Richmond Newspapers, Inc. v. Commonwealth of Virginia*, 448 U.S. 566, at 570 (1980).

76. *Gannett Co., Inc. v. DePasquale*, 443 U.S. 368 (1979).

77. *Richmond Newspapers Inc. v. Commonwealth of Virginia*, 448 U.S. 554 (1980).

78. *Globe Newspaper Co. v. Superior Court for the County of Norfolk*, 457 U.S. 596 (1982).

79. *Waller v. Georgia*, 467 U.S. 39 (1984).

80. *Press Enterprise Co. v. Superior Court of California, Riverside County*, 478 U.S. 1 (1986).

81. *Gannett Co., Inc. v. DePasquale*, 443 U.S. 368, at 382, 383, 405 (1979).

82. *Richmond Newspapers, Inc. v. Commonwealth of Virginia*, 448 U.S. 554, at 569, 571, 572 (1980).

83. *Craig v. Harney*, 331 U.S. 367, at 374 (1947).

84. *Pennekamp v. Florida*, 328 U.S. 331 (1946).

85. *Branzburg v. Hayes*, 408 U.S. 665, at 681 (1972).

86. *Waller v. Georgia*, 467 U.S. 39, at 45, 46 (1984).

87. *Press Enterprise Co. v. Superior Court of California, Riverside County*, 478 U.S. 1, at 27, 28 (1986).

88. *The Oregonian Publishing Co. v. U.S. District Court, Oregon*, 920 F.2d, 1462 (1990).

89. *Caribbean International News Corp. v. Puerto Rico*, 508 U.S. 147 (1993).

90. *Press Enterprise Co. v. Superior Court of California, Riverside County*, 478 U.S. 1, at 14 (1986).

91. *The Times Mirror Co. and The Copley Press and KCST-TV v. United States*, 873 F.2d 1210, at 1213 (9th Cir. 1988).

92. *U.S. v. Hernandez*, 608 F.2d 741 (9th Cir. 1979); *U.S. v. Eisner*, 533 F.2d 987 (6th Cir. 1976).

93. *Latimore v. Sieloff*, 561 F.2d 691 (7th Cir. 1977); *Geise v. U.S.*, 262 F.2d 151 (9th Cir. 1958); *U.S. v. Sherlock*, 865 F.2d 1069 (9th Cir. 1988).

94. *U.S. v. Aker*, 542 F.2d 770 (9th Cir. 1976).

95. *U.S. v. Northrop Corp.*, 746 F. Supp. 1002 (Dist. Ct. Calif., CD, 1990).

96. *U.S. v. Broussard*, 767 F. Supp. 1545 (Dist. Ct. D. Oregon, 1991).

97. *Associated Press and Los Angeles Herald Examiner v. U.S. District Court, Central District of California*, 705 F.2d 1143, at 1145 (9th Cir., 1983); *Seattle Times Co. and Hearst Corporation v. U.S. District Court, Western District, Washington*, 845 F.2d 1513 (9th Cir. 1988).

98. *Nebraska Press Association v. Stuart*, 427 U.S. 539, at 553 (1976).

99. Lois Forer, *A Free Press and a Fair Trial*, 39 A.B.A. J. 800, at 803 (1953).

100. *In re Oliver*, 333 U.S. 257 (1948).

NOTES TO CHAPTER 3

1. *Estes v. State of Texas*, 381 U.S. 532 (1965).

2. Ibid., 583.

3. Ibid., 614.

4. Correspondence with the author, May 5, 1997.

5. *In re Petition of Post-Newsweek Stations, Florida*, 347 Southern 2d. 404 (1977). See also *Report of Post-Newsweek Stations Florida, Inc., to Supreme Court of Florida*, Case #46,835 in its Petition to adopt the new Florida Rule for a good history of the prevailing rules.

6. *In re Petition of Post-Newsweek Stations, Florida*, 370 Southern 2d. 764 (1979).

7. *Chandler v. State of Florida*, 449 U.S. 560 (1981).

8. All references to this argument before the Supreme Court are taken from the transcript of proceedings on November 12, 1980, in *Chandler v. State of Florida* #79–1260. Joel Hirschhorn argued for the appellants, and Attorney General Jim Smith and Assistant Attorney General Calvin Fox argued for the State of Florida. The record is available in the U.S. Archives.

9. *Cameras in the Courtroom—A Two-Year Review in the State of Washington, a Project of the Washington State Superior Court Judges' Association Committee on Courts and Community* October 11, 1978, pp. 3, 4.

10. Radio and Television News Directors Association (RTNDA), *News Media Coverage of Judicial Proceedings with Cameras and Microphones: A Survey of the States*, January 1996, at A-84.

11. Judicial Planning Coordination Unit, *A Sample Survey of the Attitudes of Individuals Associated with Trials Involving Media and Still Photography Coverage in Selected Florida Courts between July 5, 1977, and June 30, 1978*, at 16.

12. RTNDA, *News Media Coverage of Judicial Proceedings with Cameras and Microphones*, A-23–A-24.

13. *Report of the Supreme Court Committee to Monitor and Evaluate the Use of Audio and Visual Equipment in the Courtroom, an Order of the Wisconsin Supreme Court*, April 1, 1979, at 73.

14. *Report of the Supreme Court Committee on the Desirability of Modifying or Dropping Rule 14*, August 18, 1970.

15. *Craig v. Harney*, 331 U.S. 367, at 374 (1947).

16. RTNDA, *News Media Coverage of Judicial Proceedings with Cameras and Microphones*, A-86.

17. *The Advisory Committee to Oversee the Experimental Use of Cameras and Recording Equipment in the Courtrooms to the Supreme Judicial Court, State of Massachusetts*, July 16, 1982, at 7.

18. RTNDA, *News Media Coverage of Judicial Proceedings with Cameras and Microphones*, A-44–A-45.

19. *Report of the Minnesota Advisory Committee on Cameras in the Courtroom to the Supreme Court*, January 11, 1982, at 18.

20. Rob Raker, *Cameras and Recorders in Arizona's Trial Courts: An Evaluation of the Experiment*, May 1983.

21. RTNDA, *News Media Coverage of Judicial Proceedings with Cameras and Microphones*, A-8–A-9.

22. *Report on the Proposed Modification of the Maryland Canons of*

Judicial Ethics to Permit Extended Media Coverage of Court Proceedings, submitted by the Public Awareness Committee of the Maryland Judicial Conference, April 29, 1980, at 20–21, 23.

23. RTNDA, *News Media Coverage of Judicial Proceedings with Cameras and Microphones,* A-42.

24. *Final Report of the Hawaii State Bar Association Committee on "Cameras in the Courtroom,"* Hawaii Bar Journal (1982).

25. RTNDA, *News Media Coverage of Judicial Proceedings with Cameras and Microphones,* A-26.

26. Advisory Commission on Cameras in the Courtroom, Nevada, *Final Statistical Report: Cameras in the Courtroom in Nevada,* May 7, 1981, at 1.

27. RTNDA, *News Media Coverage of Judicial Proceedings with Cameras and Microphones,* A-53.

28. Alaska Judicial Council, *News Cameras in the Alaska Courts: Assessing the Impact,* January 1988.

29. RTNDA, *News Media Coverage of Judicial Proceedings with Cameras and Microphones,* A-6.

30. *Report of the Supreme Court of Virginia to the General Assembly and Governor of Virginia Concerning Electronic Media and Still Photography in the Courts,* December 29, 1989.

31. RTNDA, *News Media Coverage of Judicial Proceedings with Cameras and Microphones,* A-82.

32. State of Maine Supreme Court, *Report of the Special Advisory Committee on Cameras in the Courtroom to the Supreme Judicial Court regarding the Experimental Photographic and Electronic Coverage of Trial Courts in Portland and Bangor,* November 30, 1993, at 13, 38.

33. RTNDA, *News Media Coverage of Judicial Proceedings with Cameras and Microphones,* A-41.

34. *Report of the Chief Administrative Judge to the New York Legislature, the Governor, and the Chief Judge on the Effects of Audio-Visual Coverage on the Conduct of Judicial Proceedings,* Honorable Albert M. Rosenblatt, March 1989.

35. *The Intrusion of Cameras in New York's Criminal Courts: A Report by the Public Defense Backup Center,* May 12, 1989, at 23.

36. Paula Wade, "Supreme Court Rules Cameras Can Roll during Tennessee Trials," *Commercial Appeal,* December 15, 1995; Rebecca Ferrar, "Cameras Get Trial Run," *News Sentinel,* December 15, 1995.

37. Tennessee Rules of Court, Rule 10, Code of Judicial Conduct, Canon 3A (7)(A), and Media Guidelines.

38. Scott Olson, "Cameras in the Courtroom," *Indiana Lawyer*, September 18–October 1, 1996.

39. RTNDA, *News Media Coverage of Judicial Proceedings with Cameras and Microphones: A Survey of the States*, January 1, 1995.

40. Rhode Island, Massachusetts, Nebraska, Minnesota, California, and Hawaii provide some televised coverage of government proceedings, but only California includes limited coverage of its supreme court.

41. Washington Public Affairs Network, *Planning Report*, 1993, at 19.

42. Molly Treadway Johnson and Carol Krafka, *Federal Judicial Center, Electronic Media Coverage of Federal Civil Proceedings: An Evaluation of the Pilot Program in Six District Courts and Two Courts of Appeals*, November 4, 1993, at 13, 30.

43. Molly Treadway Johnson, *Electronic Media Coverage of Courtroom Proceedings: Effects on Witnesses and Jurors: Supplemental Report of the Federal Judicial Center*, January 18, 1994, at Appendix, 1, note 1.

44. Ibid., passim.

45. Linda Greenhouse, "U.S. Judges to Decide on Cameras in the Courts," *New York Times*, September 18, 1994, 26

46. Linda Greenhouse, "Disdaining a Soundbite, Federal Judges Banish TV," *New York Times*, September 25, 1994, sec. 4, 4.

47. *Business Wire*, September 21, 1994.

48. *Marisol v. Giuliani*, 95 Civ. 10533, 929 F.Supp 660, 662 (1996).

49. Editorial, *New York Times*, March 9, 1996.

50. *Katzman v. Victoria's Secret Catalogue, et al., In Re: Courtroom Television Network*, Opinion 96 Civ. 0003 (RWS), April 29, 1996, at 23.

51. 28 U.S.C. 2071(a) 1988.

52. Jonathan Grener, "Who Rules, Which Rules?" *Legal Times*, March 11, 1996, 18.

53. *Sigmon v. Parker, Chapin, Flattau and Klimpl*, S.D.N.Y., No. 93 Civ. 7123 (PKL).

54. *Hamilton v. ACCU-TEK*, U.S. Dist. Ct. Eastern District, No. 95, CV0049, October 18, 1996.

55. News Release, Administrative Office of the U.S. Courts, March 12, 1996.

56. *Chicago Daily Law Bulletin*, June 18, 1996.

57. News Release, American Judicature Society (no date), 129.

58. Greenhouse, "Disdaining a Soundbite," 4.

59. "Cameras in International Courtrooms Project," unpublished Court TV memorandum.

NOTES TO CHAPTER 4

1. Reported in *Petition of Post-Newsweek Stations, Florida*, 370 Southern Reporter 2d 764, at 769 (1979).

2. Rosenthal Market Resources, *Report of Court TV Questionnaire*, July 25, 1995.

3. George McCall and J. L. Simmons, *Issues in Participant Observation: A Text and Reader* 42 (Addison-Wesley, 1969).

4. Buford J. Junker, *Field Work: An Introduction to the Social Sciences* (University of Chicago Press, 1960).

5. Alan E. Kadzin, "Observer Effects: Reactivity of Direct Observations," in D. P. Hartman, ed., *Using Observers to Study Behavior* (Jossey-Bass, 1982), 5.

6. Jeffrey Roth, *The Disturbed Subject: Epistemological and Ethical Implications of Reactivity in Videotape Research* (Peter Lange, 1990).

7. Derek Freeman, *Margaret Mead and Samoa: The Making and Unmaking of an Anthropological Myth* (Harvard University Press, 1983).

8. Kadzin, "Observer Effects."

9. Alan E. Kadzin, "Direct Observations as Unobtrusive Measures in Treatment Evaluations," in Lee Sechrest, ed., *Unobtrusive Measurement Today* (Jossey-Bass, 1979).

10. Rosemary O. Nelson, David P. Lipinsky, and John L. Black, *The Effects of Expectancy on the Reactivity of Self-Recording*, 3 Behavior Therapy 337 (1975).

11. Bettyann Kevles, *Naked to the Bone* (Rutgers University Press, 1997).

12. S. L. Foster and J. D. Cone, *Current Issues in Direct Observation*, 2 Behavioral Assessment 313 (1980).

13. Roth, *The Disturbed Subject* 38, 86.

14. McCall and Simmons, *Issues in Participant Observation* 90–94.

15. John Gribbon, *In Search of Schrodinger's Cat: Quantum Physics and Reality* (Bantam, 1984), p. 103.

16. Banesh Hoffamen, *The Strange Story of the Quantum* (Dove, 1959).

17. J. C. Polkinhorne, *The Quantum World* 44 (Longman, 1984).

18. Fred Alan Wolf, *Taking the Quantum Leap: The New Physics for Nonscientists* (Harper & Row, 1981), 2.

19. David Charles Cassidy, *Uncertainty: The Life and Science of Werner Heisenberg* (W. H. Freeman, 1942), 106

20. Correspondence with Professor Daniel Kevles, California Institute of Technology.

21. Gribbon, *In Search of Schrodinger's Cat*, 1–4.

22. Daniel J. Kevles, *The Physicists: The History of a Scientific Community in Modern America* 159–168 (Harvard University Press, 1987).

23. Polkinhorne, *The Quantum World* 29.

24. Books on this experiment were written by the original social scientists who conducted the studies. See Elton Mayo, *The Social Problems of an Industrialized Civilization* (Arno Press, 1977); William J. Dickson and F. J. Roethlisberger, *Counseling in an Organization: A Sequel to the Hawthorne Researches* (Howard University, Division of Research, Graduate School of Business Administration, 1966); F. J. Roethlisberger and William J. Dickson, *Management and the Worker: An Account of a Research Program Conducted by the Western Electric Co., Hawthorne Works, Chicago* (Harvard University Press, 1939; rev. ed. 1967).

25. H. McIlvaine Parsons, *What Caused the Hawthorne Effect*, 10 Administration and Society 259 (November 1978).

26. H. McIlvaine Parsons, "What Happened at Hawthorne?" *Science*, March 8, 1974, 922.

27. G. D. Gottfredson, *The Hawthorne Misunderstanding* (unpublished manuscript, 1995).

28. *Free Speech vs. the Law of Fair Trial in the English and American Law of Contempt by Publication*, 17 U. Chi. L. Rev. 540, 552 (1950).

29. Morris Gillmore Caldwell, *Sensational News in the Modern Metropolitan Newspapers*, 23 J. Crim. L., Criminology, and Pol. Sci. 191, at 198–199, 202 (1932).

30. *Publicity Scandals Demand Exercise of Authority*, 20 J. Am. Jud. Society 82 (1936).

31. Paul Lazarsfeld, *Radio and the Printed Page* 332 (Duell, Sloan, and Pearce, 1940).

32. Ibid., 332.

33. See Dorwin Cartwright, *Some Principles of Mass Persuasion*, 2 Human Relations 253, at 257 (1949); Millspaugh, "Trial by Mass Media," in Daniel Katz, ed., *Public Opinion and Propaganda* 113–114 (1954).

34. Darrell Hunt study, reported in the *Los Angeles Times*, October 9, 1995, p. S9.

35. Erwin Hovland, "Effects of the Mass Media of Communication," in Gardner Lindzey, ed., 2 *The Handbook of Social Psychology* 1062, 1071 (Addison-Wesley, 1954).

36. *Stroble v. California*, 343 U.S. 181 (1952).

37. Ibid., 201.

38. John Monahan and Laurens Walker, *Judicial Use of Social Science Research*, 15 Law and Human Behavior 571 (1991), citing Edmond Cahn, *Jurisprudence*, 30 N.Y.U. L. Rev. 150 (1955); Paul Giannelli, *The Admissibility of Novel Scientific Evidence: Frye v. United States a Half-Century Later*, 80 Columbia L. Rev. 1197 (1989).

39. Kermit Netteburg, *Does Research Support the Estes Ban on Cameras in the Courtroom?* 63 Judicature 471 (1980).

40. Karl P. Warden, *Canon 35: Is There Room for Objectivity?* 4 Washburn L. J. 211 (1965).

41. Bert Pryer et al., *The Florida Experiment: An Analysis of On-The-Scene Responses to Cameras in the Courtroom*, 45 Southern Speech Communication Journal 12, 21, 26 (1979).

42. Janet Swim and Eugene Borgida, *Public Opinion on the Psychological and Legal Aspects of Televising Rape Trials*, 17 J. Applied Social Psych. 507, at 515 (1987).

43. Laralyn M. Sasaki, *Electronic Media Access to Federal Courtrooms: A Judicial Response*, 23 U. Mich. J. Law Reform 769, at 769–770, 793, 794–796 (1990).

44. William J. Bowers and Margaret Vandiver, *Cameras in the Courtroom Make New Yorkers Reluctant to Testify*, College of Criminal Justice, Northeastern University, Boston, Mass., April 23, 1991, 1.

45. Anton Valukas, William A. Von Hoene Jr., Liza M. Murphy, "Cameras in the Courtroom: An Overview," *Communications Lawyer*, Fall 1995, 18.

46. Molly Treadway Johnson and Carol Krafka, *Federal Judicial Center, Electronic Media Coverage of Federal Civil Proceedings* 7 (1994).

47. S. L. Alexander, *"Mischievous Potentialities": A Case Study of Courtroom Camera Guidelines, Eighth Judicial Circuit, Florida, 1989* 313 (Ph.D. dissertation, University of Florida, 1990).

48. Susanna Barber, *News Cameras in the Courtroom: A Free Press-Fair Trial Debate* 87 (Ablex, 1987).

49. Paul Thaler, *The Impact of the Television Camera on Courtroom Participants: A Case Study of the Joel Steinberg Murder Trial* 34–35 (Ph.D. dissertation, New York University, 1990).

50. Barber, *News Cameras in the Courtroom* 87.

51. Ibid., 94 (quoting Joel Hirschhorn, *Cameras in the Courtroom? No*, 7 Barrister 56).

52. Dan Slater and Valerie Hans, *Methodological Issues in the Evaluation*

of *"Experiments" with Cameras in the Courts,* 30 Communication Quarterly 4 (Fall 1982) at 378.

53. Royce A. Singleton, Bruce Straits, and Margaret Straits, *Approaches to Social Research* 181 (Oxford University Press, 1993).

54. Gerald R. Miller and Norman E. Fontes, *Videotape on Trial: A View from the Jury Box* 41 (Sage Publications, 1979), (quoting E. F. Lindquist, *Design Analysis of Experiments in Psychology and Education* 6 [Houghton Mifflin, 1953]).

55. Susanna Barber, *The Problem of Prejudice: A New Approach to Assessing the Impact of Courtroom Cameras,* 66 Judicature 250 (1983).

56. Ibid., 249.

57. Barber, *News Cameras in the Courtroom,* 90.

58. S. J. Brakel, *Videotape in Trial Proceedings: A Technological Obsession?* 61 A.B.A. J. 958 (1975).

59. Miller and Fontes, *Videotape on Trial* 45–46.

60. Ralph Frasca, *Estimating the Occurrence of Trials Prejudiced by Press Coverage,* 72 Judicature, at 162, 169, 250–254 (1988).

61. Ibid., 254.

62. James L. Hoyt, *Courtroom Coverage: The Effects of Being Televised,* 24 Journal of Broadcasting 487, at 490, 494–495 (1977).

63. Slater and Hans, *Methodological Issues* 378.

64. Barber, *News Cameras in the Courtroom* 248.

65. Ernest H. Short and Associates, Inc., *Evaluation of California's Experiment with Extended Media Coverage of Courts,* 1981, 6, 114, 119, 121, 123.

66. Donald Lewis Shores, Jr., *The Effects of Courtroom Cameras on Verbal Behavior: An Analysis of Simulated Trial Witness Testimony in Courtrooms Using Television Cameras* viii–ix, 84–85, 92–93 (Ph.D. dissertation, University of Florida, August 1981).

67. Steve Robert Pasternack, *The Effects of Perceived Community Pressure on Simulated Juror Guilt Attributions: A Study* iv, 48 (Ph.D. dissertation, University of Tennessee, Knoxville, December 1982).

68. Saul M. Kassin, *TV Cameras, Public Self-Consciousness, and Mock Juror Performance,* 20 Journal of Experimental Social Psychology 336, at 337–339, 347 (1984), (citing J. D. Harris, *Habituatory Response Decrement in the Intact Organism,* 40 Psychological Bulletin 385, citing A. H. Buss, *Self Consciousness and Social Anxiety* [Freeman, 1980]).

69. Anna R. Paddon, *Television Coverage of Criminal Trials with Cam-*

eras and Microphones: A Laboratory Experiment of Audience Effects vi (Ph.D. dissertation, University of Tennessee, Knoxville, 1985).

70. Eugene Borgida, Kenneth G. Debono, and Lee A. Buckman, *Cameras in the Courtroom: The Effects of Media Coverage on Witness Testimony and Juror Perceptions*, 14 Law and Human Behavior, at 505–507 (1990).

71. Alan Punches, *The Cognitive Effects of Camera Presence on the Recall of Testimony in a Simulated Courtroom Setting* iv, 55, 56, (Ph.D. dissertation, Colorado State University, Fort Collins, 1991).

72. Valukas, Von Hoene, and Murphy, "Cameras in the Courtroom," 21.

73. Elizabeth M. Hodgkins, *Throwing Open a Window on the Nation's Courts by Lifting the Ban on Federal Courtroom Television*, Kansas Journal of Law and Public Policy 89 (Spring 1995).

Notes to Chapter 5

1. *Kavanaugh v. Courtroom Television Network*, 91 Civ. 7959 (RPP), Declaration of Steven Brill, March 3, 1992, at 30.

2. This chapter includes extensive quotes from Steven Brill, Jeff Ballabon, Fred Graham, and Joe Russin. All are based on taped conversations with them in their offices in New York City and the author's office in Washington, D.C.

3. Jim Morrison, "Law of the Land," *Sprint Magazine, Southwest Airlines*, March 1996, p. 11; Jeff Goodwell, "Steven Brill and His Court TV, Delivering Justice in the Electronic Frontier," *Wired*, March 1995, 116.

4. 13 Executive Female, 50 (1990).

5. John Lippman, "Two Cable Court Channels are Expected to Merge," *Los Angeles Times*, November 21, 1990, D2.

6. Jay Sharbutt, "Two Cable Channels Offer a Real Live Look at Our Legal System," *Chicago Tribune*, November 22, 1990, 23D.

7. Arthur S. Hayes, "Two Court TV Channels Planned as Critics Ask If One's Too Many," *Wall Street Journal*, January 30, 1990, B1.

8. Paul Marcotte, *Courts on Cable*, 76 American Bar Association Journal 19 (April 1990).

9. Stephan McClellan, "In Court," *Broadcasting and Cable*, May 28, 1990, 38.

10. For an analysis of Court TV, see David Harris, *The Appearance of Justice*, 35 Arizona Law Review 785, at 797–807 (1993).

11. TCI report on file with the author.

12. John Lippman, "We, the Jury," *Los Angeles Times*, June 30, 1991.

13. *Kavanaugh v. Courtroom Television Network*, 91 Civ. 7959, Declaration of Steven Brill, March 3, 1992.

14. Skip Wollenberg, "Proposed Courtroom Channels Plan to Merge," A.P., November 21, 1990.

15. Mark Landler, "Will Viewers Be Shouting: I Want My Court TV?" *Business Week*, June 24, 1991.

16. Steven Brill, "The Drama of Justice," *American Lawyer*, July-August 1990.

17. Steven Brill, "Cameras in the Courts and Original Intent," *Legal Times*, January 22, 1996, 24.

18. Brill, "The Drama of Justice."

19. *Court TV Viewers' Guide* (1992).

20. Morrison, "Law of the Land," 109.

21. Because it is a private company, the financial status of Court TV cannot be corroborated.

22. Correspondence with the author.

23. David Shaw, "Did the Media Overfeed a Starving Public?" *Los Angeles Times*, October 9, 1995, S10.

24. Editorial, *Broadcasting and Cable*, February 6, 1995, 74.

25. Harris, *The Appearance of Justice* 785.

26. Correspondence with the author.

27. "Money Talks, Clients Walk," *Newsweek*, April 17, 1995, 32.

28. Jeffrey Toobin, *The People v. O.J. Simpson* (Random House, 1996).

29. Quoted in David Shaw, "The Simpson Legacy," *Los Angeles Times*, October 9, 1995, S1.

30. Andy Meisler, "Bochco Tests America's New Legal Savvy," *New York Times*, October 1, 1995, H33.

31. See *Kavanaugh v. Courtroom Television Network*, 91 Civ. 7959 (RPP), Declaration of Steven Brill, March 3, 1992, at 24–28, listing examples of this coverage.

32. Alan Dershowitz, "TV Trials Thrive on Sensationalism" (editorial), *Boston Herald*, February 10, 1992.

33. Harris, *The Appearance of Justice* 826, 827.

34. In the aftermath of Brill's exclusion from Court TV's future, an article appeared speculating whether in order to boost ratings Time-Warner would diminish the standards set by Brill. Intracorporate memos surfaced disclosing that during his tenure Brill had fought off attempts by Time-Warner (which denied the accuracy of the claims) to interfere with editorial positions of the *American Lawyer*, *Corporate Control Alert*, and Court TV. Time-Warner

countered with the complaint that Court TV was not as profitable as Brill claimed, and wasn't expected to show a positive cash flow until late 1998 or 1999. Stay tuned. Jennet Conant, "Don't Mess with Steve Brill," *Vanity Fair*, August 1997, 62.

NOTES TO CHAPTER 6

1. 38 Federal Rules and Decisions 435, at 435, 436 (1965).

2. Chief Justice Moyer, "State of the Judiciary" speech, Fall 1995.

3. Kenneth Culp Davis, 1 *Administrative Law Treatise* 441 (2d edition, K. C. Davis, 1978); Kenneth F. Warren, *Administrative Laws in the American Political System* 186 (West, 1982).

4. Hon. Elliott H. Levitas, U.S. Representative (Georgia), Statement to Ad Hoc Subcommittee on Broadcasting of House Rules Committee, 94th Congress, First Session, 42.

5. Hon. B. F. Sisk, U.S. Representative (California), Statement to Committee on Rules, 94th Congress, Second Session, March 26, 1976, 9.

6. Lawrence Friedman, *Total Justice* 1597 (Russell Sage Foundation, 1985).

7. Jerome Frank, *Courts on Trial: Myth and Reality in American Justice* (Princeton University Press, 1949); see also David Harris, *The Appearance of Justice* 35 Arizona Law Review 785, at 794–796 (1993).

8. Susan Estrich, "Prime Time for Tim McVeigh," *The Washington Post*, September 20, 1996, A23.

9. *A.P. v. U.S.*, 326 U.S. 1, at 20 (1945).

10. *Shepherd v. Florida*, 341 U.S. 50, at 51 (1951).

11. Ibid., 53.

12. Ronald Goldfarb, *The Contempt Power* xvii-xx (Anchor, 1971).

13. Application of U.S. Senate Select Committee on Presidential Campaign Activities, 361 F. Supp. 1270 (U.S. Dist. Ct., 1973).

14. Walter Goodman, "Court TV: Case of the Curious Witness," *New York Times*, July 21, 1997, B5.

15. Caryn James, "Television Review," *New York Times*, September 24, 1996, 47.

16. Lois G. Forer, "A Free Press and a Fair Trial," 39 *American Bar Association Journal* 800, 845 (1953).

17. *Craig v. Harney*, 331 U.S. 367, at 376 (1947).

18. Ralph Frasca, "Estimating the Occurrence of Trials Prejudiced by Press Coverage," 72 *Judicature* 3, at 162, 169 (October-November 1988).

19. Jeffrey Abramson, *We, the Jury: The Jury System and the Ideal of Democracy* (Basic Books, 1994), Appendix.

20. Harris, *The Appearance of Justice* 821–822.

21. Judge J. Skelly Wright, *Fair Trial-Free Press*, 38 F.R.D. 435, at 437 (1966).

22. Yale Kamisar, *Essays in Law and Policy* xii (University of Michigan Press, 1980); Yale Kamisar, Fred Inbau, Thurman Arnold, *Criminal Justice in Our Time* 19–21 (University Press of Virginia, 1965).

23. Jessica Seigel, "Getting Civil with O.J.," *Buzz*, December-January 1997, 57–58.

24. Carey Goldberg, "Simpson Case Weariness Mixes with Fascination," *New York Times*, September 20, 1996, A18.

25. Carey Goldberg, "New, Likely Tauter, Simpson Trial Opens," *New York Times*, September 18, 1996, A14.

26. David A. Anderson, *Democracy and the Demystification of Courts: An Essay*, 14 Review of Litigation, 3, 627, at 641 (1995).

27. David A. Harris, *The Appearance of Justice*, 35 Arizona Law Review 785, 794 (1993).

28. Anderson, *Democracy and the Demystification of Courts* 642, 644.

29. Judge Stephen Reinhardt, *Symposium: The Sound of the Gavel: Perspectives on Judicial Speech and the Open Judiciary*, 28 Loyola of Los Angeles L. Rev. 805, at 812 (April 1, 1995).

30. Ibid.

31. Hearings before the U.S. Senate Judiciary Committee, 99th Congress, 2d session, July 29–31, August 1, 1986, 179.

32. Paul J. Martinek, "Eavesdropping on the Court," *Massachusetts Lawyers Weekly*, November 8, 1993.

33. Michael G. Radigan, "May It Please the Court," *New York Law Journal*, October 5, 1993, 2.

34. Obituary, *New York Times*, December 1, 1995, B10.

35. Speech at the Library of Congress, April 10, 1997.

36. Theo Wilson, *Headline Justice: Inside the Courtroom: The Country's Most Controversial Trials* 11 (Thunder's Mouth Press, 1997).

37. Correspondence with the author.

38. *Crowley v. Pulsifer*, 137 Mass 392, at 394 (1884).

39. *Patterson v. Colorado*, 205 U.S. 454, at 462 (1907).

40. Steven Brill, "Cameras in the Courts and Original Intent," *Legal Times*, January 22, 1996, 48.

41. Russell Wiggins, *The Public's Right to Public Trial*, 19 F.R.D. 25, at 90, 91 (1925).

42. Paul Thaler, *The Watchful Eye* xxi (Praeger, 1994).

43. Adrian Coronauer, *The First Annual Symposium on Media and the Law: Free Speech v. Fair Trial, Comments of Judge Lawrence L. Pierson*, 41 So. Dakota L. Rev. 79, at 125 (1995).

44. George Gerbner, *Trial by Television*, 63 Judicature 117 (April 1980).

45. *Westmoreland v. C.B.S., Inc.*, 596 F. Supp. 1166 (1984).

46. Frederic Lederer, *Evolution in Courtroom Technology Presents Opportunity and Risk*, Trial, November 1994, p. 8.

47. Marshall McLuhan, *Understanding Media: The Extensions of Man* 7 (McGraw-Hill, 1965).

48. See Lawrence M. Friedman, *Law, Lawyers and Popular Culture*, 98 Yale L. J. 1579 (1989).

49. Don Hardenbergh, *The Courthouse: A Planning and Design Guide to Court Facilities*, National Center for State Courts Publication R-131, Williamsburg, Va. (1991); see also American Bar Association, *Twenty Years of Courthouse Design* (1993) and American Bar Association and American Institute of Architects, *The American Courthouse: Planning and Design for the Judicial Process*, Institute for Continuing Education, Ann Arbor, Mich. (1973).

50. Hardenbergh, *The Courthouse* 52.

51. Mark Curriden, *Courtroom of the Future Is Here*, 22 A.B.A. J. 22 (January 1995).

52. Jon Katz, "Old Media, New Media and a Middle Way," *New York Times*, January 19, 1997, H43.

53. 42 USC 10608, S. 235, Public Law 104–132, 110 Stat. 1246, April 24, 1996.

54. Correspondence with the author.

55. Thomas E. Baker, *C-SPAN: A Guide for Law Professors*, 40 Journal of Legal Education 295–305 (September 1990).

56. B. Lamb and Staff, *C-SPAN: America's Town Hall* xix (Washington, D.C., 1989).

57. Ira Reiner, "Cameras Keep Justice System in Focus," *National Law Journal*, October 23, 1995, A23.

58. Raymond Hernandez, "Albany Debates Law on Cameras in Courts," *New York Times*, July 7, 1997, B4.

59. Howard Rosenberg, "The Simpson Verdicts, Valuable Lessons of TV in Courtrooms," *Los Angeles Times*, October 5, 1995, A7.

60. Paul D. Carrington, Letter to the Editor, *New York Times*, October 24, 1995, editorial page.

61. Reiner, "Cameras Keep Justice System in Focus," A22.

62. Andy Meisler, "Bochco Tests America's New Legal Savvy," *New York Times*, October 1, 1995, 433.

63. Malcolm W. Browne, Letter to the Editor, *New York Times*, December 1995, 2.

64. Christopher Isherwood, *Goodbye to Berlin* 15 (Folio Society, 1975).

65. Janet Malcolm, "The Real Thing," *New York Review of Books*, January 9, 1997, 12.

66. Bill Nichols, *Representing Reality: Issues and Concepts in Documentary* 41–43 (Indiana University Press, 1991).

67. John S. Douglas and Glenn P. Harnden, *The Art of Technique: An Aesthetic Approach to Film and Video Production* 7 (Allyn and Bacon, 1996).

68. Carey Goldberg, "Scenes from a Trial," *New York Times*, November 27, 1996, A18.

69. Nell Henderson, "The Murders That Won't Die," *Washington Post Book World*, May 26, 1996, 1.

70. Richard N. Winfield, "Courtroom Cameras: A Final Word," *N.Y. State Bar Journal*, February 1997, 18.

71. Reinhardt, *The Sound of the Gavel.*

72. Judge Jerome Frank, *Courts on Trial: Myth and Reality in American Justice* 2–3 (Princeton University Press, 1949).

73. *In re Petition of Post-Newsweek Stations*, 370 Southern 2d. 764, at 781 (1979).

74. Justice Lewis Powell used the phrase in *Nixon v. Warner Communications, Inc.*, 435 U.S. 589, at 609 (1978); see also *U.S. v. Hastings*, 695 F.2d. 1278, at 1281 (11th Cir. 1983).

75. *Westmoreland v. C.B.S., Inc.*, 752 F.2d 16, at 22 (2d Cir. 1985)

76. *Katzman v. Victoria's Secret Catalogue*, 923 F. Supp. 580, at 588, 589. (U.S. Dist. Ct., S.D., 1996).

77. Kelli L. Sager and Karen N. Frederiksen, *Televising the Judicial Branch: In Furtherance of the Public's First Amendment Rights*, 69 So. Calif. L. Rev. 1519 (1996).

INDEX

ABOUT THE AUTHOR

Ronald Goldfarb is a Washington D.C. attorney, literary agent, and author. A former government attorney in the Air Force JAG and a prosecutor of organized crime cases in the Kennedy Justice Department, he founded a law firm in the nation's capital in 1966. He is the author of nine previous books and over a hundred magazine and newspaper articles.

Goldfarb has bachelor of arts and law degrees from Syracuse University, and Master and Doctorate of Law degrees from Yale. He lectures to university and professional organizations, has consulted for national commissions and foundations, and is a frequent panelist and commentator on radio and television. He lives in Alexandria, Virginia.